Practical Software Configuration Management:

The Latenight Developer's Handbook

Hewlett-Packard Professional Books

Atchison	Object-Oriented Test & Measurement Software Development in C++
Blinn	Portable Shell Programming: An Extensive Collection of Bourne Shell Examples
Blommers	Practical Planning for Network Growth
Caruso	Power Programming in HP OpenView: Developing CMIS Applications
Cook	Building Enterprise Information Architectures
Costa	Planning and Designing High Speed Networks Using 100VG-AnyLAN, Second Edition
Crane	A Simplified Approach to Image Processing: Classical and Modern Techniques
Fernandez	Configuring the Common Desktop Environment
Fristrup	USENET: Netnews for Everyone
Fristrup	The Essential Web Surfer Survival Guide
Grady	Practical Software Metrics for Project Management and Process Improvement
Grosvenor, Ichiro, O'Brien	Mainframe Downsizing to Upsize Your Business: IT-Preneuring
Gunn	A Guide to NetWare® for UNIX®
Helsel	Graphical Programming: A Tutorial for HP VEE
Helsel	Visual Programming with HP VEE, Second Edition
Holman, Lund	Instant JavaScript
Kane	PA-RISC 2.0 Architecture
Knouse	Practical DCE Programming
Lee	The ISDN Consultant: A Stress-Free Guide to High-Speed Communications
Lewis	The Art & Science of Smalltalk
Lund	Integrating UNIX® and PC Network Operating Systems
Madell	Disk and File Management Tasks on HP-UX
Mahoney	High-Mix Low-Volume Manufacturing
Malan, Letsinger, Coleman	Object-Oriented Development at Work: Fusion in the Real World
McFarland	X Windows on the World: Developing Internationalized Software with X, Motif®, and CDE
McMinds/Whitty	Writing Your Own OSF/Motif Widgets
Mikkelsen/Pherigo	Practical Software Configuration Management: The Latenight Developer's Handbook
Norton, DiPasquale	Thread Time: The Multithreaded Programming Guide
Phaal	LAN Traffic Management
Pipkin	Halting the Hacker: A Practical Guide to Computer Security
Poniatowski	The HP-UX System Administrator's "How To" Book
Poniatowski	HP-UX 10.x System Administration "How To" Book
Poniatowski	Learning the HP-UX Operating System
Poniatowski	Windows NT® and HP-UX System Administrator's "How To" Book
Ryan	Distributed Object Technology: Concepts and Applications
Thomas	Cable Television Proof-of-Performance: A Practical Guide to Cable TV Compliance Measurements Using a Spectrum Analyzer
Weygant	Clusters for High Availability: A Primer of HP-UX Solutions
Witte	Electronic Test Instruments
Yawn, Stachnick, Sellars	The Legacy Continues: Using the HP 3000 with HP-UX and Windows NT

Practical Software Configuration Management:

The Latenight Developer's Handbook

Tim Mikkelsen
Software Technology Center
Hewlett-Packard Corporation

Suzanne Pherigo
Software Engineering Systems Division
Hewlett-Packard Corporation

To join a Prentice Hall PTR Internet mailing list, point to
http://www.prehnhall.com/register

Prentice Hall PTR
Upper Saddle River, NJ 07458
http://www.prenhall.com

Editorial/production supervision: *Mary Sudul*
Cover design: *Anthony Gemmellaro*
Cover art: *Ben Mikkelsen*
Cover design director: *Jerry Votta*
Manufacturing manager: *Alexis R. Heydt*
Acquisitions editor: *Karen Gettman*

Published by Prentice Hall PTR
Prentice-Hall, Inc.
A Simon & Schuster Company
Upper Saddle River, New Jersey 07458

The publisher offers discounts on this book when ordered
in bulk quantities. For more information, contact:

Corporate Sales Department
PTR Prentice Hall
One Lake Street
Upper Saddle River, NJ 07458

Phone: 800-382-3419
Fax: 201-236-7141
E-mail (Internet): corpsales@prenhall.com

ISBN 0-13-240854-6

Printed in the United States of America
     10 9 8 7 6 5 4 3 2 1
     Prentice-Hall International (UK) Limited, *London*
     Prentice-Hall of Australia Pty. Limited, *Sydney*
     Prentice-Hall Canada Inc., *Toronto*
     Prentice-Hall Hispanoamericana, S.A., *Mexico*
     Prentice-Hall of India Private Limited, *New Delhi*
     Prentice-Hall of Japan, Inc., *Tokyo*
     Simon & Schuster Asia Pte. Ltd., *Singapore*
     Editora Prentice-Hall do Brasil, Ltda., *Rio de Janeiro*

Dedicated to Bill
—Suzanne

Dedicated to Virginia
—Tim

Contents

Preface

It's 2 A.M. You've been working on a particularly gnarly problem in your code. You've been at it all day—but it seems like all week. You finished off your last Jolt Cola over an hour ago. You're starting to get more than a little fuzzy. (And all the o's in your code are starting to look like tiny little rye bagels.) You are surrounded by empty Jolt cans and candy wrappers and you've just made a huge mistake. You still aren't sure how it happened. One minute, you were compiling for the last time—adding that final touch. The next minute, you were staring at an empty directory. You don't panic, yet, because you make backups. But then the thought hits you that the last backup you made was over two days ago, and too much has changed. Anyway, it's too late now. The current files are gone, and you will never win the contract with nothing to show.

If you have been developing software for any time at all, something like this situation has probably happened to you. Most of us have asked ourselves, *"Why didn't I see the problem?"* or said, *"I wish I could just get back to where I was a couple of hours ago."* The feeling is terrible and a huge waste of time and effort when it does happen. In larger companies, the situation generally isn't quite as bad, because backups are done on a more frequent and consistent basis. Also, these companies generally use some sort of configuration management system to track software changes over time. You may be thinking, that's all well and good for them, but I don't have the time or money to put something like that in place.

But configuration management is not just for the big companies working on the next space shuttle. Many free or inexpensive configuration management systems will work well for the single developer or for small teams. Tools and techniques are available to help you avoid and/or recover simply and gracefully from these sorts of problems.

The aim of this book is to help you, as a "normal" developer, deal with your software development in a solid and professional fashion. You can do so without the backing of a huge software process organization or expensive tools, and without taking time you don't have. This book will help you by providing configuration management guidance in an efficient and clear manner. With this guidance you can incorporate a configuration management solution in your own environment very quickly and painlessly. This book will guide and help you in a way that will save you from yourself, from your Jolt Cola, and maybe even from others. Then the next late night won't be nearly so bad. (Sorry, but there is nothing we can do to help you with the little bagels.)

Acknowledgments

We received help early on from the friends and colleagues who reviewed the proposal (before and after it went to the publisher), including Gary Thalman, Jerry Duggan, Susan Halter, Art Heckle, Scott Kramer, and Hal Render. We received immeasurable help from Scott Jordan, Mike Juran, and Scott Kramer with reviewing early drafts.

We thank Brett Bartow, Karen Gettman, Barbara Alfieri, Christa Carroll, and Mary Sudul at Prentice Hall for their support. We also appreciate the organization support from Pat Pekary of Hewlett-Packard.

The various developers and vendors of the configuration management tools have also been very helpful. Without their help, the tool comparison section would have been all but impossible. For RCS: Walter Tichy, the developer of RCS. For CVS: Jim Kingdon of Cyclic and Paul Bame of Hewlett-Packard, reviewers of the CVS portion of this book. For QVCS: Jim Voris, the developer of QVCS. At Burton Systems Software: David Burton and Chuck Campbell. At Microsoft: David Streams. At Mortice Kern Systems: Sandy Roslyn, Debbie Mantor, and Ellyn Winters-Robinson. At INTERSOLV: Colleen Duffy and Gloria Scheuermann. At StarBase: Basil Maloney and Tim May.

How to Use This Book

This book is a practical guide that quickly gives you the information you need to start using configuration management and to use it effectively. The book does not discuss theoretical aspects of configuration management, except as absolutely, positively necessary, because we think that inaccessibility has been one of the barriers for broader use of configuration management.

We include an introductory section (Section 1: The Basics of Configuration Management) that you should read. It discusses the principles of configuration management as well as introducing a small number of necessary concepts and terminology.

What you read next depends on who you are and what sort of development environment you use. We have divided the second portion of the book into a section for the individual and then a section for the small team. Having common sections would be possible, but dividing it up this way makes it more tuned to your needs. Thus, you will not need to read the full book, in all its glory—just the introductory section and then the section that is applicable to your particular situation. Each of these sections includes examples, using software that is supplied with the book. Our goal is for you to be able to get up and running in just a few hours.

The book also includes a tool section describing many public domain, shareware, and commercial configuration management tools. The commercial tools included are all available on a PC and are priced around $500 or less.

Finally, the book has a reference section that includes descriptions of the CD-ROM contents (public domain and shareware tools and some RCS examples). It also includes the RCS *man* pages.

About the Authors

Tim Mikkelsen is a Research and Development Project Manager at Hewlett-Packard's Software Technology Center. He has bachelor of science and master of science degrees from Iowa State University (1975, 1977) in Computer Science. He also has an interdisciplinary Management of Technology master of science degree from the National Technological University (1994). He has been at Hewlett-Packard since 1977 as a software and firmware developer, marketing engineer, and manager. For the last several years, Tim has been managing CASE environment product development including configuration management. Currently, Tim is managing projects on emerging software technologies, including the Internet, software components, and reuse libraries. Tim has published a variety of articles on computers, software, artificial intelligence, and management.

Suzanne Pherigo is with Hewlett-Packard's Software Engineering Systems Division as a Research and Development Project Manager. She has a bachelor of science degree in Computer Science and Mathematics from New Mexico State University (1985) and is currently pursuing her master's degree from the University of Colorado. She has been with Hewlett-Packard since 1985, working in both software development and quality assurance. Suzanne was recently involved in the integration of third-party configuration management systems into Hewlett-Packard's SoftBench environment, and in the development of Hewlett-Packard's own configuration management solution.

The Basics of Configuration Management

". . . what the hell, let's call him Ramses, too . . ." Ramses the 1st, inventor of versioning, at the birth of his son, 1784 B.C.

An Introduction to Configuration Management

Why Me? Why Now?

Controlling source code and other development artifacts is a critical part of modern software development. This control of software source code is generally referred to as *software configuration management*. Though software configuration management has been in existence (in some form) for over three decades, it remains a poorly understood and inconsistently applied aspect of software development.

Configuration management has been receiving attention recently because of the dramatic changes made in computers and software development over the last decade. In the mid to late 70s, when configuration management really started to arrive, machines were much smaller. A mainframe consisted of maybe a quarter of a megabyte to a few megabytes of main memory. For the very few people who could afford to get one, a personal or desktop machine was 64 Kbytes of memory with 360 Kbyte or 512 Kbyte (8-inch) floppies operating at a speed of around one megahertz. Even the UNIX minicomputers were in this general class. And more importantly, although *big* programs existed, *big* was smaller than it is today. Source code was measured in thousands and possibly tens-of-thousands of lines of code. Executable code was equally modest. Editors and compilers and other tools existed, but they were rather rudimentary by today's standards. The improvement in computers, tools, and your productivity have brought the reality of larger projects down into the realm of the individual programmer or small team.

Currently, large teams of programmers have configuration management tools, organizational support, and staffing for their software configuration management needs. However, much of the software today is written on PCs or UNIX workstations by individuals or small development teams—in other words, it is being done by people like you. As a single individual or member of a small team, you write software for commercial sale, internal company use, or for your own use. You, unfortunately, do not have a huge budget or support structure in place. But you are still working on a moderate- to large-scale project.

The Reality of Software Development

For most of us, the software development process involves a few fundamental pieces: you, the code, the libraries used, the tools used, the system software, and the actual computer itself.

You can look at software development lots of other ways. The model in Figure 1-1-1 should help in understanding your needs for configuration management. Note some of the things going on in the model. You can have one or many of just about anything in the model. For example, at the very simple end of the spectrum, you can be developing a single program by yourself, on a single computer with a minimum of tools. At the other end, several of you (i.e., a team) can be working on a group of related programs (i.e., a system) that are developed on several computers using different operating systems.

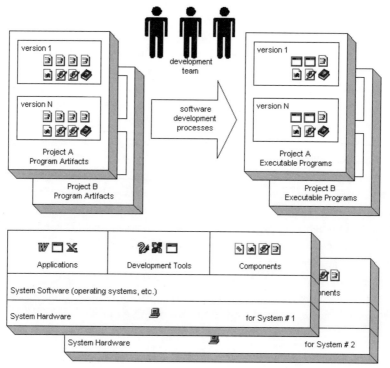

Figure 1-1-1   Software development model

It's All about Change

At its most basic level, software configuration management is about "what changes" in your development environment while you are working and programming. Other larger scale aspects (that we call "big science" configuration management) deal with managing the process you use to develop your software. For most of us, however, the majority of the problems we will encounter are at the more straightforward end of the spectrum. Thus, most of the needs can be dealt with using this approach of controlling and tracking "what changes" during development. This focus may seem really simple, but it is where and how most things go wrong in software.

This fact can be illustrated by looking at the software development model that we just described. Each of the programs you are developing changes over time. You may also have several different versions of any of these programs, each of which may change. The possibility isn't often considered, but changes in your tools and applications can really wreak havoc.

Even though the computer hardware and system software seem extraneous, you might be dealing with two types of platforms or you might have two slightly different PCs. If you are like many developers, some system configuration change has caused you trouble.

In team situations, the makeup of the team will change over time. (And not to get too metaphysical . . .) Even when you are working alone, you will change over time. A friend once said: *"Write your code for somebody who doesn't understand it, because by the time you come back to it, that somebody else will be you."*

Basic Configuration Management Concepts

The Elements of Configuration Management

We are interested in controlling and tracking "what changes" during development, and learning how configuration management can help us. At the center of software configuration management are the artifacts that you are developing and working with during development. (Some of these artifacts may be things that were created by someone else.) We describe the various types of artifacts, and the major aspects of dealing with these artifacts—artifact versioning, changes, build, and group versioning.

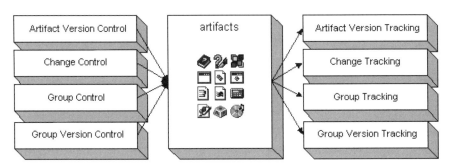

Figure 1-2-1 Aspects of configuration management

Artifacts of Software Development

Jennifer develops software for restaurant menu design. She includes templates with her software for different types of restaurants, including color schemes, font schemes, layout alternatives, and graphics. These templates give someone designing a menu for an Italian restaurant a different start from someone designing a menu for a Japanese restaurant. The templates are a very important part of the software program that Jennifer sells—even though they are not source code. For Jennifer, it is important to manage these template files along with her source code in the configuration management system.

Generally, a software system includes artifacts other than source code as an important part of the system. Each individual's or group's situation is different: Some people spend a lot of time developing graphics for their programs, and some have help files included with their programs; some keep information about code defects along with the source files where the fixes were made. All of these types of files are artifacts of software development. These artifacts are things you might consider managing, along with the source code, with the configuration management solution you choose.

You might also want to manage other files that you store on your computer. Some of these files give information about the setup of your computer. For instance, your CONFIG.SYS file gives information about the environment you are running on your PC. By storing these types of files in the configuration management system, you can determine how your environment is changing over time. If a program you haven't changed stops working, you can see not only if the program really changed, but also how the environment changed.

You probably also have other information stored on your computer that has nothing to do (at least directly) with the software you are developing. You might store customer information or accounting information, for instance. Even though these files don't affect your software development, you might want to manage some or all of them with your configuration management solution. You will have already spent the time setting up the system, so the addition of a few more files won't be too hard. It also might save you some grief later!

As you implement and become more comfortable with a configuration management solution for your environment, you will probably modify the types of artifacts that you store in the system. You might determine that you never need access to (or even know about) previous versions of some types of artifacts. These artifacts don't need to be stored in the configuration management system. You also might find yourself wishing that you had stored and managed other types of artifacts in the configuration management system. You will adapt your own methodology over time, but you don't have to stop with just code.

This list won't include every type of file that you might store in a configuration management system, but should help you get started:

- Source files
- Header files
- Data files
- Build scripts
- Documentation files (i.e., Word documents)
- Help files
- Icons
- Bitmaps
- Other graphics
- Configuration files
- Defect files
- System files (i.e., `CONFIG.SYS`, `AUTOEXEC.BAT`)
- Customer data
- Spreadsheets
- Financial information (i.e., Quicken files)

Artifact Versioning

> *Bill writes home control software for use in his home and business. Although he doesn't sell the software, it is very important for him, because it controls all aspects of his home and business, from temperature control and lighting to a sophisticated alarm system. A defect in the code can cause something as benign as a light not turning on when it should to something as serious as an alarm going off when it shouldn't—or perhaps even more serious, an alarm not going off when it should. Thus, Bill is very careful about all changes he makes to the code. Before making any change to a file, he first creates a backup copy. He likes to keep the various backup copies around for a long time (maybe forever) to help him analyze any defects that do manage to sneak into the code. He started out naming the backup copies with extensions like .bak, .old, .sav, .really-old. . . . This system got quite cumbersome, as you can imagine, so he went to a better system of using the date as an extension (e.g., 0406). Unfortunately, now he is running out of disk space. . . .*

Bill needs help with the most basic element of configuration management—artifact versioning. All configuration management systems provide a mechanism for creating and managing different versions, or revisions, of the files stored within them. As you make changes to a file, you will want to store snapshots of the file. This will allow you to recreate these snapshots later. Each of these snapshots is referred to as a version, or revision, of the file. To allow you to recreate a particular snapshot, the configuration management system must provide a naming scheme so that you can find the exact revision of the file you want. (And, of course, you want a naming scheme that is better than adding a .bak extension to the file name!)

Files stored on your file system are uniquely identified by their full path name. For instance, you might have a file on your system named C:\AUTOEXEC.BAT. Only one file can exist on your system with that exact name, although you might have files named AUTOEXEC.BAT stored on other directories of your file system (for example, C:\BACKUP\AUTOEXEC.BAT or D:\AUTOEXEC.BAT).

Files stored in a configuration management system require a revision string as well as a full pathname to uniquely identify them. All configuration management systems use a numbering scheme to identify the different revisions of a file. This numbering scheme generally gives some indication of the order that the files were created and stored in the system.

> *Dennis[1] created a file called hello.c. This file, hello.c, is stored in a configuration management system. The initial revision Dennis created was given the revision number 1.1.[2]*

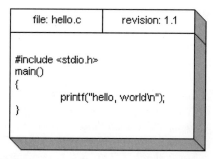

Figure 1-2-2   The initial file

> *The next revision that Dennis created was given the revision number 1.2. Dennis made this change with an intentional error to show how the C language works. He made this revision by modifying the initial revision.*

---

1.   These example programs for hello.c, if you didn't recognize them, are from Brian Kernighan and Dennis Ritchie's second edition of *The C Programming Language.*

2.   In this example we are using the numbering scheme used by RCS. All configuration management systems have some sort of numbering scheme, but not necessarily the same as the one used by RCS.

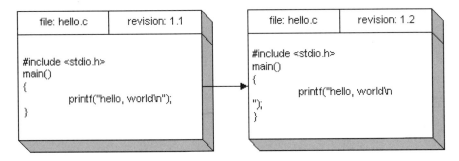

Figure 1-2-3   The file is revised with an error

The third revision was given the revision number 1.3, because it was created by modifying revision 1.2. Dennis created revision 1.3 to correct the errors introduced in version 1.2.

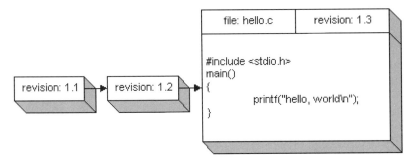

Figure 1-2-4   The file is fixed

Then Dennis creates two more revisions, both by modifying revision 1.3. The first of these revisions, numbered 1.4, split up the printing of the string used in the hello message.

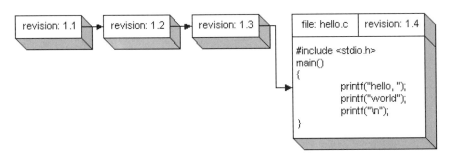

Figure 1-2-5   The file is revised with formatting changes

The second version, numbered 1.3.1.1, was created later but was a variation of 1.3 to show minor changes in capitalization.

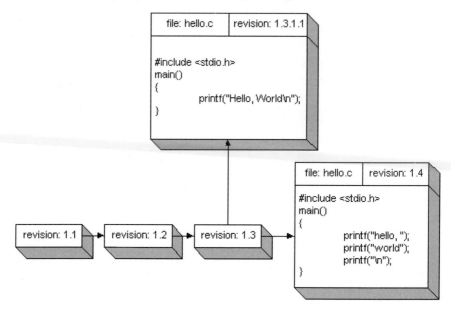

Figure 1-2-6   A branch is created for capitalization

Note that the revisions of a file can be represented by a tree, with the initial revision at the root. Each subsequent revision is created by starting with a revision already stored in the system and modifying it. As long as you only create one new revision from each revision already stored in the system, you will have a single line revision tree. If you need to create more than one new revision from a revision stored in the tree, you will create a branch in the tree. In Figure 1-2-6, we saw an example of a branch coming out of revision 1.3. Once a branch has been created, you can create new revisions on that branch, just as you can create new revisions on the main line of the tree. For instance, Figure 1-2-7 shows that revision 1.3.1.2 has been created from 1.3.1.1.

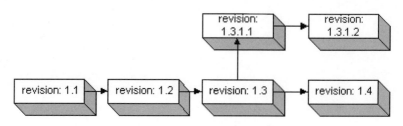

Figure 1-2-7   An example of a revision created from a branch

A numbering scheme for storage of the different revisions of files is the central element of artifact version control. You now have the ability to retrieve any of the stored revisions from the system.

To help with the disk space problem, most configuration management systems do not store each revision separately. Rather, they generally store deltas, or change information, that allow them to recreate one revision from another. For instance, complete information might be stored for revision 1.1 of the file, hello.c. Then, when it is time to store revision 1.2, only the differences between revision 1.1 and revision 1.2 are stored.

Configuration management systems also help with artifact version tracking. They record relationships between versions (e.g., the order the versions were created and how two versions differ from each other), and document how files have changed over time. Most configuration management systems provide some sort of mechanism to automatically store the version identifier of a file within the contents of the file, as we will see in the next topic, Artifact Identification. They also allow you to determine who created a particular version and when it was created. All of this information can help you find out how and when that elusive bug slipped into your code.

Artifact Identification

> Ben and Amanda are in charge of creating and maintaining their organization's internal Web documents – documents such as the organizational chart, project status sheets, sales information, etc. Most of the time, people want to look at the latest versions of the documents. However, sometimes they need to review historical information and thus want to look at and compare older versions. In any case, something that is very important to many people reading the documents is knowing when they were last updated, and who is in charge of each document (in case changes need to be made to a document). Ben and Amanda recently started using a configuration management system to archive their Web documents and keep track of older versions of the documents. But they are still entering the author and date of each version of the documents by hand, and many times they accidentally enter it wrong, causing themselves endless grief and time in going back to straighten it all out. . . .

Although Ben and Amanda got part of their problem under control by using a configuration management system, they still were having to enter data in "by hand" to describe each document they created in the document itself. What they didn't realize is that many configuration management systems provide a method for self-identification of documents. In order to provide this self-identification, a specific string (commonly called a *keyword*) can be embedded in a file that is then stored in the configuration management system. Whenever a specific version of the file is retrieved from the system, the string is replaced with the value for that particular version.[3] If the file is a document, this value then becomes part of the document. If the file is a source file, the value can be used in a comment, or even assigned to a program variable and used within the program. This can be useful if you want to print out the versions of each of the source files used to create a particular instance of the program.

The exact information that you can embed in a file depends on the configuration management system that you use. Also, the format of the keyword varies with the system that you choose. Some common keyword values used by almost all of the tools include:

- Author—the id of the person who checked in the version
- Date—the date the version was checked in (often both a date and a time can be given)
- Revision—the revision number for this particular version
- Source—the pathname to the file
- Log—a comment the author gave describing why this particular version of the file was created

Change Control and Coordination

The Alpha team designs sales order-tracking software. All of the software is stored in a directory on a machine accessible by all of the Alpha developers. Each of the developers owns some of the source files and expects that other developers will not mess with files that they do not own. Three files exist that all of the developers need to modify at one time or another, however. In order to manage the changes made to these three files, the Alpha team has developed the soda can system. The team has three different soda cans—a Coke, a Pepsi, and a Sprite. When a developer needs to make a change to the first of the three common files, she first must find the Coke can. Only the person holding the Coke can is authorized to make changes to the first file (the Pepsi and Sprite cans are needed to modify the second and third files). Although the system has worked better than no system, the developers have found that they waste a lot of time looking for the correct can and negotiating over its possession. Also, late at night, developers often sneak in

---

3. Yes, you can indicate that you don't want the string replaced with the value, if what you really wanted was the actual string in the file.

changes without getting the can, because they often think they are the only one who could possibly be working. And to top it off, one night, the system almost fell apart when someone in a sleep- and schedule-induced state of confusion drank the Coke!

Earlier in this chapter, we talked about artifact versioning. We didn't talk about how the configuration management system controls and tracks the creation of the various revisions of files from different team members. The model used by most systems is the check-out/check-in model, similar in principle to the model used by the Alpha team.

In the check-out/check-in model, files are stored in a central location. Users can either work directly with files in this central location, or, more commonly, each user can have a personal workspace with copies of the files. Before a user can modify a file, he or she must check out the file (i.e., gain possession of the soda can for that file). The action of checking out the file will put a lock on the file and provide the user with a writeable (modifiable) version of the file. After the user is finished with the modification, the file is checked back in (i.e., the user relinquishes control of the file's soda can). The action of checking in the file will create a new revision of the file and remove the lock, thus allowing other users access to the file.

The check-out/check-in model provides change control by allowing controlled access to the files managed by the system. For teams of developers, it provides an automated method to make sure users are not accidentally removing their colleagues' changes. For the single developer, it provides the ability to track the changes made to a file (e.g., if the developer has several bugs to fix, she may want to have each fix made in a different version of the file to keep the fixes as independent as possible).

Two users, Chris and Pat, are working on the same project. They both want to work on the same file (see Figure 1-2-8).

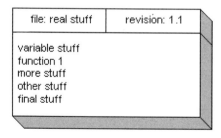

Figure 1-2-8   The file that Chris and Pat both want to work on

Figure 1-2-9 shows how they both copy the file to their own personal workspaces without checking to see if anyone is accessing the files.

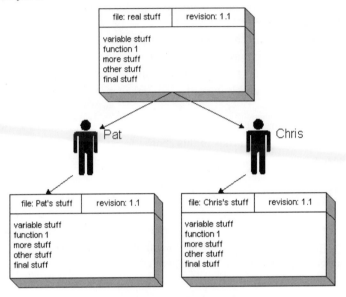

Figure 1-2-9   Chris and Pat start down the road to ruin. . . .

Pat adds a new function to the file (see Figure 1-2-10).

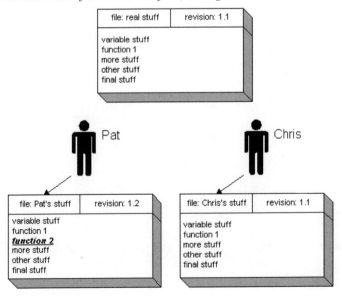

Figure 1-2-10   Pat adds a function

Pat then copies the changed file back to the central location as you see in Figure 1-2-11.

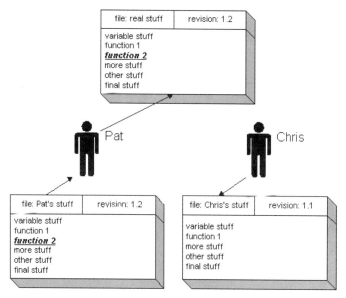

Figure 1-2-11   Pat puts the file back in the central location

Meanwhile, Chris deletes a no-longer-used function (see Figure 1-2-12).

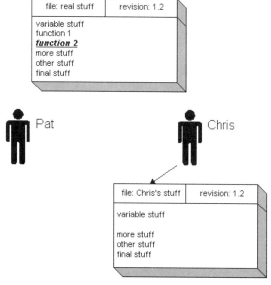

Figure 1-2-12   Chris deletes the function

Chris then copies the changed file back to the central location (see Figure 1-2-13). When Chris copies this file, this action erases the changes that Pat had made to the file, because Chris's version did not have the new function.

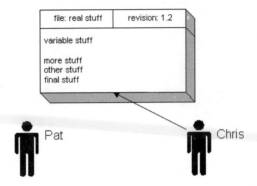

Figure 1-2-13   Figure 1-2-13: Chris overwrites Pat's work

If Pat had locked the file before making the change, Chris would not have copied the file until Pat's change was in place.

The check-out/check-in model is often used to control and track the changes made to a file. For instance, if you are fixing defects, you might want to check out a file, make a defect fix, and then check the file back into your configuration management system. This approach keeps each of the fixes easily separable from the others. Then, if you later find out that you really didn't fix a defect, you know exactly where to look for it. This capability is useful for both team and individual development situations.

Along with the actual information stored in the file, most configuration management systems also store information about the revision, such as when it was created, who created it, and author comments (hopefully indicating why the new revision was created). This additional information allows you to easily track the changes made to files stored in your configuration management system. Thus, when you need to figure out why you (or someone else) changed a file, you can just look at the comments instead of analyzing all of the changes. The information can also help you figure out which revision of a file you care about, without hunting through each of the revisions individually.

Grouping

Mary-Sue is the support programmer for the research station on the Galapagos Islands. The users of the software are not programmers and are actually pretty much computer illiterate. Thus, Mary-Sue developed a collection of standard graphical front-ends and common routines so that the various pieces of software operated in at least a similar fashion. Last year Mary-Sue was working on tracking the mating habits of the giant horned tortoise, whereas this year she is tracking the migration paths of iguanas. Much of her iguana software is similar to what she used for the tortoises, so she made several changes to the tortoise software to create the iguana version. Today, she got an urgent call—an error in one of the statistical calculations used in the tortoise tracking software needs to be fixed today. The only problem is that her current version of the software isn't in a state to be sent out and she has no idea what versions of each file were used last year!

We have talked about how a file is modified over time and how the modifications are preserved in the configuration management system. We saw how to create new versions of a file, both on the main line and on branches, and got a quick glimpse of a simple version numbering scheme.

Usually components are logically grouped together into a composite that represents the finished program. Just as each component can be versioned, versioning these groups of components is desirable, as is keeping track of variants at this level. This grouping is generally accomplished using a concept calling *tagging*. A *tag* is a unique name given to a revision of a file. You can use the tag instead of the sometimes long revision number to access the named revision of a file.

Larry is developing some new code. As Figure 1-2-14 shows, he uses the tag Release 1 *to mark the version of each source file used in the first release of the new code.*

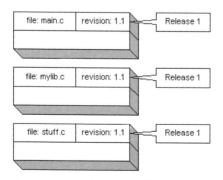

Figure 1-2-14   Larry's original files tagged for Release 1

Then Larry makes some changes and comes up with a new release. In this process, he has replaced `mylib.c` *with* `newlib.c`. *He has also made changes and come up with a new revision of* `stuff.c`. *The main program,* `main.c`, *is exactly the same (see Figure 1-2-15).*

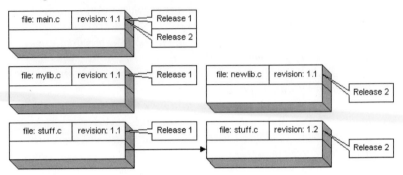

Figure 1-2-15   Larry's files tagged for the two releases

Now, when Larry wants to recreate the first release, he just needs to access the version of each file that is marked with the tag Release 1.

Most configuration management systems support this grouping and tagging ability. This is much easier than remembering the version number of each file that went into the release and accessing them individually.

Group version control is similar to artifact version control. You have not only the ability to retrieve a revision of any one file, but also the ability to retrieve a unique revision of a group of files. Tagging also helps with group version tracking. You can determine who made changes, as well as when and why, to different files that make up the group.

Build

Bobby develops custom software for running FM radio stations. He needs to take into account four major brands of station control hardware when constructing software. In addition to the different hardware, he also is continually adding new features in the new versions he releases. Bobby is going to the annual NAB (National Association of Broadcasters) meeting in Las Vegas. He is working feverishly to get his next release ready for NAB. He goes through and runs his automated build scripts on the four variations of his new release. When he arrives at the show, the software for the Namaguchi controller doesn't work. Fortunately, it is the least popular of the controllers. When he gets back, he discovers that his build script for the Namaguchi system was using the libraries for the Ronkiput 5000 controller.

Although not all of the development you may do involves a compilation step, all software development includes the concept of constructing or coalescing the components into the completed deliverable program. Examples other than building source code into a program include building help files or publishing Web documentation. This can be done by using a batch file, typing commands "by hand," or some other method. No matter what form the compilation step takes, we refer to it as "building" your program. A "build script" is any batch file or other method that helps automate your build process. Some of the common build problems include building using the wrong revisions of files (and not knowing it), and being unable to reproduce built programs because you aren't sure how they were built.

Many of the larger, more sophisticated configuration management systems provide very good support for the build process and help alleviate these problems. They help in three areas: preparing for the build, executing the build, and tracking the build. They help in preparing for the build by assuring that the correct revision of each file needed for the build is available for building. They help in executing the build by running an automated build script to execute each step necessary in the process. They help in tracking the build by recording each element that went into the build. Many record the version number of each file used in the build, the version number of the build script, and what tools (e.g., a C compiler) were used in the build process.

Willy is getting ready to create a release of his program (Figure 1-2-16 shows his files). Willy does use an automated script but not an automated tool (like make). He is developing on a PC and is using the GNU[4] editor, compiler, and debugger. He uses the RCS configuration management tools from the set of GNU tools. His BUILD.BAT *script does the job, most of the time. The script includes the following lines:*

```
cd c:\project
cc -v -g -o gui_lib.o gui_lib.c
cc -v -g -o myio_lib.o myio_lib.c
cc -v -g -o sysit.exe main.c
```

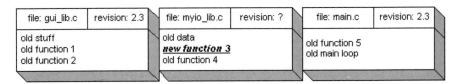

file: gui_lib.c	revision: 2.3	file: myio_lib.c	revision: 2.3	file: main.c	revision: 2.3
old stuff old function 1 old function 2		old data old function 3 old function 4		old function 5 old main loop	

Figure 1-2-16   Contents of Willy's files

This method of building is okay most of the time, but Willy made some recent changes to his source files (see Figure 1-2-17) without checking them in.

file: gui_lib.c	revision: 2.3	file: myio_lib.c	revision: ?	file: main.c	revision: 2.3
old stuff old function 1 old function 2		old data ***new function 3*** old function 4		old function 5 old main loop	

Figure 1-2-17   Willy makes some quick changes

---

4.   If you are not aware of the set of development tools from the Free Software Foundation (also referred to as the GNU tools), they are worth checking out. They are free, full featured, and include source.

The build went just fine (see Figure 1-2-18), since it was just pick-
ing up the local files in the project directory.

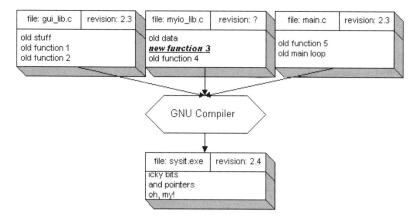

Figure 1-2-18   Willy runs his build script

Willy went on vacation for a week. After he came back, he made
some additional changes and then checked the files in under a new
version (see Figure 1-2-19).

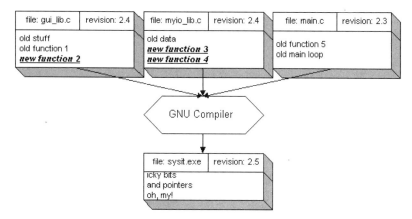

Figure 1-2-19   Willy builds a new release

He is now missing the intermediate set of revisions and is unable
to recover that release.

Most of the configuration management systems we are going to talk about
don't provide much automated build support. Still, these systems can help with your
build process. We'll get to that possibility later in the book.

What Next?

What Are Your Real Needs?

We have covered the basic elements of configuration management. Now, stop and think for a few minutes about what your fundamental software development problems and issues are. This way, you have your specific problems in mind as you learn more about the various topics. And, as you proceed, you can come back and refine, extend, or enhance your software configuration management techniques. This set of questions may help you characterize your situation.

- From an overall point of view, what are the major problems, issues, or events that you have encountered during your software development?
- What problems, issues, or events have you had with the various parts of your development environment?
  - System hardware
  - Operating system
  - System configuration
  - Development tools
  - Applications
  - Libraries
- What problems, issues, or events have you had with people in the development process—either yourself or team members (or even family members and pets)?
- What problems, issues, or events have you had with the various development artifacts in your software development?
  - Source files

- Binary files
- Data files
- Graphics
- Icon bitmaps
- User documents
- Help files
- Tests
- Design documents
- Other . . .

Integrating Configuration Management with Your Daily Development

Another thing to think about is how to integrate your configuration management steps with your daily development steps. Depending on your tools and approach, much of the configuration management can be automatic and relatively painless. However, you can also do things in a fairly manual fashion, if you desire.

Normally, you will change how you do your configuration management over time. You will be learning the basic approaches, learning more about one or more tools, and changing how you do software development. Thus, not everything you do at the start is going to be correct. Don't get worried or bothered by this. The best thing to do is to go ahead and get started. The great thing about starting with configuration management is that, in general, you don't lose by getting started. Even if you have laid out your files and versions in a nonoptimal (i.e., stupid) fashion, you can still get at the information and reconstruct it later into a different (and hopefully) better model.

Changing models and tools as you go can be a challenge. Many times, in the larger firms, they stay with a moderately ineffective tool just because of the transition costs. However, for you as an individual or as part of a small team, this transition is really not bad. Most of the transition problems faced by the large firms are due to people and sociological aspects. As the team size scales down, these problems are much less severe.

Where Do I Go Now?

Hopefully, you now have a good handle on the basics and your needs. The real bottom line is to go ahead and get started.

One thing to think about as you get started is how deep you go when you start. This decision can be a tough trade-off of a minimalist (i.e., fast) start that may require additions later, versus a more complete start that may have you doing too much and keeping too much information and data (i.e., baggage). The best bet is to err slightly on the baggage side as you go. Gathering too much information should not get in your way, and going back and trying to reconstruct data or information that you need is almost always harder. You are the best judge of this trade-off, of course. If you have only a few problems—start simple. If you have a lot of things that are potential issues—start with a slightly more complex model.

The upcoming chapters will get you started. If you are primarily an individual developer (either at home or in an industrial or commercial setting), you should read Section 2, "Configuration Management for the Individual." If many of you work together on project artifacts, you should read Section 3, "Configuration Management for the Team." Note that even if you are the only developer on a team, but you still share development artifacts (for example, with a documentation person), you should probably read the team section. Reading through both the individual and team sections won't hurt, but unless you operate in both domains, it isn't necessary.

Before you jump to one section or the other, read Chapter 1-4. It recommends that you use RCS to experiment. Remember, although this subject isn't rocket science, you really should experiment with configuration management on something other than the only copy of your precious code!

What Tool Do
I Use to
Get Started?

Which Comes First . . .

You have many options for a configuration management tool. However, if you are new to the area (or mostly new), you need to get far enough into configuration management in order to know what you want and the issues you are going to face. Afterward, you will be able to choose a tool effectively. A classic chicken and egg problem: You need to use a tool before you can choose a tool.

What we will be doing is using a public domain tool—RCS[5] (the Revision Control System)—as our vehicle for describing the basics of configuration management. We recommend that you start with RCS as well. The discussion here will get you part of the way, but trying some of the examples and experimenting is worthwhile. Thus, using RCS is a reasonable thing to do for several reasons. First, since RCS is freeware, it is inexpensive (i.e., free). Second, it is available for your machine (PC or UNIX or whatever). Third, the basics of operation are the same for RCS as they are for almost all existing configuration management tools—i.e., you can scale up to the other tools without trouble. And fourth, we have provided it (for the PC) on the included CD-ROM.[6]

---

5.   We are using RCS version 5.7. If you use a different version, some of the commands may be slightly different – or give different results.
6.   RCS has drawbacks. The most painful one is that it is a command line tool. If you are running a Windows system, you will have to use a DOS window to access the RCS commands. This process makes incorporating RCS commands into scripts easy, but isn't that user-friendly in a Windows-oriented environment.

If you already have another tool or preference, don't feel compelled to use RCS. Most any tool should work as well as (or even better than) RCS. However, you should pay attention to terminology differences.

In the next two sections, we will come back to the topic of choosing a tool.

Installing RCS

The RCS tool is available on the enclosed CD-ROM. It includes the code, documentation, source code, and some examples. The CD is readable on most computers and operating systems (DOS, Windows 3.1, Windows 95, and Windows NT).

The general organization of the CD is a collection of directories for the various tools. Within each tool directory exist several directories—for sources and for precompiled executables. The **rcs** directory has a subdirectory **dos** for PC executables. Also, the **rcs-5.7** subdirectory exists for the original sources. (If you have a UNIX or LINUX system you can compile from these original sources.)

These instructions are for PC users running MS-DOS, Windows 3.1, Windows 95 or, Windows NT. To install the files from the CD-ROM to your hard drive, complete the following steps:

1	Insert the CD-ROM into your CD drive.

2	If you are using MS-DOS: Assuming that the CD-ROM drive is the **D:** drive, type the following DOS commands to examine the RCS directory:
	
	`CD D:\RCS`
	`DIR`
	
	If you are using Windows: Use File Manager or Windows Explorer to locate the CD and the RCS directory (at the top directory level on the CD).

3	Read the **rcs\readme** file on the CD, which contains the copyright information and a discussion of new features and defect fixes.
4	Read the **rcs\readme.txt** file on the CD (written by Marc Singer, the person who did this port to DOS). This file contains the specific DOS port information and a discussion of new features, suggestions, additional installation information, and defects.
5	Read the **rcs\rcs-5.7\rcs-5.7\man\Copying** file on the CD, which contains the "GNU General Public License," the legal copyright information.
6	Create a directory on your hard drive. I would recommend (assuming C: as your drive letter) **C:\rcs**. You can use something other than this, but be sure you set the appropriate path information (as described later). If you are using MS-DOS, execute the following command: `MKDIR C:\RCS`

7	Copy all the files on the CD under **rcs\dos\bin** into the directory on your hard drive. If you are using MS-DOS, execute the following command: `COPY D:\RCS\DOS\BIN\* `**`C:\RCS`**
8	Copy all the files on the CD under **rcs\dos\util** into the same directory on your hard drive. If you are using MS-DOS, execute the following command: `COPY D:\RCS\DOS\UTIL\* `**`C:\RCS`**
9	Edit your `autoexec.bat` file and add the following lines: `SET RCSBINPATH=`**`C:\RCS`** `SET RCSBIN=`**`C:\RCS`** `SET USER=`*`YourLoginName`* `SET TZ=`*`YourTimeZone`* If your system already has a USER and a TZ environment variable set, you do not need to add those here. MS-DOS (not running from Windows 95 or Windows NT) requires that files be of the *XXXXXXXX.yyy* form (filename and file type extension). This causes problems in RCS because of the addition of a **,v** suffix to filenames. So, if you are using MS-DOS, you should turn this name extension feature off by adding the following line to your `autoexec.bat` file: `SET RCSINIT=-x`
10	Edit your `autoexec.bat` file and add the RCS directory to your path by adding the following line to the file: `SET PATH=%PATH%;`**`C:\RCS`**
11	Reboot to allow the changes to take effect.

Be careful with RCS when it is installed with some other configuration management tools, because they may be based on RCS technology and commands. Similar commands may conflict, and you will end up using whichever command is found first in the path search.

After You Have Your Sea Legs . . .

As mentioned, you have many options for a configuration management tool. Once you are further along and better understand your issues and needs, you will be able to determine what tool suits you. Of course, you face the normal danger of staying with the first tool you use. However, as mentioned, RCS is a great foundation; many tools are actually based on an RCS foundation. Thus, even if you end up moving to a different tool, understanding the basics of RCS will come in handy. It should help speed your learning of other tools, and most tools provide a migration path from RCS. Chapter 2-6, "Choosing a Tool for Yourself," or Chapter 3-9, "Choosing a Tool for Your Team," describe the trade-offs and help in choosing a tool.

Configuration Management for the Individual

"... have I, perchance, not penned this story line? I feel, oft, that I have writ it anon." William Shakespeare, 1597, 1599, 1608, and 1615.

Introduction to Configuration Management for the Individual

Y ou are doing software development, on your own. You have determined that you need *software configuration management.* And because you aren't a large team, you don't have the configuration management tools, organizational support, and staffing for your software configuration management problems. You might write software for commercial sale, internal company use, or for your own use. Each of these situations has different characteristics and presents different levels of risk and effort for you. The expectation is that you do not have much money for tools.

This section takes you through the basics of configuration management. We start by presenting the configuration management model for the individual. Then we give information on how to choose a configuration management tool. Finally, we go through the basic operations and use models you are likely to need as you implement and use a configuration management system.

A Configuration Management Model for the individual

Generally, for the individual, the software development process is somewhat simplified. You will be working by yourself. Usually you will be working on a single machine (usually a reasonably healthy PC). But beyond this simplification of the general process, you have multiple pieces of code, multiple components in the code, and multiple libraries.

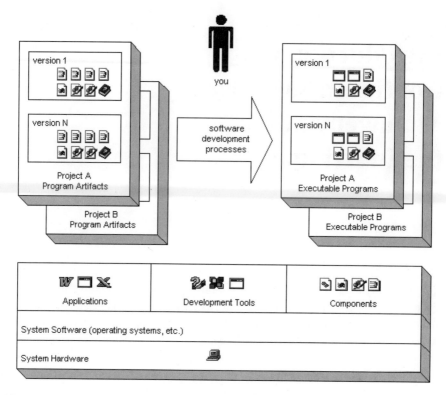

Figure 2-1-1　Configuration management model for the individual

What do you need to control and track what changes during development? Of course your code changes. *You* are also going to "change." You are going to be filling different roles (how many and how different depends on your development process). As mentioned previously, your tools, applications, and system software can and do change. Even though you probably don't want to version the full operating system (although that would be really handy!), you probably do want to version configuration files and the operating system version number.

Nightly Development Operations with RCS

$\mathbf{I}$n the rest of this section, we are going to follow our friend Ric[7] as he develops a nutrition analysis package using RCS. We start with the nightly operations—those that Ric performs on a daily (or nightly) basis as he develops his software. Then we look at the release operations and maintenance operations that Ric does on a periodic basis. Although we use RCS as our example system, the basic operations can be done using any of the configuration management systems—you just have to use the commands that are specific to the system you choose.

Ric has developed a nutrition analysis package that he sells primarily through local health clubs. He created the package on a 486 machine, running Windows 95, and has about 500 customers, with the number growing. He works on the software in his spare time, since he has a "real job"[8] that takes up most of his time.

Recently, he started working on a major modification to the software and was about halfway through when he had to go on a two-week business trip for the real job. When he returned, he took forever figuring out what he had changed already and what still needed to be done. It finally convinced him to give a configuration management system a try, and he has chosen RCS as the system to use, once he finishes up the changes in progress.

---

7. Ric has decided to spell his name without the 'k,' in order to save a byte each time his name is stored in a computer somewhere.
8. A "real job" is something that someone else pays you for; a "spare time job" is something you enjoy.

Artifacts

Any type of artifact, whether text or binary, can be stored in RCS. When an artifact (referred to as a *working file* in RCS terminology) is stored in the RCS system for the first time, a configuration management information file, called an RCS file is created for its storage. The RCS file contains all of the information necessary to re-create any of the versions of the file that have been created and stored in RCS. The RCS file is given the name *artifactname*,**v**. This **,v** suffix indicates a file is an RCS file containing versioned file information. Although the RCS system can store the RCS file in the same directory as the working file, we recommend that you store it in a subdirectory named **RCS**.

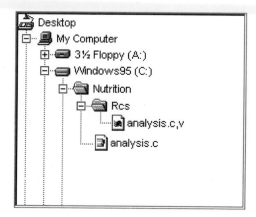

Figure 2-2-1   RCS directory

Figure 2-2-1 shows how the file **analysis.c** is stored in an RCS file, named **analysis.c,v**. We use the subdirectory **RCS** to store the RCS files in order to help keep the working environment cleaner and easier to understand and use.

What, you may ask, does *stored in the RCS system* really mean? RCS does not consist of or contain a central database. *Storing a file in RCS* merely creates an RCS ",v" file corresponding to the working file. All of the RCS files for a working directory are stored together, either in the RCS subdirectory or directly in the working directory. We recommend storing the files in the RCS subdirectory to minimize the clutter in your working directory. Storing the files together allows you to easily manage them collectively or individually.

RCS does not store each version of a working file separately, since this method is not very space-efficient. Only the most recent revision on the main line is stored intact. All other revisions are stored as *reverse deltas*. A *reverse delta* describes how to produce a previous revision from a revision that was created directly from one of them. This technique makes the retrieval of the latest revision fast, since that revision is stored intact by RCS.[9] This fact is good, since you will usually be working with the latest revision of files.

Note that the **,v** suffix is just fine in Windows 95 and Windows NT. However, it does present a problem on MS-DOS and Windows 3.1. The examples in this section use the **,v** suffix, but turning this suffix off is straightforward. The lack of a **,v** suffix requires the use of a subdirectory (otherwise the filenames would be in conflict). If you don't use the **,v** suffix, be sure to know which file you are looking at—your *work ing file* in your working directory or the *RCS file* in your RCS directory. If you aren't careful, you could destroy your *RCS file* and lose all of your previous versions.

> *Ric works with several different types of artifacts. He has C source and include files, data files containing nutrition information that are used by the program, a user manual (written using Microsoft Word), and a customer database built out of a spreadsheet (created using Lotus 1-2-3). For now, he has decided just to store the source and data files used by the program in RCS. He figures that once he has figured that out, he will be ready to store the user manual and spreadsheet in RCS as well.*

Putting Newly Created Files into RCS

Putting a new file into a configuration management system involves "checking in" the file. In RCS, you use the **ci** ("check in") command. This will create an RCS file for your working file, which contains one revision (the initial revision) of that file, along with a description about the file that you provide. If you are already working on a project (like Ric), the first thing you will want to do when you start using a configuration management system is to store all of your existing files in it. Then, as you create new files, you will store those into the system as well.

> *Before he starts, Ric creates a directory and stores a copy of his original files there, just in case he misconfigures something when he starts with the configuration management system. He lives by the philosophy that "just because you are paranoid doesn't mean they aren't out to get you." Three of the files Ric wants to store into RCS are:* `calories.c`, `graph.c`, *and* `food.h`. *All of these files are contained in the same directory. Because this is the first time Ric is using RCS, he first creates the RCS subdirectory to hold the RCS files:*

```
mkdir RCS
```

> *With the RCS subdirectory created, Ric's file structure now looks like Figure 2-2-2.*

---

9.   The storage mechanism for versions on branches is different, but we won't get into that here.

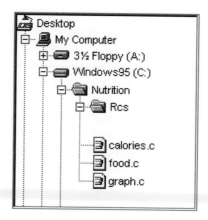

Figure 2-2-2   RCS directory creation

Again, the three files Ric wants to store into RCS are: calories.c, graph.c, and food.h. With the RCS subdirectory created, he can now use the ci command (executed from the Nutrition directory in a DOS window) to check them in:

```
ci -u calories.c
 RCS/calories.c,v <-- calories.c
 enter description, terminated with single '.' or end of file:
 NOTE: This is NOT the log message!
 >> This is the file that computes calorie counts of meals
 >> .

ci -u graph.c
 RCS/graph.c,v <-- graph.c
 enter description, terminated with single '.' or end of file:
 NOTE: This is NOT the log message!
 >> This is the file that graphs calories per day
 >> .

ci -u food.h
 RCS/food.h,v <-- food.h
 enter description, terminated with single '.' or end of file:
 NOTE: This is NOT the log message!
 >> This file stores common food with info on
 >> calories and serving sizes.
 >> .
```

With the three files checked in, Ric's file structure now looks like Figure 2-2-3.

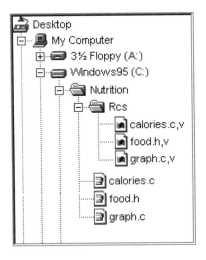

Figure 2-2-3   RCS initial check-in

With the directory creation and the initial check-in, Ric has created the initial versions of his files in RCS.

The **ci** command creates an RCS file for the given working file and stores it into the RCS subdirectory. Each RCS file contains an initial revision of its working file, which is numbered 1.1.[10] As new revisions are created, they will be numbered 1.2, 1.3, and so on. When you use the **ci** command to create a new RCS file, you are prompted for a description of the file. You can enter any text you want, ending it with a single period (.) on a line by itself. The **-u** option indicates that you want to keep a nonwriteable copy of the working file in your directory. If you don't use the **-u** option, the RCS file will be created, and the working file will be deleted. (Of course, you can get it back at any time because it is now stored in RCS. The caveat is that if you delete the configuration management files—the **,v** files in the RCS system—you won't be able to get any revision back, because they will all be gone. Remember that a configuration management system is not a backup system. You still need to back up the configuration management files!).

---

10.   This numbering scheme is the default used by RCS. If you really want to, you can choose another number for any revision of the file. This can be useful in certain instances; for example, if you want to re-sync the version numbers of each of your files before starting on a new release (e.g., number them all 2.0). In this chapter, we will stick with the default numbering scheme used by RCS.

.	More about the ci command[a]
The ci (checkin) command is used to create new files in RCS and to create new versions of existing files. The simplest invocation is **ci <filename>**.[b] This will check in the file—either creating a new RCS file with one revision, or adding a new revision to the existing RCS file for this working file—and remove the current working copy of the file. Some of the more useful command line options include:	
-l	Checks in the file, creating a new revision. Then checks out this new revision with a lock. Basically, this process stores your changes and then lets you keep on working, making more changes to the same file.
-u	Checks in the file, creating a new revision, and then checks out this new revision in read-only mode (no lock). Without options, your working copy of the file is deleted.
-r <rev>	Checks in the file and specifies a revision number to give the newly created revision. <rev> can be of the form: **<number>**, **.<number>**, or **<number>.<number>**. Assume your current checked out revision (and the revision at the top of the tree) is numbered **1.3**. Then a **<rev>** of **2** will create a new revision numbered **2.1**, a **<rev>** of **.5** will create a new revision numbered **1.5**, and a **<rev>** of **2.1** will create a new revision numbered **2.1**. The restriction on the numbers is that you cannot create a revision with a number lower than current revisions. Other, more complex forms of **<rev>** can be used, but we won't discuss them here.
-n <name>	Marks the new revision with the symbolic name **<name>**. **<name>** cannot currently be assigned to a revision of the file.
-N <name>	Marks the new revision with the symbolic name **<name>**. If **<name>** is currently assigned to a revision of the file, it will be moved to the new revision.

a.   In this and future tables, we will give a little more information about the options that can be
     given to the standard RCS commands. We are not covering all options, or all information on
     how to use the commands. We have included the man pages for RCS as an appendix, which go
     into much more detail.

b.   In all of the commands, you can give more than one filename, and the command will be exe-
     cuted for all files given.

Making a Change

Making a change to a file or set of files using a configuration management system is
really a three-step process:

- **Check-Out:** First, you get the correct version in your workspace of each file
  you are going to change. You do so by checking out the correct version of each
  file from the configuration management system.

- **Modify:** Second, you make the change (just like you would before you started using configuration management).
- **Check-In:** Third, you check in the changed files to your configuration management system.

In RCS, the **co** (check-out) command is used to check out files. Once you have made your changes to your files, you use the **ci** command to check the changes back into RCS.

The first change Ric is going to make to his software once he has all of the files checked into RCS, is to the file calories.c. He found that he wasn't computing the average calories burned based on weight and body fat percentage correctly. His customers were complaining about feeling really hungry when they tried to follow his guidelines!

Because Ric needs to make a change to the file, rather than just look at it, he needs a writeable copy of the file. Before he begins, calories.c is read-only and the directory structure looks like Figure 2-2-4.

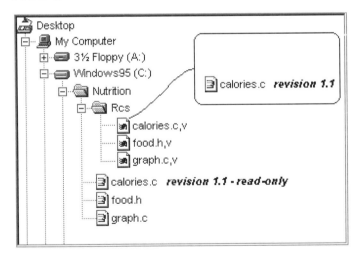

Figure 2-2-4   Structure before file check-out

*So the first thing he uses is the **co** command with the lock option (-l), to get a locked, writeable version of calories.c:*

```
co -l calories.c

RCS/calories.c,v --> calories.c
revision 1.1 (locked)
done
```

After doing the check-out, his directory structure looks like Figure 2-2-5.

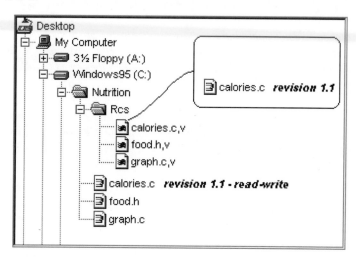

Figure 2-2-5   Structure after file check-out

Ric uses his normal source code editor to make modifications to the file (Ric personally likes the ed editor, but he is a little strange). Once he is satisfied with the change, he checks in his file:

```
ci -u calories.c

RCS/calories.c,v <-- calories.c
new revision: 1.2; previous revision: 1.1
enter log message, terminated with single '.' or end of file:
>> fixed the formula to compute average calories burned
>> .
```

Now his directory structure looks like Figure 2-2-6.

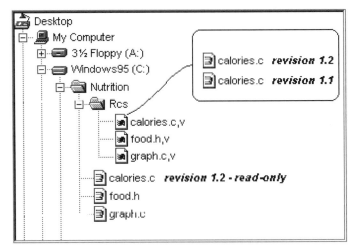

Figure 2-2-6   Structure after file check-in

The **co** command retrieves a specified revision of the RCS file and creates a working file for you to use. If you don't specify a revision, the revision retrieved is the default revision. Generally, the default revision is the one at the top of the revision tree, not on a branch. If you have not created a branch, this will be the most recent revision. If you are using branches, you may want to change the default revision using the **rcs** command, which is described later.

By default, RCS is set up to require that you *lock* a file before you make changes to it, although it can be set to not have this requirement. If you use the default setting, you have to use the **-l** option, to lock a file for modification. Although the lock requirement is not absolutely necessary for the single developer like yourself, we do recommend that you use it to help keep track of which files you have modified and to help avoid accidentally losing changes. In our examples, we assume that you are using the locking.

If a modifiable working file already exists when you perform the **co** command, RCS informs you that a writeable copy of the file exists and asks if you want to remove it. If you respond with a "yes," the working file will be overwritten and your changes will be lost.

The **ci** command used to check in changes operates differently from when it is used to initially check files into RCS. Instead of creating a new RCS file, it will create a new revision of your file in the existing RCS file. You will also be asked to enter a comment describing the change you made to the file. This comment will be kept with the new revision being created, giving you a log of what you changed in each of your files and why you made the changes. You can type as much text as you like in the comment—a line consisting of a single period (.) ends the check-in comment.

More about the co command	
The co (check-out) command creates a working copy of one revision of any RCS file. The simplest invocation is **co <filename>**. This will check out a read-only copy of the default version of the file and put it in the working directory. Some of the more useful command line options include:	
-l <rev>	Checks out a revision of the file with a lock. Basically, this creates a writeable copy of the file in your working directory, and marks the revision in the RCS file with a lock.
-r <rev>	Checks out a given revision of the file. **<rev>** can either be a revision number or a symbolic name. All of the numeric forms given under the **ci** command can be used. If you have marked a revision with a symbolic name, that symbolic name can be used for **<rev>**. Other, more complex forms of **<rev>** can be used that we won't discuss here.
-u <rev>	Same as the **-r** option, except that it unlocks the retrieved revision if it was locked by the caller. If no **<rev>** is given, this option will retrieve the revision locked by the caller if one exists, otherwise it retrieves the latest revision on the default branch.
-d <date>	Checks out a revision of the file based on the date. Basically, it checks out the latest revision on the selected branch whose check-in date is less than or equal to the date given. The date can be given in several forms: **4-Jan-1996**, **1996/03/17**, **1996-12-09 13:00:00**, etc.

Building Your Software

Building your software is the act of constructing or coalescing the components into the completed deliverable program. You will probably be doing two types of builds while developing your software—intermediate builds that you do as you are working on changes, and release builds that you use to create the releases of your software. Depending on how you work, you may do several intermediate builds a night, or you may only do one every once in a while. For instance, you may want to build each time you make a change (to make sure you don't have any syntax errors), and then run some tests on the change to see how things are going. Or you may work on several changes before doing a build, so you can catch several errors at once. You will probably do release builds less frequently, although usually you will end up doing more than one release build per release (because you find that last-minute error that just has to be fixed before you really release your program).

Most people these days use some sort of mechanism to help with their build process, rather than just typing commands one at a time to complete the build. Many systems (like Microsoft's Visual C++) try to insulate the users from the build process as much as possible—you create files to be used in the build, and the system takes care of building the project for you. Also, *makefiles* are used quite frequently to help with builds. Makefiles are files that contain rules for building a program—then a make program (of which several exist) is run using the makefile.

RCS and most of the more inexpensive, lower-end configuration management systems don't provide much additional help in the build process. You can still take advantage of the system to help execute and keep track of your builds.

> *Ric uses Microsoft's Visual C++ to build his software. When he is doing intermediate builds, he wants to use the latest files in his directory and he really doesn't care about keeping track of the intermediate builds. When he gets ready to do a release build, however, he does want a little help. He has created a batch file that will check out (read-only) the latest version of each file from RCS, and store the revision number of each file in another file he has named* buildinfo. *Then he again uses Visual C++ to build the software. If the build succeeds, he checks in the buildinfo file to RCS to keep the history of what went into the build.*

Most people will be more concerned with capturing information about release builds than they are about capturing information about intermediate builds. By using configuration management functions in a batch file or script, you can be quite flexible about what you do and the information you capture. One of the ways you can use a configuration management system to help with release builds is by setting up a script to check out the latest versions of each of the files you need to create the build. Then, if you keep track of what each of those versions is, you can check to make sure you have included everything you expected, and you can recreate the build later, if necessary. In Chapter 2-3, "Release Operations," we discuss grouping files, which will help make some of the capture of all of this information easier.

If you are using a makefile or another type of build script to help with your build process, you want to make sure you check that file into your configuration management system, and keep track of its version number as well. If you are using a system like Visual C++ to help with the builds, you want to keep track of which version of the system you are using, as well as any other attributes of the system that might change. You may also have environment settings that affect the results of your build. If so, you want to make sure these are set correctly when you create the build, and that the settings are captured. Any information that you capture should be stored in the configuration management system, so that you can retrieve it later.

If you have bigger build problems, at some point you may choose to look at one of the higher-end configuration management systems.

Identifying Versions

When you are using the configuration management system, checking files in and out, you can easily see what version of each file you are using. You can also use the system to see both when different revisions were checked in and the check-in comments you entered for each revision. If the files are somewhat removed from the configuration management system (e.g., you have used them to build a program or you have given your document files to someone else), easily getting that information about the particular revision that you have is harder.

One way to get around this problem is to embed the information directly in the files you are creating and using. This way, no matter where the files are, you have the information with them. RCS provides several *keywords* that you can embed in your files. When a particular revision of a file is checked out of the system, the keywords are expanded to the actual information for that revision.

Ric has a hidden option for his program that will print out the version of each data file used in his program. The data files contain calorie information, and he can update these files without recreating the program. In each of the data files, he has embedded the string: $Revision$ in a known location of the file, and when he executes his hidden option, the program reads the values from each of these strings.

The data files each contain a line like the following:

```
Revision = $Revision$
```

The program uses the following function to retrieve the revision information from each data file. (This function returns the value of an element stored in a data file—Ric uses it to return calorie information as well).

```
rev = get_data(Revision, data_file);
```

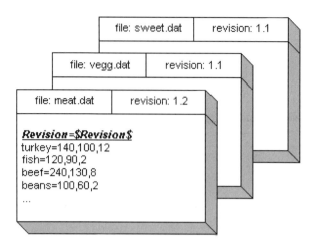

Figure 2-2-7   Embedded keywords in data files

RCS keywords are of this form: $*keyword*$*. When the file is checked out of RCS, you can indicate whether or not the keyword should be expanded. If the keyword should be expanded, the $*keyword*$* string will be replaced with the value of the keyword, enclosed in $ signs. If it should not be expanded, it will be left as is.

More about keywords	
RCS provides several keywords that can be embedded in your files. Options are available for each of the RCS commands that you can use to indicate what to do with the keywords when the command is executed.	
$Author$	The login name of the user who checked in this version of the file.
$Date$	The date and time this version of the file was checked in to the system.
$Header$	A string that contains the full pathname of the RCS file, the revision number, the date and time this version of the file was checked in, the author, the state, and the locker of the file (if it is locked). This is a consolidation of several other keywords, and a shortcut for providing all of that information.
Id	The same information as provided by $Header$, except that only the name of the RCS file (not the full path) is given.
$Locker$	The login name of the user who has the file locked, if it is locked. If the file is not locked, the string is empty.
Log	The check-in comment, entered by the author when the version was checked into RCS. The check-in comment is preceded by a header containing the RCS filename, the revision number, the author, and the date and time. Existing log messages are not replaced; rather the new message is appended to the existing ones. Thus, you can accumulate a complete change log in the source file—note that this can get quite long after a while, however.

More about keywords	
$Name$	The symbolic name used to check out the file, if a symbolic name was used.
$RCSfile$	The name of the RCS file without the full path.
$Revision$	The revision number of the given revision.
$Source$	The full pathname of the RCS file.
$State$	The state assigned to the given revision.[a]
-kkv	Generates keyword strings using the default form. The keyword $Revision$ is expanded to *$Revision: 1.2$* for revision 1.2, for example. The locker's name is inserted into the generated value for $Header$, Id, and $Locker$ only when the file is being locked (e.g., using ci -l). This form is the default for keyword expansion.
-kkvl	Like -kkv, except the locker's name will always be inserted if the given revision is locked.
-kk	Generates only the keyword names, not the values. The keyword $Revision$ will be left as $Revision$. This option is useful if you are checking for differences between two revisions, and don't care about differences in keywords. Log messages are still inserted for Log.
-ko	Generates the old keyword string that was present in the working file just before it was checked in. This is useful for binary files, in which you don't want to accidentally change a part of the file that just happened to look like a keyword.
-kv	Generates only the keyword values, not the names. The keyword $Revision$ will be expanded to *1.2* for revision 1.2, for example. Note, if you used this form on check-out, the keyword would be removed from the file and no further expansions could take place. Thus the option is not allowed when locking a file.

a.   We don't spend any time talking about state. This is another field in RCS that can be used to capture the state of the file. The default is Exp, for Experimental, but you can give any value you like to the state attribute. We tend to prefer symbolic names over state.

Identifying Changes

After you have been working with a file for hours (or days), you sometimes forget exactly what you have done to it. This lapse is especially a problem when you somehow can't get your program to compile no matter what you do, and of course *you* haven't changed anything that could possibly have any impact!

Usually, you will want to compare your working copy of a file to the revision you last saved in your configuration management system. Configuration management systems provide a command to allow you to do so, as well as to compare any two revisions of a file against each other. The command in RCS is called **rcsdiff**.

Ric made several changes to his calories.c file and now has created four revisions of the file. He has not worked on the file for a few days, though, and has forgotten exactly what changes he made. He first wants to see what is different between his working revision and the last revision he saved. Then he wants to go back a couple of revisions and see what he has changed since his last stable system. He starts by using the rcsdiff command to see what is different:

```
rcsdiff calories.c

 RCS file: RCS/calories.c,v
 retrieving revision 1.4
 diff -r1.4 calories.c
 3c3,4
 < tot_cal += this_cal
 --
 >
 > tot_cal = this_cal

rcsdiff -r 1.3 -r 1.4 calories.c

 RCS file: RCS/calories.c,v
 retrieving revision 1.3
 retrieving revision 1.4
 diff -r1.3 -r1.4 calories.c
 3c3
 < tot_cal = this_cal
 --
 > tot_cal -= this_cal
```

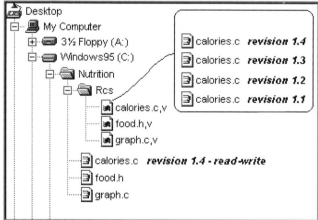

Figure 2-2-8   Structure with many revisions

The **rcsdiff** command with no options compares the working copy of the file specified with the default for the file (usually the revision last checked into the configuration management system, although if you are using branching it may be another revision). If you give one **-r <revnumber>** option, the comparison will be made between the working copy of the file and the revision with the given revision number. If you give two **-r <revnumber>** options, the comparison will be made between those two revisions of the file.

More about the rcsdiff command
The **rcsdiff** command compares two revisions of an RCS file, or the working copy of the file to a revision of the RCS file. The simplest invocation is **rcsdiff <filename>**. This will compare the working copy of the file to the default version of the file. Some of the more useful command line options include:

-r <rev>	If you give one **-r <rev>** option, it compares the current working copy of the file with the given revision. If you give two **-r <rev>** options, it compares those two revisions. All of the numeric and symbolic forms described under the **ci** and **co** commands can be used for the **<rev>** fields. Other, more complex forms of **<rev>** can be used that we won't discuss here.
-i	Ignore case when doing the comparison (treat upper- and lowercase the same). Thus, a difference between an 'a' and an 'A' would not be flagged.
-B	Ignore blank lines when doing the comparison.
-w	Ignore white space when doing the comparison. Thus, a difference between 'cat' and 'c at' would not be flagged.
-b	Ignore changes in amount of white space. Thus, if you changed two spaces to one, this difference would not be flagged.

Retrieving a Previous Version

Sometimes after you have made some changes to a file, you realize that you have really messed up! You look at the history of the file and perhaps use the **rcsdiff** command to see how the file has changed over time. Finally, you figure out that the best thing to do is just get back to where you were a few days ago. This situation is one in which a configuration management system can really help.

In order to get back to a previous revision of a file, you need to:

• Determine the number of the revision you want
• Check that revision of the file out of the configuration management system
• Check the file back into the configuration management system as the "latest" revision

Once Ric looks at what he has changed in the calories.c file, he re-alizes that he has made a big mistake. He really wants to get back to a revision he had a couple of months ago. He uses the rlog com-mand to determine exactly which revision he wants.

```
rlog calories.c
RCS file: RCS/calories.c
Working file: calories.c
head: 1.5
branch:
locks: strict
access list:
symbolic names:
keyword substitution: kv
total revisions: 5;selected revisions: 5
description:
----  ----------------------
revision 1.5
date: 1996/09/10 21:38:13; author:ric; state: Exp;
lines: +4-1
fixed the formula to compute average calories burned
--------------------------
revision 1.4
date: 1996/08/12 23:18:19; author:ric; state: Exp;
lines: +10-20
really fixed the problem with calories per pound for people over
300 lbs
--------------------------
revision 1.3
date: 1996/08/12 21:22:13; author: ric; state: Exp; lines: +30-3
fixed the problem with calories per pound for people over 300 lbs
--------------------------
revision 1.2
date: 1996/07/10 23:45:21; author: ric; state: Exp; lines: +6-0
better error messages when don't know calorie count
--------------------------
revision 1.1
date: 1996/07/8 22:45:18; author: ric; state: Exp;
Initial revision
```

At this point, his directory structure looks like Figure 2-2-9.

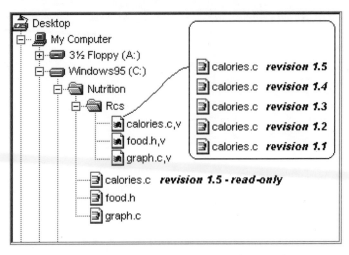

Figure 2-2-9   Structure with even more (wrong) revisions

Ric determines from the log (and the revision comments) that he wants to go back to revision 1.2. So he does a checkout:

```
co -l -r 1.2 calories.c
```

After the checkout, the directory structure looks like Figure 2-2-10.

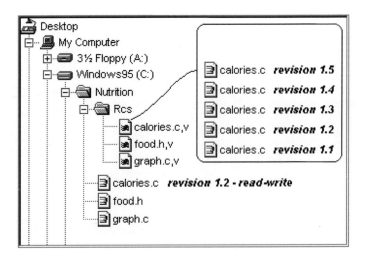

Figure 2-2-10   Structure after getting a previous revision

Now that he has a good version of his file, he makes his "real" change to it. When he checks it back into the system, he wants to make sure it is checked in at the top of the revision tree, not as a branch, so that he will get it by default the next time he checks out the file. Doing this procedure is kind of tricky. First, he has to unlock his current revision of the file. Then he locks the revision at the top of the tree (lock only—not check out, or his changes will be overwritten). Finally, he checks in his version of the file as the new top of the tree. He makes the following changes to bring about this goal:

```
rcs -u calories.c

 RCS file: calories.c,v
 1.2 unlocked
 done

rcs -l calories.c

 RCS file: calories.c,v
 1.5 locked
 done

ci -u calories.c

 RCS/calories.c,v <- calories.c
 new revision 1.6; previous revision 1.5
 enter log message, terminated with single '.' or end of file:
 >> got back good revision
 >> .
```

With the changes completed, the directory structure now looks like Figure 2-2-11.

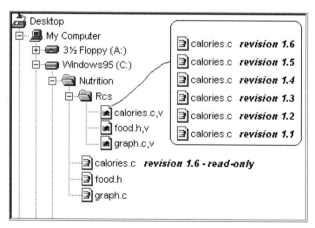

Figure 2-2-11   Structure after checking in modifications to a previous revision

To figure out the revision number of the revision you want, you need to look at the history of the file. The history includes revision numbers and check-in comments that you entered describing your changes. The history also includes the date and time you checked in each revision, and some other useful information. In RCS, use the **rlog** command to look at the history of a file. You might also want to use the difference command (**rcsdiff** in RCS) to see the exact changes you made in a particular revision of the file, especially if the check-in comments aren't very helpful.

Once you know what revision you want to check out, you once again use the check-out command to check out the desired revision. In RCS, all you have to do is provide an **-r** option to the **co** command, giving the revision number that you want to check out. For instance, the command **co -r 1.2 calories.c** will check out revision 1.2 of the file calories.c. Remember, when you check out a new revision of a file, it will overwrite the file in your working directory. Thus, any changes you had made in your working directory will be lost.

Because you checked out a version other than the version at the top of the revision tree, the default on check-in is to create a branch in the revision tree (see Figure 2-2-12).

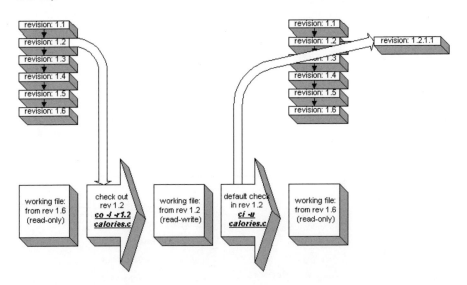

Figure 2-2-12   Default check-in of previous revision creates a branch

If you create a branch, the newly checked-in revision is not created at the top of the revision tree for the file. The next time you check out a file, unless you specify the revision number for the newly created revision, this is *not* the revision that will be checked out. As before, the revision that is checked out by default is the one at the top of the revision tree for the file.

In some cases, you don't want to create a branch. You really want to put the revision at the top of the revision tree, and make it the new default revision. The trick to this outcome is that you first have to lock the revision that is currently the top of the tree in order to create a new revision from it. So you first unlock the revision you have locked (don't delete the modified file though!), and then lock the revision at the top of the revision tree. Locking the file, rather than checking it out, leaves your working copy of the file. Then when you check it in, it will be created as the new top of tree revision (see Figure 2-2-13).

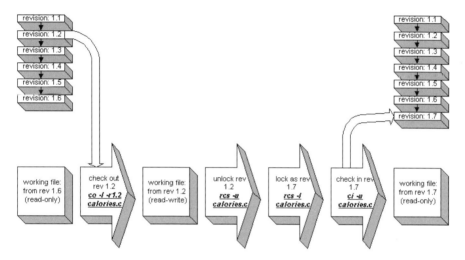

Figure 2-2-13   Specific revision check-in of previous revision does not create a branch

More about the rlog command	
The **rlog** command is used to print information about an RCS file or files. The simplest invocation is **rlog <filename>**, which will print all of the known information about the file. Some of the more useful command line options include:	
-L	Prints only information about files that have locks set. If you give the command **rlog -L *.***, you will get information only about files you have locked.
-R	Prints only the name of the RCS file. If you use this with the -L option, you get only the names of the files you have locked.
-r <revs>	Prints only information about the specified revisions. They can be specified as **<rev1>:<rev2>**, **:<rev>**, or **<rev>:**. The first form gives information about all revisions between **<rev1>** and **<rev2>**, inclusive. The second form gives information about revisions up to and including **<rev>**. The third form gives information about revisions later than and including **<rev>**. All of the numeric and symbolic forms described under the **ci** and **co** commands can be used for the **<rev>** field. Other more complex forms of **<rev>** can be used that we won't discuss here.

Release
Operations

O n a daily (or nightly) basis, you make your changes, merrily checking out and checking in files. At some points in time, however, you will want to create some sort of release of your software and distribute it to your customers.

Two important activities that are typical parts of release operations are marking all of the files used to create the release and writing release notes, which talk about what has changed since the last release. Configuration management helps with both of these activities.

Grouping Files

When you create a release, you want to keep track of the versions of each file that went into that release. You do this by marking the appropriate version of each file with a symbolic name or tag that is specific to the release you are creating. Once you have marked a version of a file with a symbolic name, you can use that symbolic name in other configuration management operations, such as checking in and out files, so you don't have to remember the specific version number of each file you need to access.

You can mark a version of a file with a symbolic name when you create the version (by checking it in), or you can mark it after the version has already been created and stored in the configuration management system.

*Ric has been working on his program for a few weeks and has fixed several defects. He is ready to package up another version to start selling to new customers. This version is the third that he has created for sale, and he has decided to use the symbolic name **rev3** to mark all of the versions of the files that went into the release. Because he has checked in all of the changes to RCS already, he is going to mark the last checked-in version of each file with his symbolic name, **rev3**. He executes the following command:*

```
rcs -nrev3: *.*
 RCS file: RCS/calories.c,v
 done
 RCS file: RCS/graph.c,v
 done
 RCS file: RCS/food.h,v
 done
```

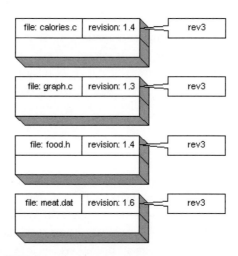

Figure 2-3-1   Files tagged with **rev3** symbolic name

As soon as he has marked all of the changes, however, he realizes that he had one more thing to do to the file, calories.c. So, he has to check out the file, make the change, and check in a new version of the file. Because he wants this last change to be part of his release, he needs to move the symbolic name on calories.c to the newly created version. He uses the following command:

```
co -l calories.c
 RCS/calories.c,v --> calories.c
 revision 1.4 (locked)
 done
```

Ric then makes the necessary changes to the calories.c file and checks it in, as follows:

```
ci -u -Nrev3 calories.c
 RCS/calories.c,v <-- calories.c
 new revision: 1.5; previous revision: 1.4
 enter log message, terminated with single '.' or end of
file:
 >> oops! Forgot fat notice!
 >> .
 done
```

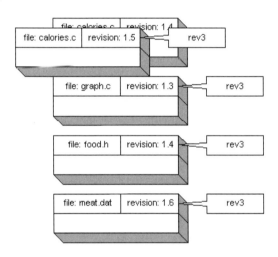

Figure 2-3-2 New **calories.c** tagged with **rev3** symbolic name

Symbolic names can really make your life easier if you have to deal with groups of files for any reason. When you first check in files, they all have the same version number (e.g., version 1.1). But as you change files over time, you will usually be working with different version numbers of each file. (Rarely will every file have to be changed exactly the same number of times.) If not for symbolic names, you would have to remember the version number you wanted for each file that you needed to group together. With symbolic names, all you have to remember is the symbolic name that stands for the release of the software you need to access.

Another thing to remember when grouping your files to mark a release: Your software often depends on other things on your system. Usually, you are using someone else's tools (e.g., Microsoft's Visual C++) to build your software or to create some of the artifacts that you use. Also, you may depend on some configuration files or variables set on your machine. As your machine environment changes over time, it might make reproducing a release very hard, even if you have marked all of your software files with a symbolic name. An easy way to capture and save the information about the tools you are using is to create a file in which you manually enter the data you need. Then you check this file in (and mark it with the symbolic name) along with your software. Another way you can capture information about configuration files, is to put those files under configuration management (again, making sure to mark them with appropriate symbolic names).

More about the rcs command	
The **rcs** command is used to change various attributes of an RCS file. Used without any options, the command does nothing. Some of the more useful command line options include:	
-l <rev>	Locks the revision numbered **<rev>**. You can use the same forms for **<rev>** as given under the **ci** and **co** commands.
-u <rev>	Unlocks the revision numbered **<rev>**. This is useful if you lock a file, make a bunch of changes, and then realize you don't want any of them. All you have to do is unlock the file, remove the working copy of the file, and start over. (The **co -u** command is another way you can do the same thing—this command will unlock the file, remove the working copy of the file, and check out the given revision.)
-L	Sets locking to strict, meaning you have to lock the file before checking in a new revision.
-U	Sets locking to nonstrict, meaning you don't have to have a lock before checking in a new revision. This is not recommended.
-n<name>:<rev>	Marks the given revision with the symbolic name **<name>**. If no **<rev>** is given, assigns **<name>** to the default revision. If no **:<rev>** is given, deletes the symbolic name. An error occurs if **<name>** is already assigned to a revision.
-N<name>:<rev>	Behaves the same as the -n option, except that if **<name>** is currently assigned to a different revision of the file, it will be moved to the given revision.
-b <rev>	Sets the default branch to **<rev>**. The default revision for RCS commands is usually the revision at the top of the revision tree. If you usually want to work with the last revision on a branch, using this option to set that revision to be the default revision is easier, rather than having to give the revision as an option to each RCS command.
-V	Prints the revision number for RCS. This option is available for all of the RCS commands.

Writing Release Notes

Often one of the things you want to include with a second (or third or fourth or . . .) release of a software program is a description of what has changed since the last release. Customers are interested in what is new with this release (i.e., why should they buy it?), what problems have been fixed, and any other changes you have made. Since you are the one that made all of the changes, you will likely remember most of what you have done. But, if it has been weeks or months (or even years) since your last release, some chance exists that you will forget one small detail that really should be included as part of your release notes.

One thing you can do to help you remember what you have changed is to make good use of the check-in comments. Then, to figure out what has changed, all you need to do is take a look at the check-in comments of your files and create the release notes from those. Another method you can use is to record the changes in a file as you make them, writing the release notes as you go. If you use this method, you can store the release note file in the configuration management system along with your other project files. You can group it (mark it with a symbolic name) along with the other files, so that you always know what version of the release notes goes with each version of the software.

Ric procrastinated writing release notes, but he was good about entering his check-in comments when he checked in files. Now that he is ready for a release, he needs to create the release notes. He wants to examine all of the check-in comments for his files since the last release, and build his release notes from those. He uses the following command:

```
rlog -rrev2:rev3 *.*

RCS file: RCS/calories.c
Working file: calories.c
head: 1.5
branch:
locks: strict
access list:
symbolic names:
rev1: 1.3
rev2: 1.5
keyword substitution: kv
total revisions: 5;selected revisions: 3
description:
---------------------------
revision 1.5
date: 1996/09/10 21:38:13; author:ric; state: Exp;
```

```
lines: +4-1
fixed the formula to compute average calories burned
----------------------------
revision 1.4
date: 1996/08/12 23:18:19; author:ric; state: Exp;
lines: +10-20
really fixed the problem with calories per pound for
people over 300 lbs
----------------------------
revision 1.3
date: 1996/08/12 21:22:13; author: ric; state: Exp;
lines: +30-3
fixed the problem with calories per pound for people over
300 lbs
----------------------------
```

  . . .

Of course, you could also take a look at the files themselves, to see exactly what has changed in them. We have seen how in Chapter 2-2, and sometimes you will want to take this approach. Generally, however, you don't want to pore over your source code, line by line, trying to determine from your customers' point of view what has changed in this release of your program. If you have put good comments in your files, you won't have to pore over the source code!

Maintenance Operations

Fixing Bugs in a Previous Release

Unfortunately, we don't know of any programs that are perfect the first time out. Unless you start over from scratch each time you work on a program, you will spend time finding and fixing defects after you have released a version of your software. Many times you can fix defects as part of your work for the next release of your software. Thus, you just incorporate the fix in with the other changes you are making to your source files. Other times, you need to fix a defect before your next scheduled release. If you are in the middle of a huge change to your software and an important customer calls in with a really big problem, you don't want to have to wait for a month or more before you can get the customer back up and running.

Finding a Defect

The first step in fixing a defect is to find it. Usually, the first thing to do to find the defect is to try out your latest version of the program to see if you can reproduce the defect. If you can, the next step is to start hunting through the code to figure out where it went wrong. If you can't, you want to go back to the version of the program that was being used when the defect was found, in order to track down the problem. In the last chapter (topic "Grouping Files"), we talked about how to group files. If you created a symbolic name that represents all of the files that were used to create your release, you can easily recreate that release and search for the defect.

After Ric released the third version of his program, he decided to rewrite many of the slower portions and add some better graphics capabilities. He was deep in the middle of this massive change when one of his biggest customers—a local health club—called in a panic. One of his calorie counting routines was subtracting when it should have been adding, and some of the health club members were gaining weight because of it and breaking all of the expensive machines. They obviously needed a fix right away. There is no way for Ric to wrap up all of the changes he has been making and give them new software, so he needs to recreate the **rev3** *version of the software and fix the defect there.*

First, Ric saves all of his current work by checking in all of the files he has been modifying.

```
ci *.*
```

Then, he checks out the **rev3** *versions of all of the files.*

```
co -rrev3 *.*
```

Once he has all of the files that went into making **rev3** *of his program, Ric's job is to find and fix the defect.*

Rebuilding a Fixed Release

Once you have fixed the defect, you want to be able to give your customers a new version of the software (otherwise, why would you have bothered?). Just like any release of your software, you want to keep track of what went into the release (so that if you find another problem the customer really needs fixed right away, you can add that fix to this version, instead of starting over with the original one). Thus, you want to re-group the files and add information to your release notes. We recommend that you mark the files with a symbolic name that gives you some information about why you created this release. For instance, you might want to name it *rev3_1*, if the original release was named *rev3* and this bug fix is the first you have made to that release.

After Ric has found and fixed his defect, he rebuilds the software and rushes a new copy over to the health club. He also marks each of the files he used in this release rev3_1, to help him remember that he created this version to fix the fat problem at the health club. Finally, he stores a few extra copies of the new version on floppy disks so that he can give updates to any of his other customers who stumble across the problem.

Merging Your Fix with Your Current Version

Many times, if you make a change in an old version of your software, you also want that change incorporated into the current version. Each file you changed as part of your defect fix needs to be updated in the current work you are doing, to include the defect fix information. Of course, you can't just check in the changed files in place of the current ones, or you will lose any of the changes that you have made since your last release. You instead need to *merge* the two versions of the files to come up with a version that includes the defect fix as well as any later changes you have made. You can use the **rcsmerge** command to accomplish this.

In order to merge two versions of a file, you start with a common ancestor revision. In many instances, you are merging the changes made on a branch with those made on the default revision tree. In these cases, the common ancestor is the revision from which the branch was derived. For instance, if you have a revision numbered 1.2.1.2 that you want to merge with the current default version, numbered 1.4, the common ancestor is revision 1.2. The merge determines the changes made from revision 1.2 (the ancestor revision) to revision 1.2.1.2 and from revision 1.2 to revision 1.4. If the changes are disjoint—they don't affect the same lines in the file—all changes are accepted. If the changes overlap, the merge cannot be completed automatically, and you have to determine what you want the final file to contain. Even in cases where the merge can complete automatically, however, you probably want to scan the changes to make sure they all make sense together.

Ric just changed one file in his fix—calories.c (of course). He had already made changes to this file as part of his new work, so when he checked it out, made the changes, and checked it back in, a branch was created. The revision checked in as part of the fix is numbered 1.7.1.1. The current default revision is numbered 1.9. Ric checks out the default revision and then executes the merge. The merge command takes two version numbers—the common ancestor version and the version to merge with the current working copy of the file.

```
co -l calories.c

 RCS/calories.c,v -->calories.c
 revision 1.9 (locked)
 done

rcsmerge -r1.7 -r1.7.1.1 calories.c

 RCS file: RCS/calories.c,v
 retrieving revision 1.7
 retrieving revision 1.7.1.1
 Merging differences between 1.7 and 1.7.1.1 into calories.c
```

In Ric's case, the changes were disjoint. The merge completed successfully, and both the changes from the fix and the changes he has been making in his new work are now included in the working copy of calories.c. (If the changes were not disjoint, the merge command would have issued a warning and Ric would have had to do the merge "by hand.") Ric wants to make sure the changes work together, however, so he uses the rcsdiff command to see how the file has changed:

```
rcsdiff calories.c

RCS file: RCS/calories.c,v
retrieving revision 1.9
diff -r1.9 calories.c
2c2
< tot_cals = new_cals
--
> tot_cals += new_cals

rcsdiff -r1.7.1.1 calories.c

RCS file: RCS/calories.c,v
retrieving revision 1.7.1.1
diff -r1.7.1.1 calories.c
15a15
> //I need to do something to speed this up!
```

Ric decides that the changes work fine together, so he checks in the modified, merged file.

The **rcsmerge** command merges two versions of a file. The first **-r** option to rcsmerge, which is required, specifies the common ancestor revision to use in the merge. The second **-r** option specifies the revision to merge with the current working copy of the file. If no working file exists, the **rcsmerge** command fails. The results are put in the working file (overwriting it!), unless you use the **-p** option (which will send the results to the standard output).

More about the rcsmerge command	
The **rcsmerge** command merges two different revisions of an RCS file. You must give one **-r** option, indicating the ancestor revision of the revisions to be merged. Usually, you also give a second **-r** option, indicating the revision to merge with the current working copy of the file. Given these two options, the command will merge the specified revisions and store the results in the working copy of the file. Some of the more useful command line options include:	
-r <rev>	The first **-r** option indicates the common ancestor revision. The second **-r** option indicates the revision to merge with the current working copy of the file. If the second **-r** option is not given, the default is the default revision. The **<rev>** can be any of the numeric or symbolic forms described under the **ci** and **co** commands.
-p	Rather than overwriting the working copy of the file with the merge results, the results are printed to the standard output.

Beyond the Basics

W e thought a few topics would be important to mention, without going into great depth. These are topics that will not be of interest to everyone—you can do a lot with a configuration management system without addressing any of these topics. These are some of the areas in which the various systems can be most differentiated. The topics we discuss here are projects, change management, and the copy-merge configuration management model.

Projects

We have discussed how to group files to better manage releases of products, or other events of interest. Some configuration management systems go even farther in grouping files: Many systems have the concept of a *project*. With projects, you don't just check a file into the configuration management system; rather, you *add it to the project*. Adding a file to a project stores the file in the configuration management system, and it also associates it with a particular project. The project model is useful if you are dealing with a large number of files across several directories or if you are creating more than one program or product.

Systems that support the project model usually have commands that allow you to work with projects, in addition to working with individual files. For example, in many systems you can "check out a project," creating copies of all of the files contained in that project in your local workspace. Projects usually have revisions (just like files). So usually each time you make any change to the project (e.g., check in a file, create a new file, etc.), the project revision changes. Also, you can tag the project when you are ready for a release, rather than tagging each individual file.

This capability effectively captures the current revision of each file used in the project. Then, if you ever need to get back, you just check out that particular revision of the project, and you get the correct version of each file used in the project.

For systems that don't have project support, you can mimic some of the ideas by storing all of the files for a project in one location. Although you won't have built-in capabilities for project support, you can use commands on groups of files to get a similar result. In general, though, if you are interested in project capabilities, your best bet is to use a system that supports them directly.

Change Management

Something that is important to many software development individuals and teams is the ability to track defects in their software and to easily know when and in which version a particular defect has been fixed. When you have a defect, you want to know:

- Is it fixed?
- If it is fixed, what files were modified to fix it (and what revisions were created as part of the fix)?
- If it is fixed, what release of your product contains the fix (or is it waiting to be released)?
- If it is not fixed, have you done anything yet to start fixing it (e.g., have any files been modified)?

Some configuration management systems now provide defect tracking support along with configuration management, which can help keep track of the information necessary to answer these types of questions. In some systems, if you check out a file as part of the work to fix a defect, that filename and revision are added to the information stored about the defect. Sometimes, the defect number or identity are also added to the check-in comments when the file is checked in, so that the reason for the change is kept with the file.

If you are very disciplined in your use of any configuration management system, you can annotate the check-in comments with this information, and you can store filenames and versions with the defect information that you manage. This approach can get to be a big pain quickly, however. Thus, if this is something that you would find useful, you might want to find a configuration management system that has the built-in capabilities already.

The Copy-Merge Configuration Management Model

We have used a "check-out/check-in" configuration management model in this book. In this model, if you want to make a change to a file, you lock the file, creating a modifiable version of the file for you to change. After you are finished with your change, you check in the file, creating a new revision in the configuration management system. This model is the one used by RCS and by many other configuration management systems.

Another configuration management model used by some systems is a *copy-merge* model. In this model, you don't lock files to make modifications to them. Rather, you check out files without locking them, and you can make modifications whenever you want. When you want to save a modification, you check in the file. If the file has not changed in the system since you checked it out, your changes will be stored to the system and a new revision for the file created, much like before. If, however, the file has changed in the system (e.g., a new revision has been created), a merge must take place before you can check in your changes.

For teams, the implications of the two models can make how the team functions together different, depending on the model used by the system they have chosen. For an individual, the implications don't matter as much. In the check-out/check-in model, seeing what files you have locked (and potentially changed) is easier when you get ready to do a backup or release. In the copy-merge model, you don't have to explicitly check out a file before changing it. Usually, you won't run into the problem of merging, since you are the only one changing files, so the check in will be the same as in the check-out/check-in model. Really, no "right" answer exists as to which model is better. If you are interested in the second model, the CVS system is a good system to examine, since it uses this model (and it's free!).

Choosing a Tool for Yourself

By now, you may be ready to choose your configuration management tool. First of all, don't be afraid of moving off or staying on RCS. What you have been going through is just a warmup. Let your needs and the characteristics of the tools determine which is the appropriate tool.

You have many options for a configuration management tool. An important question to think about is what are your real needs and boundary conditions. In Section 1, The Basics of Configuration Management, we introduced a series of questions that we suggested you look at and consider. It's time to come back to that and rethink some of your answers.

- From an overall point of view, what are the major problems, issues, or events that you have encountered doing your software development?
- What problems, issues, or events have you had with the various parts of your development environment?
  - ❏ System hardware
  - ❏ Operating system
  - ❏ System configuration
  - ❏ Development tools
  - ❏ Applications
  - ❏ Libraries
- What problems, issues, or events have you caused yourself during the development process?

- What problems, issues, or events have you had with the various development artifacts in your software development?
    - ❑ Source files
    - ❑ Binary files
    - ❑ Data files
    - ❑ Graphics
    - ❑ Icon bitmaps
    - ❑ User documents
    - ❑ Help files
    - ❑ Tests
    - ❑ Design documents
    - ❑ Other . . .

Now, having reconsidered some of the issues you are dealing with, what are the characteristics of your environment and what are your boundary conditions?

- How much do you want to spend?
    - ❑ Nothing   ($0)
    - ❑ A small amount   (<$100)
    - ❑ A moderate amount   ($100–$500)
    - ❑ Whatever it takes   (give us a call . . .)

- How technically competent are you?
    - ❑ Beginning
    - ❑ Moderate
    - ❑ Advanced

- How easy should the tool be to use?
    - ❑ Very easy   (need a graphical interface)
    - ❑ Moderately easy   (would like a graphical interface)
    - ❑ Not an issue   (command line/guru)

- How complex are your configuration management needs?
    - ❑ Very simple   (simple versioning)
    - ❑ Moderate   (like branching)
    - ❑ Very complex   (like multiple projects)

- What is your hardware configuration (assuming a single computer environment)?
    - CPU: _____
    - RAM size: _____
    - Hard drive size: _____
    - Operating System: _____ver___

- What is your software development environment?

    Language: _____

    Development tools: _____

- How critical is support to you and your software development?
    - ❑ Not critical   (you can deal with problems yourself or can get along without solutions)
    - ❑ Moderate   (want or need some help from time to time)
    - ❑ Critical   (you need solutions, probably in a timely fashion)

Given the answers to these key questions, you can now go to the tools section (Section 4) of the book and compare your characteristics with the tools' characteristics.

Characteristic	Heading Found Under
How much do you want to spend?	Tool comparisons: *Price*
What is your HW configuration?	Tool comparisons: *Platforms*
How critical is support?	Tool comparisons: *Support*
What is your SW environment?	Tool comparisons: *Bindings*
How technically competent are you?	Tool overviews: *Best suited for*
How easy should the tool be to use?	Tool overviews: *Best suited for*
How complex are your CM needs?	Tool overviews: *Best suited for*

The recommended approach is to presort the choices (and any other tools that you may find) based on price, hardware, and support needs. Note software bindings are a nice feature, but just because a tool does not have your development environment as a binding is not a good reason to remove it from the list. However, for two otherwise similar configuration management tools, having bindings can be a deciding factor. Next go through the set of tools in Chapter 4-2, look at the *Best suited for* portion of the specific tool overview, and see if the tool is reasonable for you based on your technical skills, ease of use, and problem complexity.

After you have reached this point, look at the tool-specific information and make sure that the tool is a reasonable match to your needs.

After You Have Narrowed Your Choices . . .

If possible, get an evaluation copy and use the tool or tools that interest you. We have made every attempt at providing useful and correct information. However, tools change and you should check the vendors' current releases. Also, these tools have a lot of features—more than we can cover in this book. Nothing can substitute actually looking at and using the real tool.

After You Have Made Your Choice . . .

As you start using a tool, be sure to pay attention to terminology differences. Most tools use similar terminology—but some of them can be fairly subtle—like version versus revision.

Recommendations for Projects and Problems

$\mathbf{I}$n this section, we have gone through the basic operations and use models you are likely to need as you implement and use the configuration management system in your environment. In addition to that information, we want to give a few recommendations on using a configuration management system to develop and manage projects, and to address potential problems you may encounter. This chapter is really a set of recommendations—not requirements. We know that every project is different and not all of the recommendations are applicable. Use the ones you like and don't worry about the rest.

How Do You Structure Your Projects?

Most configuration management systems do not have a detailed set of requirements regarding how you structure your projects, and how you name the files and directories that are part of those projects. Most of this section discusses things that you might consider about the structure of your projects, regardless of whether or not you use a configuration management system. Some of them you may have already thought about before, and you most likely already have a structure in place for your projects. Putting a configuration management system in place will cause you to make some changes, however, and it is an ideal time to reconsider what you have already done and to make changes as appropriate.

Following are some of our recommendations:

* *Create a root directory for all of your projects, with a subdirectory for each project below it.* Usually, you want to keep all of the files associated with a

project separate from everything else you store on your computer. If you are working on more than one project, you can more easily back up and share files across projects if you have a shared root directory for all of them. Even if you only have one project now, you might consider making a root directory, in case you expand what you are doing in the future. Once you have created a shared root directory for all of your projects, you usually want to create a separate subdirectory under that for each project. This subdirectory will be the root directory for a single project.

- *Use a hierarchical directory structure for each of your projects.* Once you have created a root directory for a project, you probably want several subdirectories under that root, in which you will logically group all of the files that belong to your project. For instance, if you are building one executable and a couple of libraries, you might want to put the source for each library in its own directory, and the source for the executable in a separate directory. You might find separating the documentation files from the source files easier as well. That way, when you are working on documentation, you only have to browse through the documentation files, and when you are working on source, you only have to browse through the source files. A good rule is: "When in doubt, add another level in the hierarchy." Many people start out putting too much in the top-level directory, and over time they end up with unnecessary top-level clutter. Adding another level in the hierarchy can help alleviate this situation.
- *Make sure each subdirectory contains a manageable set of files.* For instance, don't store 100 files in one directory!
- *If you share source or libraries among projects, create a subdirectory for the shared code directly under the root directory, rather than under one project.* Also, if you are creating something (a library, for instance) that you currently only use in one project, but think you may use several places in the future, we recommend creating a separate location for its files. This will make reuse of that code easier—it will be easier to find (since you won't have to remember which project you stored it with), and it should be easier to merge with all of your projects that need it.
- *Use names and a structure that are meaningful to you so that you can find things easily.* The separation into subdirectories will cause confusion if you find yourself hunting through all of the subdirectories to find the one file you need!
- *Reduce clutter!* Most of the configuration management systems you will deal with store the configuration management files either in the same directory as the working files or in a subdirectory below it. In order to reduce clutter, you should store the configuration management files in a subdirectory (if that capability is supported by your configuration management system), rather than in the same directory as your working files.

How Often Do You Check in Your Files?

Telling you how often to check in your files is like trying to tell you how often to do a save in an editor—no matter what we tell you, you will do what you want. Most people almost never save while editing, until they lose something. Then they start saving every minute or so. Gradually, they come to some sort of workable compromise. We have a feeling that the same sort of pattern will apply when trying to figure out how often to check in (i.e., save) your files to your configuration management system. Nevertheless, here are some suggestions to keep in mind:

- *If you are going to experiment with your files, check in everything first, so you can keep track of where you are.* Often, you will be involved in a change and realize that you aren't exactly sure how to proceed. So you start trying a little of this and a little of that, and pretty soon you realize that you have no idea what you are doing and you just want to go back to something you had before you started experimenting. If you had checked in the files, going back would be easy to do.

- *Check in meaningful chunks together, so that you generally have something that works together.* Most changes involve more than one file. If you are working on several changes over the course of a night, check in all files involved with the first change before you jump into the second change—even if you will be modifying some of the same files in the second change. The reason is that even if you screw up completely while working on the second change, you will at least have the first change completed and saved.

- *Check in before backing up.* We are going to talk about backup strategies next, but in general, you want to check in your changes before you do backups, in order to make sure the changes are included in your backup.

- *If you are going to be gone for three weeks, check in and back up!* This recommendation is an obligatory "good sense" one. Just like you wouldn't leave your editor open with five hours of work unsaved for a long period of time, don't leave your modified files unprotected (i.e., not checked in).

- *It never hurts to check in.* This recommendation is another obligatory "good sense" one. Even if you aren't sure if the changes you made are entirely correct or even complete, saving them by checking them in won't hurt. One of the beauties of the configuration management systems, as we have seen, is that you can get back to any previous version of your files easily. Most systems even allow you to "obsolete" specific versions if you really want to get rid of them forever (although in most cases, the disk space you save is not really worth the effort). Thus, checking in is even less destructive than saving in your editor—you can always go back![11]

What Files to Store

We have mainly focused on how to manage your source files in the configuration management system. Remember that you do need other information besides the source to re-create old versions of your projects. Also, for most people, source files aren't the only type of information that you create and need to manage. Once you get comfortable with a configuration management system, consider *all* types of information you may want to store there—not just source files. Although this list isn't comprehensive, it may help trigger your memory about something else you should store in the system:

- Tool versions (or the tools themselves), even if you didn't create them
- Accounting information
- Customer data
- Documentation
- System configuration files
- Makefiles or other batch files or scripts

Backup strategies

We really can't stress enough that a configuration management system is not a backup system. No matter how many times you check in a working file, if your disk crashes and you lose the configuration management file associated with it, your information will be gone. You probably (hopefully) already have some sort of backup strategy (you do backups, right?). But having a configuration management system will change that strategy somewhat.

We recommend that you just back up your configuration management files, and not the working files. If you check in before backing up, your configuration management files will contain all of the information found in the working files. If you lose your disk, you can re-create both the configuration management files and the working files from your backups, and yet, you have managed to keep your backups as small as possible[12].

---

11.   Of course, we realize that this recommendation contradicts the second recommendation (check in meaningful chunks . . .). Which one you use depends on the circumstances. If you are going to take weeks to create a meaningful chunk, don't wait to check in the pieces!

12.   This recommendation does assume that you check in as frequently as you back up. If this assumption is not the case, backing up just the configuration management files will not always get the latest changes. We do recommend that you check in all files before doing a backup, or at least back up very frequently so the amount you lose in a catastrophe is small.

If you have stored the configuration management files in their own subdirectories, you can just back up relatively easily the configuration management files.

Because the configuration management files include all of the historical information directly in the files, you won't need to keep several different versions of your backups (because from today's backup you can not only re-create what you had today, but you can also re-create what you had last week). Thus, although we do recommend that you keep a few of your last backups, you don't need to keep every single backup since the beginning of time. And, since you can recycle your backup disks or tapes more often, you should consider doing backups more often than before.

One caveat is that we do recommend keeping a backup of each real release you create. That way, if you need to get to it quickly, you don't have to rebuild everything from the master backups. Rather, you can just copy it off and you are ready to go.

System Errors

Most of the available configuration management systems are fairly good. Like all software, unfortunately, these tools have defects that can cause you trouble. If you are just getting started with a system and it doesn't seem to work well, you may have something misconfigured. Some common problems include:

- The PATH variable is not set correctly
- Other environment variables have not been set correctly
- Another tool installed on your system is causing the new tool to function incorrectly. Many of the configuration management systems use RCS as a base. These systems sometimes have utilities named with the same name as RCS utilities (e.g., co, ci, etc.). If you have installed RCS and the new system, you need to make sure the correct utility is in your PATH first. If it is not, an incorrect version of each utility might be called mistakenly, causing the system to malfunction.

If you have been using the system without problems for a while, it has probably been installed correctly. If you run into a problem in these cases, it might be harder to troubleshoot. If you are using a graphical user interface, you might try using the command line function to see if the error message is more informative. Sometimes, you might want to even check out the available documentation or online help! Also, news forums are dedicated to configuration management (see the Appendix for more information), in which you can pose questions.

Next Steps for the Individual . . .

Hopefully we have given you enough information about configuration management to help you understand how you can use it in your environment. You have several ways to proceed from here: You might want to learn more about RCS, you might want to review some of the other tools available, or you might want to just jump in and get started.

If you are interested in learning more about RCS, we have included some sample RCS files on the CD to help you with this. You can use these files to play around with RCS and the commands that we have described. This will give you a feel for how the system really works, and allow you to watch files changing over time. These files have different versions, check-in comments, branches, etc. The structure of the files is similar to files that have been stored in RCS for a while and have undergone various changes in that time. See Appendix A for instructions on how to install the sample files.

Once you have installed the files on your disk, you can practice with any of the commands we have described. For example, try doing some (or all) of the following:

- Show the history of a file
- Show the differences between two revisions of a file
- Take a look at the symbolic names that are defined on a file
- Check out the default version of a file
- Check out a particular version of a file, given by a revision number
- Check out a particular version of a file, given by a symbolic name
- Check in a file

We realize, however, that RCS is not the ideal system for everyone. One of its drawbacks is that it is a command line system, without a user-friendly interface. In this section, we discussed what to consider when choosing a tool. In Section 4, we describe some of the tools (both public domain and for sale) that are available to use. We have not done complete reviews of any of the tools, but do provide information on what they can and cannot do for you. We also include directions on how to get information on each of the tools.

Regardless of the tool and methods you choose, we wish you good luck in using configuration management in your late-night development situation!

Configuration Management for the Team

". . . you know, I preferred the way you had the pyramid yesterday . . ." Ramses the 5th, inventor of the vault, shortly before his entombment, 1637 B.C.

Introduction to Configuration Management for the Team

Y ou are a member of a team, doing software development. You have determined that you and your team need *software configuration management*. Hopefully your team members agree, since the usage of a configuration management system won't be very effective if all team members aren't using it. Chapter 3-2 talks about convincing your team to buy in if you do have some team members that are skeptical.

Using configuration management in a team is a little harder than if you were doing software development on your own—you really do need team agreement on which configuration management system to use, when to use it, and how to use it. The benefits, however, can be much greater than if you were doing development on your own, since your team development environment and projects are probably much more complex than for an individual.

Since you are the one reading this book, we assume that you are a team member who is driving or contributing to the decision to move to a configuration management system. You may need to support the implementation of the configuration management system in your team, and teach the other team members how to use it. (If you are one of the team members being taught, good job! Reading this book will help you, too!)

The rest of this section of the book describes a model for using configuration management in a team environment. We start by discussing both how to choose an appropriate configuration management tool for your team and methods for getting the rest of the team involved in the process. Then we go through the use model—discussing individual operations, team operations, and operations for building and releasing your products. Finally we give some recommendations for teams and team projects and talk about some common enhancements you might find useful.

Getting the Rest of the Team Involved with the Process

Software Is a Team Sport

Using a configuration management system within a development team is not easy, or very effective, if the whole team has not bought into it. Even if you have distinctly divided up your project—with the responsibilities of each team member well defined and separable, and with each team member "owning" their own files and their own pieces of the project—at some point you have to pull it all together. You have to be able to build the complete project, make sure all of your changes are compatible with everyone else's, back up all of the sources, etc. Although you could use configuration management in your own private workspace, without the rest of the team using it in a consistent manner, you won't see most of the benefits achievable from using it.

Who Is on the Team?

In making a move to a configuration management system you need to make the decisions to both acquire and use the software. Thus, two types of people may need to be convinced that this is a good idea—those that are part of the decision to acquire and support the configuration management system, and those that will be using the system once it is in place.

If you are interested in purchasing a commercial configuration management system, you probably have to convince someone to sign the check. If you have system administrators who help maintain and back up your systems, you probably need some sort of buy-in from them (or at least a promise to them that you will provide training). If you share code with other teams, you may need to change the way that sharing takes place (or convince them to use the same configuration management system as your team). Although these people probably won't be using the configuration management system on a daily basis, they can have an impact on the decision to acquire the system in the first place. Thus, their buy-in is important, and you need to understand and be able to address their concerns and questions.

You also need to understand and address the concerns and questions of those who will be using the system on a daily basis. They usually include more people than just those writing software. You might also have documentation writers, testers, and others who need to be able to access and update files that you plan on storing in the configuration management system. Thus, one of your first challenges is to determine whom you need to convince that configuration management is a necessary element in your development environment. Once you know whom to convince, you need to know how.

Convincing Skeptical Team Members

Our most important advice is to try it before you sell it.[13] Before you try to convince team members that you need configuration management, make sure you understand how you want to use it, what it can do for you in your unique situation, and how much it will cost.

We recommend that you go through this book (surprise, surprise) and follow the examples. Take notes about your development environment. Try to find examples of problems that have arisen and determine how configuration management could have helped alleviate those problems. Take a subset of your project files (or all of the files if the project is small) and put them into a configuration management system—this trial will help you determine how best to structure the files and what kinds of rules you will need to follow. Don't be afraid to experiment and don't lock yourself in too early—be willing to throw out all of your early attempts so that you can do something better before you get too far. Once you like how things are going, give a demo to team members to show them how easy it will be for them to use. Make sure you bring up specific examples of where configuration management can help all of you.

If you have some very skeptical team members, you might want to convince some of the more receptive members first. If your boss is convinced that all it will do is disrupt the schedule, you might want to get the rest of the developers on board first and then go to the boss as a team (again making sure you mention past problems that could have been avoided). In general, most managers with a software

---

13.   Otherwise, it could be like saying *"watch this"* before diving off the high dive and ending up doing a huge belly flop!

development background will probably appreciate the value of configuration management. If you have a manager with a different background, you might want to try to relate it to something they are familiar with, such as manufacturing specifications. Of course, we don't recommend trying to implement configuration management the week before an important release is supposed to be done. So find a time that is as good as possible for all (or at least most) of the team, and then give it a shot.

Daily Individual Development Operations with RCS

W e hope you can get the rest of the team on board or at least willing to give configuration management a try. In the next few chapters, we follow our team—Jerry, Elaine, Cosmo, and their manager, George—as they develop an order entry system for their company, "Stuff I Need, Inc.," using RCS as their configuration management system. We start with the daily operations—those that individual team members do as they develop their software, and those that they do as a team. Then we look at the release operations and maintenance operations that the team does on a periodic basis. Throughout, we will show how configuration management helps keep the team members in sync as they do both the daily and periodic operations. Although we use RCS as our example system, the basic operations can be done using any of the configuration management systems—you just have to use the commands that are specific to the system your team chooses.

The "Stuff I Need" company is a catalog company that sells leisure products to young middle- and upper-class professionals. The company has been using a very outdated order entry system for some time and it is causing problems for them. George, the manager of the order processing group, has decided that a new order entry system is needed. He has picked three of the developers in the software group—Jerry, Elaine, and Cosmo—to create the new system. Their plan is to use Microsoft's Visual C++ and Microsoft's Access running under Windows 95 for their development environment. George has repeatedly reminded them that the company is not a software com-pany, but it is a catalog company. Therefore,

*they won't have a bunch of money to spend to develop the system,
and they won't have a bunch of time. Rather, they need to get going
quickly and get it done quickly, too. After they have the design done
and jump into coding, Jerry quickly realizes that they need a better
method to manage this team development environment. They are
constantly overwriting each other's changes (by accident) and
having to spend much of their time in rework. Jerry has read something about configuration management, and now wants to give it a
try. He is going to experiment with RCS and if it is useful, he'll try
to get Elaine's and Cosmo's (and George's) buy-in to start using
it in the team.*

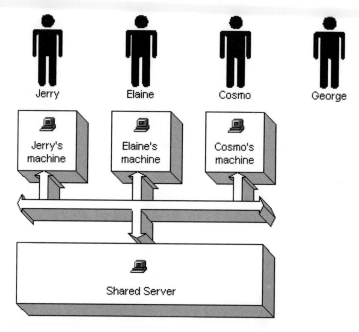

Figure 3-3-1   System model for the Stuff I Need company

Artifacts

Any type of artifact, whether text or binary, can be stored in RCS. When an artifact
(referred to as a *working file* in RCS terminology) is stored in the RCS system for
the first time, a configuration management information file, called an *RCS file* in the
RCS system, is created for its storage. The *RCS file* contains all of the information
necessary to re-create any of the versions of the file that have been created and
stored in RCS. The RCS file is given the name *artifactname*,**v**.

In a team environment, the RCS files need to be accessible to all team members. Generally, team members want private copies of the working files. By not shar-

ing working files, team members can each work individually, making necessary changes to the files, without affecting the other team members. So each team member will work in a private workspace. When a team member is ready to share changes, the files can be checked back into RCS so that other team members can access them.

RCS can store an RCS file in the same directory as its default working file or in a subdirectory named RCS (see Figure 3-3-2). Using the RCS subdirectory helps keep track of all of the RCS files and makes for a cleaner, easier-to-use environment.[14]

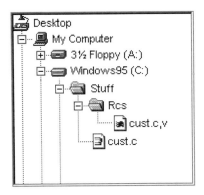

Figure 3-3-2   File **cust.c** and its RCS file **RCS/cust.c,v**

Figure 3-3-2 shows how the file **cust.c** is stored in an RCS file, named **cust.c,v**.

We have been talking about *storing files in the RCS system*. At this point, you might have the question, what does *stored in the RCS system* really mean? RCS does not consist of or contain a central database. *Storing a file in RCS* merely creates an RCS file for that working file. You can collect a set of RCS files together in an RCS subdirectory, which will allow them to be easily managed collectively or individually.

RCS does not store each version of a working file intact, since this method is not very space-efficient. Only the most recent revision on the main line is stored intact. All other revisions are stored as *reverse deltas*. A reverse delta has sufficient information to produce a previous revision from a revision that was created directly from it. This technique makes the retrieval of the latest revision fast, since that revision is stored intact by RCS.[15] This storage is good, since you are usually working with the latest revision of files.

---

14.   Since team members work in their own private workspaces, several copies of the working file can exist for each RCS file—at most one should be writeable, and the rest read-only.

15.   The storage mechanism for versions on branches is different, but we won't get into that here.

Jerry, Elaine, and Cosmo have divided the new order entry system into three major chunks: entry forms, database interfaces to the customer and inventory databases, and output order forms and invoices. The source files are Visual C++ and Access files. The three team members also are working on a manual for the operators who will have to use the system (in Microsoft Word) and are putting together some testing information. Jerry thinks that putting all shared information under configuration management control makes sense—although he is convinced that the team will need separate archive directories for source, user manual, and test information.

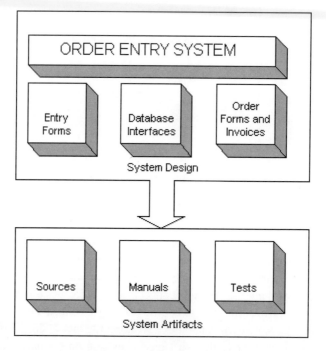

Figure 3-3-3   Stuff I Need order entry design and artifacts

Accessing the Archive Files

Generally in a team, one member is responsible for getting the configuration management system installed and running on everyone's machines (or at least coordinating those activities). Once this is done, each team member needs to get access to the files. Each team member should work in his or her own separate working directory on his or her own machine. This way they can test things out independently of what others are doing and control their working environments. Changes are coordinated through the configuration management system, as you will soon see.

The method you use to get access to the archive files depends on the operating system you are using. On any platform, you can give the complete pathname to the files stored in the archive directory. Or, in order to avoid typing, you can create a link to the RCS archive directory. The way you create the link varies across platforms. On UNIX platforms, you actually create a link from your working directory to the RCS archive directory. For example:

```
cd workingdir
ln -s RCS archivedir/RCS16
```

Once the link has been created, the RCS directory seems like a subdirectory of the working directory. This setup allows files to be created, accessed, and modified in RCS.

Although you can create links (or shortcuts) to directories in Windows 95 and in Windows NT, the link is not named RCS, but is given a different name (such as "Link to RCS"). Thus, you can't just create the link and use it directly. Instead, RCS provides another mechanism to specify the link. You create a file in your working directory named "RCS." In this file, you include a single line containing the pathname of the RCS archive directory. For example, the file c:\workingdir\rcs might contain:

```
c:\archivedir\RCS
```

Note that if you have subdirectories within your working directory, you need to create a file named RCS in each of the subdirectories to point to the appropriate RCS archive directory.

> *Jerry and his team have one PC that they are using to store all shared files, and to build the system as it is developed. The shared PC and all of the team PCs are running Windows 95. Jerry uses the Explorer tool to create three RCS directories on the shared system—one for the sources, one for the manual information, and one for the tests. He shares the directories using the Network Neighborhood so that all of the team members can access the archive files. He sets the G:/ drive on each team members' machine to point to the archive directories.*

---

16.   Note that this command may vary slightly depending on the version/type of UNIX you are using.

He then sets up a working directory on each of their machines, named c:\working. Within the c:\working directory, he creates a file named rcs containing the following line:

```
g:\sources\RCS
```

(They are starting out just working with the source files—when they start using the user manual and test files they will need to create working directories to correspond to those RCS archive directories and create the rcs files in each of those directories as well.)

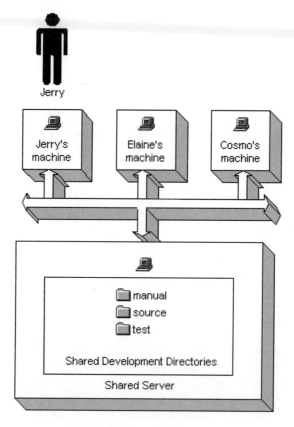

Figure 3-3-4   Stuff I Need shared directories structure

Putting Newly Created Files into RCS

Once your team has a shared archive directory, you want to store some files in it. Putting a new file into a configuration management system involves "checking in" the file. In RCS, you use the **ci** command (ci stands for "check-in"). Checking in a file creates an RCS file for the working file, which contains one revision (the initial revision) of that file, along with a description about the file that the person checking it in provides. If your team is already working on a project (like Jerry, Cosmo, and Elaine), the first thing you want to do when you start using a configuration management system is to get the existing files stored into the system. In a team, either you can have members store their own existing files into the system or you can designate one member to put all of the existing files into the system. Then, as the team creates new files, you (the team members) will store those into the system as well.

> *Jerry's part of the project is to work on the database output order forms and invoices. Elaine works on the entry forms, and Cosmo works on the database interfaces to the customer and inventory databases. Cosmo likes to see what Jerry and Elaine are doing with their forms, and to make modifications to them based on what he is doing in the database interfaces. Unfortunately, he usually does so without telling them and usually overwrites all of the work that they have done in the meantime. Jerry decides to check in his files to RCS first. Then the next time Cosmo overwrites one of Elaine's changes, he thinks he'll have an easy convert in her and be able to get her help in converting Cosmo to use RCS along with him. The directories (Jerry's working directory and the shared archive directory) looks like Figure 3-3-5 before Jerry creates his initial versions.*

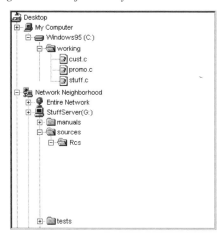

Figure 3-3-5   Shared directories before initial check-in

Jerry has three files to check in: cust.c, stuff.c, and promo.c. He is going to check these into the archive directory for the source files (g:\sources\RCS). Remember, he created the rcs file to point to that archive directory, so he doesn't have to include the full path in his RCS commands. He executes the RCS commands from his working directory in a DOS window:

```
cd c:\working
ci -u cust.c

  g:\sources\RCS\cust.c <-- cust.c
  enter description, terminated with single '.' or end of file:
  NOTE: This is NOT the log message!
  >> This file contains the customer entry form
  >> .

ci -u stuff.c

  g:\sources\RCS\stuff.c <-- stuff.c
  enter description, terminated with single '.' or end of file:
  NOTE: This is NOT the log message!
  >> This file contains the order entry form
  >> .

ci -u promo.c

  g:\sources\RCS\promo.c,v <-- promo.c
  enter description, terminated with single '.' or end of file:
  NOTE: This is NOT the log message!
  >> This file contains the promotion display form
  >> .
```

Now Jerry has created his initial versions of his files (see Figure 3-3-6).

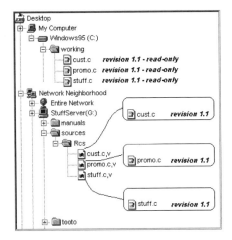

Figure 3-3-6   Shared directories after initial check-in

The **ci** command creates an RCS file for the given working fileworking file and stores it in the RCS subdirectory. Each RCS file contains an initial revision of its working file, which is numbered 1.1.[17] As new revisions are created, they are numbered 1.2, 1.3, and so on. When you use the **ci** command to create a new RCS file, you are prompted for a description of the file. You can enter any text you want, ending it with a single period (.) on a line by itself. The **-u** option indicates that you want to keep a read-only copy of the working file in your directory. If you don't use the -u option, the RCS file will be created, and the working file is deleted. (Of course, you can get it back at any time because it is now stored in RCS. The caveat is that if you delete the configuration management files—the **,v** files in the RCS system – you won't be able to get any revision back, because they will all be gone. Remember that a configuration management system is not a backup system. You still need to back up the configuration management files!)

---

17.   This numbering scheme is the default used by RCS. If you really want to, you can choose another number for any revision of the file. This can be useful in certain instances, for example, if you want to re-sync the version numbers of each of your files before starting on a new release (e.g., number them all 2.0). In this chapter, we stick with the default numbering scheme used by RCS.

More about the ci command[a]	
The ci (check-in) command creates new files in RCS and new versions of existing files. The simplest invocation is **ci <filename>**.[b] This checks in the file—either creating a new RCS file with one revision, or adding a new revision to the existing RCS file for this working file—and removes the current working copy of the file. Some of the more useful command line options include:	
-l	Checks in the file, creating a new revision. Then it checks out this new revision with a lock. Basically, this stores your changes and then lets you keep on working, making more changes to the same file.
-u	Checks in the file, creating a new revision, and then checks out this new revision in read-only mode (no lock). Without options, your working copy of the file is deleted.
-r <rev>	Checks in the file and specifies a revision number to give the newly created revision. <rev> can be of the form: **<number>**, **.<number>**, or **<number>.<number>**. Assume your current checked out revision (and the revision at the top of the tree) is numbered **1.3**. Then a **<rev>** of **2** creates a new revision numbered **2.1**, a **<rev>** of **.5** creates a new revision numbered **1.5**, and a **<rev>** of **2.1** creates a new revision numbered **2.1**. The restriction on the numbers is that you cannot create a revision with a number lower than current revisions. Other more complex forms of **<rev>** can be used that we won't discuss here.
-n <name>	Marks the new revision with the symbolic name **<name>**. **<name>** cannot currently be assigned to a revision of the file.
-N <name>	Marks the new revision with the symbolic name **<name>**. If **<name>** is currently assigned to a revision of the file, it is moved to the new revision.

a.   In these tables throughout the book, we give a little more information about the options that can be given to the standard RCS commands. We are not covering all options, or all information on how to use the commands. We have included the manual pages for RCS as Appendix B, which goes into much more detail.

b.   In all of the commands, you can give more than one filename and the command will be executed for all files given.

Any team member can create new files in the RCS system, as long as he or she has permission to write in the shared archive directory. Once a new file has been stored in the RCS system, it is available for other team members to access. When you are working in a team environment, you want to make sure that you use strict locking. Strict locking assures that only one person can have a file locked at one time. This mode is generally the default for all files checked into RCS. However, if necessary, you can use the **rcs** command to make sure that the files have strict locking set.

Jerry is a little paranoid. Even though he thinks that his files are created with strict locking turned on, he wants to make sure. Thus, once he has checked in his files, he uses the rcs command to assure that strict locking is set for his three files:

```
rcs -L cust.c

 RCS file: g:/sources/RCS/cust.c
 done

rcs -L stuff.c

 RCS file: g:/sources/RCS/stuff.c
 done

rcs -L promo.c

 RCS file: g:/sources/RCS/promo.c
 done
```

If Jerry had wanted to turn off strict locking, he would have used the -U parameter, rather than -L. Of course, Jerry would never turn it off (unless maybe Cosmo was on vacation).

More about the rcs command	
The **rcs** command changes various attributes of an RCS file. Used without any options, the command does nothing. Some of the more useful command line options include:	
-l <rev>	Locks the revision numbered **<rev>**. You can use the same forms for **<rev>** as given under the **ci** and **co** commands.
-u <rev>	Unlocks the revision numbered **<rev>**. This is useful if you lock a file, make a bunch of changes, and then realize you don't want any of them. All you have to do is unlock the file, remove the working copy of the file, and start over. If you unlock a revision that someone else has locked, this breaks their lock on the file—leaving it open for someone else to lock. Exercise this option with extreme care! (The **co -u** command can be used to unlock a file that you have locked—this command unlocks the file, removes the working copy of the file, and checks out the given revision.)
-L	Sets locking to strict, meaning you have to lock the file before checking in a new revision.
-U	Sets locking to non-strict, meaning you don't have to have a lock before checking in a new revision. We do not recommend this option.

More about the rcs command	
-n<name>:<rev>	Marks the given revision with the symbolic name **<name>**. If no **<rev>** is given, it assigns **<name>** to the default revision. If no **:<rev>** is given, it deletes the symbolic name. An error occurs if **<name>** is already assigned to a revision.
-N<name>:<rev>	Behaves the same as the -n option, except that if **<name>** is currently assigned to a different revision of the file, it is moved to the given revision.
-b <rev>	Sets the default branch to **<rev>**. The default revision for RCS commands is usually the revision at the top of the revision tree. If you usually want to work with the last revision on a branch, using this option to set that revision to be the default revision is easier than having to give the revision as an option to each RCS command.
-V	Prints the revision number for RCS. This option is available for all of the RCS commands.

Making a Change

Making a change to a file or set of files using a configuration management system is really a three-step process:

1. **Check Out:** First, you get the correct version in your workspace of each file you are going to change. You do so by checking out the correct version of each file from the configuration management system.
2. **Modify:** Second, you make the change (just like you would before you started using configuration management).
3. **Check In:** Third, you check in the changed files to your configuration management system.

In RCS, the **co** (check-out) command checks out files. Once you have made your changes to your files, you use the **ci** command to check the changes back into RCS.

> *Jerry is currently working on developing the entry form for customer data. This form includes fields for the customer's name, address, phone number, and credit card information, as well as a field to indicate if the customer has an unpaid balance or a bad credit history. Cosmo recently created a query interface to the database that would return the amount of any unpaid balance, and Jerry wants to make his form display that amount, rather than just indicating that the customer has an unpaid balance. The file he*

needs to change is cust.c. The file looks like Figure 3-3-7 before check-out.

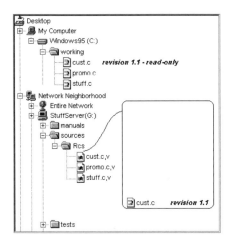

Figure 3-3-7   File **cust.c** prior to check-out

Jerry uses the co command to get a locked version of this file from the database:

```
co -l cust.c
```

```
g:/sources/RCS/cust.c --> cust.c
revision 1.1 (locked)
done
```

This command puts a working copy of cust.c in his current working directory. He uses Visual C++ to make the modifications to the file. He makes the balance flash red if it contains an unpaid amount. The file looks like Figure 3-3-8 during this time.

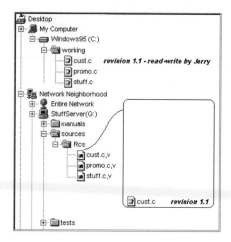

Figure 3-3-8   File **cust.c** during check-out

*Cosmo comes over while Jerry is working and badgers him until
he also adds a loud bell that sounds when the balance is over $100.
He figures he can take it out later. Once he is satisfied with the
change, he checks in his file:*

```
ci -u cust.c
```

```
g:/sources/RCS/cust.c <-- cust.c
new revision 1.2; previous revision 1.1
enter log message, terminated with single '.' or end of file:
>> Added a cool bell!
```

*The checked-in file appears in Figure 3-3-9. Now, he is done with
the change—waiting only for Cosmo to leave and forget about the
request.*

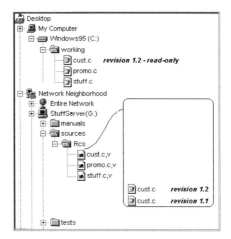

Figure 3-3-9   File **cust.c** after check-in

In RCS, the **co** (check-out) command checks out files. In a team environment, when you are making changes to a file, you want to make sure some other team member isn't changing it at the same time. Thus, you want to check out the file locked. This approach gives you a writeable version of the file. As long as you have strict locking turned on, it also prevents other team members from checking out the same file with a lock—although they can still check out an unlocked copy of the file, to be used in read-only mode.

The **co -l** command retrieves the latest revision of a file from the RCS file and creates a writeable working file for you to use. It also locks the file so that no one else can get a writeable version of the file while you are making your modifications.

Once you have made your changes to your files, you use the **ci** command to check the changes back into RCS.

The **ci** command that checks in changes operates differently from when it initially checks files into RCS. It creates a new revision of your file in the existing RCS file. It also asks you to enter a comment describing what you changed in the file. This comment is kept with the new revision being created, so you have a log of what you changed in each of your files, and why you made the changes. If you are still going to make modifications to the file, you can use the **-l** option with **ci**. This option checks in your changes, and then re-locks the file, so that you still have a writeable, modifiable version with which to work. Lots of times you might want to use this— for example, if you have several different areas in the file you want to change, you might want to check in each change separately so that you don't lose one change while you are working on another.

More about the co command
The co (check-out) command creates a working copy of one revision of any RCS file. The simplest invocation is **co \<filename\>**. This checks out a read-only version of the default version of the file and puts it in the working directory. Some of the more useful command line options include:

-l \<rev\>	Checks out a revision of the file with a lock. Basically, this creates a writeable copy of the file in your working directory, and marks the revision in the RCS file with a lock.
-r \<rev\>	Checks out a given revision of the file. **\<rev\>** can either be a revision number or a symbolic name. You can use all of the numeric forms given under the **ci** command. If you have marked a revision with a symbolic name, you can use that symbolic name for **\<rev\>**. Other more complex forms of **\<rev\>** can be used that we won't discuss here.
-u \<rev\>	Same as the **-r** option, except that it unlocks the retrieved revision if the caller locked it. If no **\<rev\>** is given, this option retrieves the revision that the caller locked if one exists; otherwise it retrieves the latest revision on the default branch.
-d \<date\>	Checks out a revision of the file based on the date. Basically, it checks out the latest revision on the selected branch whose check-in date is less than or equal to the date given. The date can be given in several forms: **4-Jan-1996, 1996/03/17, 1996-12-09 13:00:00**, etc.

Identifying Versions

When you are using the configuration management system, checking files in and out, you can easily see what version of each file you are using. You can also use the system to see when different revisions were checked in and the check-in comments that were entered for each revision. If the files are somewhat removed from the configuration management system (e.g., you have used them to build a program or you have given your document files to someone else) getting that information about the particular revision that you have is harder.

One way to get around this problem is to embed the information directly in the files you are creating and using. This way, no matter where the files are, you have the information with them. RCS provides several *keywords* that you can embed in your files. When a particular revision of a file is checked out of the system, the keywords are expanded to the actual information for that revision.

> *The team has decided to embed the $Header$ keyword in each file*
> *that they create, so that they can easily see the configuration man-*
> *agement information about the file directly in the file. This infor-*

mation is especially useful during the integration phase, because it tells who the last person (author) was to touch the file—which, of course, points to who is causing the current problems! The keywords look like Figure 3-3-10.

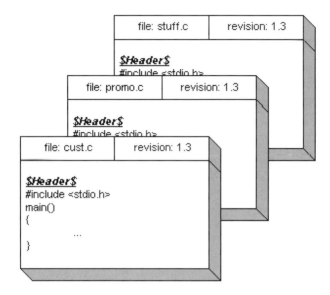

Figure 3-3-10   Files with embedded keywords

RCS keywords are of the form **$**keyword**$**. When the file is checked out of RCS, you can indicate whether or not the keyword should be expanded. If the keyword should be expanded, the **$**keyword**$** string is replaced with the value of the keyword, enclosed in $ signs. If it should not be expanded, it is left as is.

More about keywords	
RCS provides several keywords that you can embed in your files. You can use options for each of the RCS commands to indicate what to do with the keywords when the command is executed.	
$Author$	The login name of the user who checked in this version of the file
$Date$	The date and time this version of the file was checked in to the system
$Header$	A string that contains the full pathname of the RCS file, the revision number, the date and time this version of the file was checked in, the author, the state, and the locker of the file (if it is locked). This is a consolidation of several other keywords, and a shortcut for providing all of that information.
Id	The same information as provided by $Header$, except that only the name of the RCS file (not the full path) is given.

More about keywords	
$Locker$	The login name of the user who has the file locked, if it is locked. If the file is not locked, the string is empty.
Log	The check-in comment, entered by the author when the version was checked into RCS. The check-in comment is preceded by a header containing the RCS filename, the revision number, the author, and the date and time. Existing log messages are not replaced; rather, the new message is appended to the existing ones. Thus, you can accumulate a complete change log in the source file—note that this can get quite long after a while, however.
$Name$	The symbolic name used to check out the file, if a symbolic name was used.
$RCSfile$	The name of the RCS file without the full path.
$Revision$	The revision number of the given revision.
$Source$	The full path name of the RCS file.
$State$	The state assigned to the given revision.[a]
-kkv	Generate keyword strings using the default form. The keyword $Revision$ is expanded to *$Revision: 1.2$* for revision 1.2, for example. The locker's name is inserted into the generated value for $Header$, Id, and $Locker$ only when the file is being locked (e.g., using ci -l). This form is the default for keyword expansion.
-kkvl	Like -kkv, except the locker's name is always inserted when the given revision is locked.
-kk	Generates only the keyword names, not the values. The keyword $Revision$ is left as *$Revision$*. This option is useful if you are checking for differences between two revisions, and don't care about differences in keywords. Log messages are still inserted for Log.
-ko	Generates the old keyword string that was present in the working file just before it was checked in. This is useful for binary files, in which you don't want to accidentally change a part of the file that just happened to look like a keyword.
-kv	Generates only the keyword values, not the names. The keyword $Revision$ will be expanded to *1.2* for revision 1.2, for example. Note, if you used this form on check-out, the keyword is removed from the file and no further expansions can take place. Thus the option is not allowed when locking a file.

a.   We don't spend any time talking about state. This is another field in RCS that can capture the state of the file. The default is Exp, for Experimental, but you can give any value you like to the state attribute. We tend to prefer symbolic names over state.

Identifying Changes

Usually you want to keep a file checked out and locked only while you are actively working with it. In a team environment, you are usually considered rude if you "hog" a file (e.g., keep a file locked when unnecessary), because no one else can check it out and make their own changes to it. Of course, some changes do take a long time to finish, and after you have been working with a file for hours (or days), you sometimes forget what exactly you have done to it. This forgetfulness is especially a problem when you somehow can't get your program to compile no matter what you do, and of course *you* haven't changed anything that could possibly have any impact (and you can't blame anyone else since you have the file locked)!

Usually, you will want to compare your working copy of a file with the revision that was last saved in the configuration management system. Configuration management systems provide a command to allow you to do this comparison, as well as compare any two revisions of a file against each other. The command in RCS is called **rcsdiff**.

Jerry has been working on the customer entry form for a few days now. Each time he thought he was finished, either Cosmo or Elaine came over to request one more absolutely necessary change—either to be able to interface with the database or to be consistent with the forms Elaine is developing. Jerry has made six different revisions of the file cust.c since he first checked it in. Now, Cosmo is asking for a change that Jerry is sure he just removed a couple of days ago at Cosmo's request! Jerry wants to review the last couple of revisions to see just exactly what he has changed. He uses the rcsdiff command:

```
rcsdiff cust.c

 RCS file: g:/sources/RCS/cust.c
 retrieving revision 1.6
 diff -r1.6
 3c3,4
 < color = red
 --
 >
 > color = blue
 >

rcsdiff -r 1.5 -r 1.6 cust.c

 RCS file: g:/sources/RCS/cust.c
 retrieving revision 1.5
 retrieving revision 1.6
 diff -r1.5 -r1.6
```

```
3c3
< color = red
--
> color = blue
```

Jerry sees that he has made the color change before. He decides to wait a couple of days to see if Cosmo is going to change his mind again before making the change.

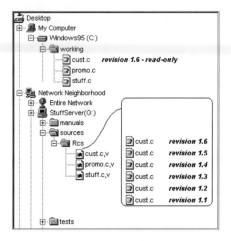

Figure 3-3-11   The sequence of revisions

The **rcsdiff** command with no options compares the working copy of the specified file with the default for the file (usually the revision last checked into the configuraton management system, although if you are using branches this default pattern may not be true). If you give one **-r <revnumber>** option, the comparison is made between the working copy of the file and the revision with the given revision number. If you give two **-r <revnumber>** options, the comparison is made between those two revisions of the file.

More about the rcsdiff command	
The rcsdiff command compares two revisions of an RCS file, or compares the working copy of the file to a revision of the RCS file. The simplest invocation is **rcsdiff \<filename\>**. This will compare the working copy of the file to the default version of the file. Some of the more useful command line options include:	
-r \<rev\>	If you give one **-r \<rev\>** option, it compares the current working copy of the file with the given revision. If you give two **-r \<rev\>** options, it compares those two revisions. You can use all of the numeric and symbolic forms described under the **ci** and **co** commands for the **\<rev\>** fields. Other more complex forms of **\<rev\>** can be used that we won't discuss here.
-i	Ignores case when doing the comparison (treats upper- and lowercase the same). Thus, a difference between an 'a' and an 'A' would not be flagged.
-B	Ignores blank lines when doing the comparison.
-w	Ignores white space when doing the comparison. Thus, a difference between 'cat' and 'c at' would not be flagged.
-b	Ignores changes in amount of white space. Thus, if you changed two spaces to one, this difference would not be flagged.

Retrieving a Previous Version

Sometimes after you have made some changes to a file, you realize that you have really messed up! You look at the history of the file and perhaps use the difference command to see how the file has changed over time. Finally, you figure out that the best thing to do is just get back to where you were a few days ago. This situation is one in which a configuration management system can really help.

In order to get back to a previous revision of a file, you need to:

- Determine the number of the revision you want
- Check out that revision of the file from the configuration management system
- Check the file back into the configuration management system as the "latest" revision

Remember, though, that you aren't always the only one making changes to a file. Before you revert to a previous version, make sure you aren't going to inadvertently delete someone else's changes.

*After Jerry argues with Cosmo for a couple of hours, they decide
that what they really want is the version that Jerry had checked in
three days ago (revision 1.4)! So Jerry typed in the following commands:*

rlog cust.c

```
rlog cust.c
RCS file: g:/sources/RCS/cust.c
Working file: cust.c
head: 1.6
branch:
locks: strict
access list:
symbolic names:
keyword substitution: kv
total revisions: 6;selected revisions: 6
description:
--------------------------
revision 1.6
date: 1996/10/10 11:38:13; author:jerry; state: Exp;
lines: +4-1
changed the background color for the form again
--------------------------
revision 1.5
date: 1996/10/09 08:18:19; author:jerry; state: Exp;
lines: +10-20
changed the background color for the form
--------------------------
revision 1.4
date: 1996/10/08 12:18:19; author:jerry; state: Exp;
lines: +10-20
made the display flash when overdue balance
--------------------------
revision 1.3
date: 1996/08/12 21:22:13; author: cosmo; state: Exp; lines: +30-3
--------------------------
revision 1.2
date: 1996/07/10 23:45:21; author: jerry; state: Exp; lines: +6-0
fixing up the form
--------------------------
revision 1.1
date: 1996/07/8 22:45:18; author: jerry; state: Exp;
Initial revision
```

co -l -r 1.4 cust.c

*Now that he has a good version of his file again, he makes his real
change to it (after kicking Cosmo out of his office). The file looks
like Figure 3-3-12.*

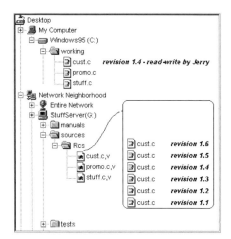

Figure 3-3-12   Checking out a previous version of **cust.c**

When he checks it back into the system, he wants to make sure it is checked in at the top of the revision tree, not as a branch, so that it will be the new default version for everyone on the team. This check-in is kind of tricky. First, he has to unlock his current revision of the file. Then he locks the revision at the top of the tree (lock only—not check out, or his changes will be overwritten). Finally he checks in his version of the file as the new top of tree. See those three steps below:

```
rcs -u cust.c

 RCS file: g:/sources/RCS/cust.c,v
 1.4 unlocked
 done

rcs -l cust.c

 RCS file: g:/sources/RCS/cust.c,v
 1.7 locked
 done

ci -u cust.c

 g:/sources/RCS/cust.c,v <- cust.c
 new revision 1.7; previous revision 1.6
 enter log message, terminated with single '.' or end of file:
 >> got back good revision
 >> .
```

Now the new revision is at the top of the tree as you see in Figure 3-3-13.

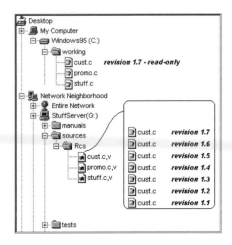

Figure 3-3-13   Checking in the updated file **cust.c** derived from revision 1.4

To figure out the revision number of the revision you want, you need to look at the history of the file. The history includes revision numbers, the name of the person who checked in that revision of the file, and the check-in comments that the author entered upon check-in. The comments are (hopefully) useful in helping you figure out what changed in that version of the file. The history also includes the date and time the revision was checked in, and some other useful information. In RCS, the **rlog** command looks at the history of a file. You might also want to use the difference command (rcsdiff in RCS) to see the exact changes that were made in a particular revision of the file, especially if someone else made those changes.

After you know what revision you want, you once again use the check-out command to check out the desired revision. In RCS, all you have to do is provide a **-r** option to the **co** command, giving the revision number that you want to check out. For instance, the command **co -r 1.4 cust.c** checks out revision 1.4 of the file **cust.c**. Remember, when you check out a new revision of a file, it overwrites the file in your working directory. Thus, any changes you made in your working directory will be lost.

Because you checked out a version other than the version at the top of the revision tree for the file, the default on check-in is to create a branch in the revision tree (see Figure 3-3-14).

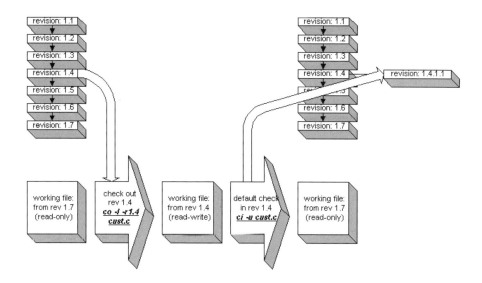

Figure 3-3-14   Default check-in of previous revision creates a branch

If you create a branch, the newly checked-in revision is not created at the top of the revision tree. The next time someone checks out the file, unless he or she specifies the revision number for the newly created revision, this is *not* the revision that is checked out. As before, the revision that is checked out by default is the one at the top of the revision tree for the file.

In some cases, you don't want to create a branch. You really want to put the revision at the top of the revision tree and make it the new default revision. The trick to this process is that you first have to lock the revision that is currently the top of the tree in order to create a new revision from it. So you first unlock the revision you have locked (don't delete the modified file, though!) and then lock the revision at the top of the revision tree. Locking the file, rather than checking it out, leaves your working copy of the file. Then when you check it in, it is created as the new top-of-tree revision (see Figure 3-3-15).

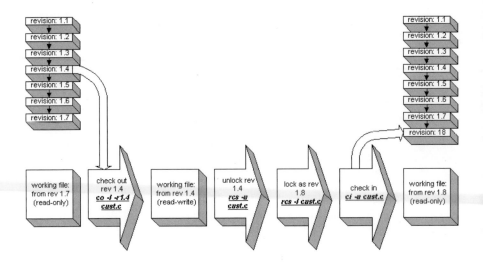

Figure 3-3-15   Specific revision check-in of previous revision does not create a branch

More about the rlog command
The rlog command prints information about an RCS file or files. The simplest invocation is **rlog <filename>**, which prints all of the known information about the file. Some of the more useful command line options include:

-L	Prints only information about files that have locks set. If you give the command **rlog -L *.***, you get only information about files you have locked.
-R	Prints only the name of the RCS file. If you use this with the -L option, you get only the names of the files you have locked.
-r <revs>	Prints only information about the specified revisions. The revisions can be specified as **<rev1>:<rev2>**, **:<rev>**, or **<rev>:**. The first form gives information about all revisions between **<rev1>** and **<rev2>**, inclusive. The second form gives information about revisions up to and including **<rev>**. The third form gives information about revisions later than and including **<rev>**. You can use all of the numeric and symbolic forms described under the **ci** and **co** commands for the **<rev>** field. Other more complex forms of **<rev>** can be used that we won't discuss here.

Daily Team Interactions

Synchronizing with the Team

When you are working on a team project, you can't ignore the rest of the team for-ever (much as you sometimes want to!). A configuration management system allows you to have a private workspace in which to make your changes. It also allows you to synchronize your changes with those of the rest of the team. For example, con-sider a couple of instances:

1. You and another team member both are making changes to the same file.
2. Your team members are modifying different files from you, but you need their source files to build the complete product (e.g., to run tests, etc.).

Usually, on one project and team, you run into both of these cases.

> *George has asked Elaine for a demo of her work. Although she would really love to tell him to get lost, she knows that is not the politically correct thing to tell your boss. In order to build some-thing that makes a reasonable demo, she needs to update some of the files that Cosmo has been creating. Also, she and Jerry have both made modifications to the stuff.c file, and she wants to make sure she incorporates Jerry's latest changes (making blaming him easier, if something goes wrong in the demo). In order to update the changes, Elaine needs to do a checkout of all of the files. Note, she doesn't want to lock them; she just wants read-only copies to*

use in her build. In this case, Elaine uses the full path to the files
so that she can use the *.* wildcards:

```
co g:\sources\RCS\*.*

g:/sources/RCS/cust.c,v --> cust.c
revision 1.9
done

g:/sources/RCS/promo.c,v --> promo.c
revision 1.2
done

g:/sources/RCS/stuff.c,v --> stuff.c
revision 1.7
done
```

Since both the stuff.c file and all of Cosmo's files are in the sources
directory, Elaine just needs the one command, above. Figure 3-4-
1 shows the files she checked out but didn't lock.

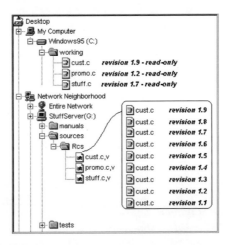

Figure 3-4-1   Files checked out for demo, but not locked

Even if you aren't going to change a file, you often want the latest version of
it in your local workspace—either to build with it, to test with it, or maybe just to
look at it. If other team members are checking files into the configuration management system, the version in your local workspace becomes out of date, unless you
explicitly refresh your workspace with the latest version. Remember that the latest
version of a file is the one that was last checked in. Thus, if a teammate has a file
checked out and is working on it, you don't see those changes in your local work-

space. You just see the changes that were made before the last time the file was checked into the configuration management system—probably what your team-mate (and you) would prefer.

Generally, you want some formal or informal process that you follow to update your files—e.g., you might update them each morning when you get to work, or after a successful build has taken place. You might even want to have an auto-mated script run each night that updates your files for you.

Isolation from the Team

Although you usually want the latest versions of working files, you don't want to update your local workspace with a half-fixed file that a teammate checked in before going on vacation. You also don't want to disallow check-ins from team members for long periods of time, or you will start losing some of the benefits of the configu-ration management system. If a team member checks in a file with an incomplete change or one that will not compile, other team members have problems when they update their local workspace with this file. A solution to both of these problems is to use symbolic names to define a promotion scheme.

In a promotion scheme, symbolic names are used to mark files. For example, the symbolic name **goodrev** could be used to mark the last tested version of a file. Until a team member has tested the latest changes, the latest version is not marked with the **goodrev** symbolic name. Team members usually want to update their local workspaces with the **goodrev** versions of most of the files, rather than the latest ver-sions. Each one still wants the latest versions of the files that he or she is modifying, of course.

You can use several different symbolic names to signify versions of files in several different states. You might care about a demo version, a tested version, a ver-sion that went out to selected customers, a version with a given defect fixed, etc. Once the symbolic names have been defined and attached to the files, the other team members can easily update their local workspaces with exactly the version they want. Using a promotion scheme allows team members to check in files as often as they like, without adversely affecting their team mates.

The discussion on grouping (in Chapter 3-6) gives information on manipulat-ing symbolic names.

What Did My Buddy Change?

In Chapter 3-3, we talked about seeing how you had changed a file over time. When working in a team environment, you sometimes want to know what other team members have changed in a file. This knowledge is particularly useful when a change one of your teammates makes breaks your code! The method you use is essentially the same as that used to determine what you have changed, although more information might be useful to you when you are checking up on a teammate (such as who made the change, when it was made, etc.).

> *Jerry has been working all night on a cool addition to the customer entry form—he wants the ability to tell them about a daily special based on what they have already ordered. He gets it all working around 3:00 A.M. when Cosmo wanders in and says that he has made a cool change of his own. If the customer has an unpaid bill, a flashing stop sign appears on the screen with the amount of the unpaid bill in the middle of the sign. "Check it out, Jerry," he says. "I'm going home to get some sleep. Before trashing his workspace with Cosmo's changes, Jerry decides to see what Cosmo changed. Cosmo has told him only two files—dialogs.c and errors.c—have changed. So Jerry looks at the differences to see if the changes will break anything for him:*

```
rcsdiff dialogs.c

RCS file: g:/sources/RCS/dialogs.c
retrieving revision 1.4
diff -r1.4
10a11
> flashtime = 2.5
> showstop(flashtime);

rcsdiff errors.c

RCS file: g:/sources/RCS/errors.c
retrieving revision 1.3
diff -r1.3
13a14
> if (stop_error)
> ; // need to do some error checking here
```

> *Jerry decides that until Cosmo puts in some real error checking, he will leave the cool change out!*

You still use the **rcsdiff** command to see differences in two versions of a file. When you are the only one making changes, the file in your local workspace is usually the most recent version of the file (especially if you have it checked out locked). When you are working in a team, however, often the file in your local workspace is older than the last one checked in. If you don't give a revision argument to the rcsdiff command, you are still comparing the latest checked-in version with the one in your local workspace.

In addition to the **rcsdiff** command, the **rlog** command is also useful. We saw the rlog command when we talked about viewing the history of a file in "Retrieving a Previous Version" in Chapter 3-3. The **rlog** command is also useful in determining how your teammates have changed a file. The **rlog** command not only tells you when revisions were made to a file, but also *who* made them. This information is very useful in helping you decide whom to blame when something goes wrong!

Breaking Locks

If someone has a file locked and disappears for days or weeks, you often can't wait until the offending person returns to unlock the file so that you can make your own changes. Most systems provide a capability to break someone's lock on a file. Use this option very carefully, however, because you can cause someone to lose their changes if he doesn't realize that he used to have a file locked and then you broke his lock when he wasn't looking.

> *Cosmo decides to take off for two weeks in the Caribbean in the middle of the development of the system. He leaves a file locked that Jerry desperately needs to change. Although he wouldn't normally do it, Jerry decides to break Cosmo's lock on the file so that he can get some work done in the next two weeks. He leaves Cosmo a voice mail message, several notes on his desk telling him that the lock was broken, and sends him some e-mail telling him about it, too.*

In RCS, the **rcs -u** command breaks a lock. It really should be used only in extreme cases, and good team etiquette says that when you do use it, you need to make sure you inform the team member who used to have the lock that her lock is now gone.

Merging Changes

Sometimes you really need to be changing a file at the same time as another team member. For instance, you may both be fixing defects that have to get done before the end of the day, and both defects just happen to be in one file. This case can cause a bunch of grief if you don't have a configuration management system. Many times, the person who last copies over their changes will "win," and the other's changes will inadvertently be discarded. With a configuration management system, a better chance exists that this won't happen—although it is still not normally automatic.

The basic method is the following:

- One person checks out and locks a file.
- The second person can't check out the file in a locked state. Thus, she checks out the file in an unlocked state and then uses an operating system command to make her local copy writeable.
- The first person checks back in his changes.
- The second person now locks her copy of the file (without checking it out, so that it doesn't overwrite her changes) and then merges those changes with the last checked-in version.

If the two sets of changes don't overlap each other (e.g., the same line was not changed by both person one and person two) the merge can be automatic and includes all of the changes both people made. If the two sets of changes do overlap, however, someone needs to make the decision about how the file really should be changed in the merge.

George is getting really anxious to get a beta version of the soft-ware into use. He came in at 3:00 on Friday and told the team that whatever they had by Wednesday at noon was going to be used for the beta. Jerry, Elaine, and Cosmo have been fixing defects madly for the past two days and are almost done. Jerry and Elaine both have one more thing to fix, and they both need to modify promo.c. Jerry checks out a locked version of the file to make his change:

```
co -l promo.c

g:/sources/RCS/promo.c --> promo.c
revision 1.3 (locked)
done
```

The results appear in Figure 3-4-2. Jerry then starts to make his changes on his locked version of promo.c.

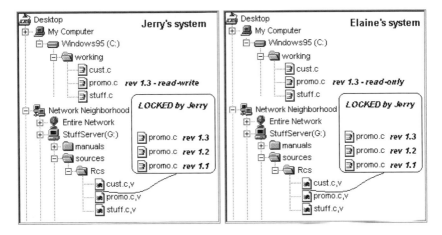

Figure 3-4-2   Jerry checks out **promo.c** for the beta release

Elaine checks out an unlocked version of the file:

```
co promo.c

g:/sources/RCS/promo.c --> promo.c
revision 1.3 (unlocked)
done
```

Now her system looks like that in Figure 3-4-3. Elaine now makes the file writeable, using Windows Explorer, and starts making her changes.

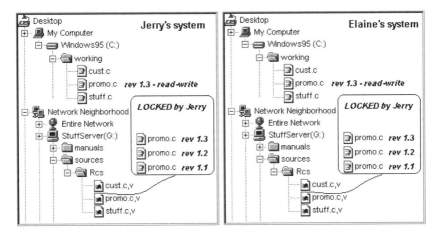

Figure 3-4-3   Elaine checks out her own working copy of **promo.c** for the beta release

Once Jerry has made his change, he checks it in (unlocking the file).

```
ci -u promo.c

g:/sources/RCS/cust.c <-- cust.c
new revision 1.4; previous revision 1.3
enter log message, terminated with single '.' or end of file:
>> Changed the dialog label to "new Customer"
>> .
done
```

The new revision appears, as you see in Figure 3-4-4.

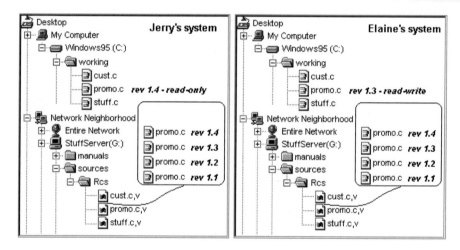

Figure 3-4-4   Figure 3-4-4: Jerry checks in the locked version of **promo.c**

After Jerry checks in the file, Elaine then uses the rcs command to lock it (see Figure 3-4-5).

```
rcs -l promo.c

RCS file: g:/sources/RCS/promo.c
locked
done
```

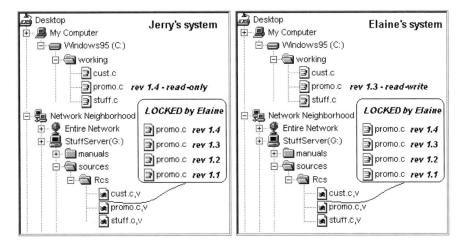

Figure 3-4-5   Elaine locks her version of **promo.c**

She then merges her changes with the ones Jerry made.

```
rcsmerge -r1.3 promo.c

RCS file: g:/sources/RCS/promo.c
retrieving revision 1.3
retrieving revision 1.4
Merging differences between 1.3 and 1.4 into promo.c

ci -u promo.c

g:/sources/RCS/cust.c <-- cust.c
new revision 1.5; previous revision 1.4
enter log message, terminated with single '.' or end of file:
>> Changed the dialog label to "New Name"
>> .
done
```

The results of the merge appear in Figure 3-4-6.

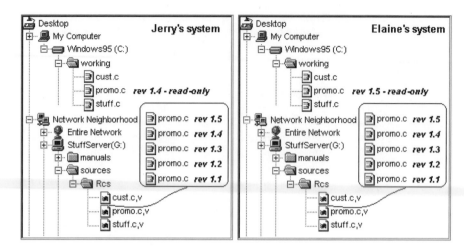

Figure 3-4-6   Elaine merges Jerry's and her versions of **promo.c**

> *Luckily, Jerry and Elaine were changing different parts of the file,
> so their changes didn't overlap. The merge completes successfully
> and both changes make it into the new, latest version of the file.
> Just to be safe, Elaine uses the rcsdiff command to see exactly how
> the file changed due to these two changes.*

```
rcsdiff -r 1.3 -r1.5 promo.c

retrieving revision 1.3
retrieving revision 1.5
2c2
< "Customer"
--
> "New Customer"
15c15
< "Name"
--
> "First Name"
```

In order to merge two versions of a file, you start with a common ancestor revision. In the case just described, the common ancestor is the common revision that both team members checked out and modified. If the changes are *disjoint*—they don't affect the same lines in the file—all changes are accepted. If the changes overlap, the merge cannot be completed automatically, and you have to determine what you want the final file to contain. Even in cases where the merge can complete automatically, you should scan the changes made to make sure they all make sense together.

In RCS, the **rcsmerge** command merges two versions of a file. The first **-r** option to rcsmerge, which is required, specifies the common ancestor revision to use in the merge. The second **-r** option specifies the revision to merge with the current working copy of the file (if no working file exists, the **rcsmerge** command will fail). The results are put in the working file (overwriting it!), unless you use the **-p** option (which sends the results to the standard output).

More about the rcsmerge command	
The **rcsmerge** command merges two different revisions of an RCS file. One **-r** option, indicating the ancestor revision of the two revisions to be merged, must be given. Usually, a second -r option, indicating the revision to merge with the current working copy of the file, is also given. Given these two options, the command merges the specified revisions and stores the results in the working copy of the file. Some of the more useful command line options include:	
-r <rev>	The first -r option indicates the common ancestor revision. The second **-r** option indicates the revision to merge with the current working copy of the file. If the second **-r** option is not given, the default is the default revision. The **<rev>** can be any of the numeric or symbolic forms described under the **ci** and **co** commands.
-p	Rather than overwriting the working copy of the file with the merge results, the results are printed to the standard output.

Group Activities—
Pulling It All Together

W e have described the common daily individual development operations using a configuration management system. At some point, however, you need to start pulling together all of the "stuff" that the team members have been creating to make one product. Generally, you have to go through some sort of integration cycle. In this chapter, we give some suggestions on how to make the integration cycle a little easier—taking advantage of the capabilities of the configuration management system. We realize that this exact process won't work in every team situation, but hopefully it will at least give you some ideas on how to proceed.

Integration Activities

Regardless of what type of product you are creating, the integration usually involves:

- Creating a *clean* environment
- Gathering together a *consistent* set of files and tools
- *Building* using a known, repeatable process
- Finding and fixing problems that are discovered
- Doing it over and over until you get it right

By a *clean* environment, we mean one that doesn't have old versions of files or environmental settings that affect the results of the integration cycles. Depending on your product, creating a clean environment might be fairly easy or fairly hard. In most cases, one of the things you want to do in creating your clean environment is to remove all of your old working versions of source and data files that are being created as part of your product. This helps assure that you don't use old versions of them in building your product.

By a *consistent* set of files and tools, we mean the correct version of each of the pieces and tools used to create your product. These include all of the source files, any libraries you may use, any tools (such as Visual C++), etc. Generally, for the files that are being created or modified as part of the product, you want to get the latest versions. This scenario is not always the case, however, so you need to make sure you do get the versions you expect.

The way a product is built depends on the product. If you are creating a Visual C++ product, you probably have a build step for both the executable and for the associated help files. You want to make sure that you can build in a known and repeatable fashion, or re-creating the product over and over will be hard (usually you need to rebuild as you find and fix problems). Some of the higher-end configuration management systems help you with the build process. If you use the systems we talk about here, you are generally on your own as far as creating and maintaining a build process.

You are also on your own as far as finding and fixing problems (sorry).

Creating an Integration Environment

The way we have described the team development environment, each team member works in his or her own private workspace, and the archived files are stored in a central location. Team members decide independently when and how to update their local workspaces. In some teams, team members can work in relative isolation from each other, whereas in other teams more interaction occurs between team members.

When the time comes to get serious about integration, we recommend that you create a new integration workspace to use for your integration activities. Having a workspace that meets the requirements we described above is very useful, and maintaining those requirements in a workspace that an individual is using to get his or her work done is usually hard. You would really upset a hard-working team member if you decided to clean out all of her source files when she was in the middle of an important change.

If you have an integration workspace, you can often create automated scripts that clean out the integration workspace and update it with the correct versions of all of your files. You can sometimes also have automated scripts that build the product for you. This way, when you get to work in the morning, you can get started right away.

A sensible setup is to have one team member who is the owner of the integration workspace. This person can decide which versions of files and libraries are installed into the workspace and when and how often to update and build in the workspace. Although all team members need access to the workspace, having one owner responsible for maintaining it keeps it more stable and usable.

Having an integration workspace can also help when you get serious about testing your product. Because you have a *clean* environment, you know that problems found are real problems and not ones that were fixed weeks ago (but you still see them because you have an old version of something). It is also a great environment to verify that defects have been fixed, or to verify that defects really exist in the current version before you spend hours trying to track them down. Team members want to update their local workspaces occasionally, to be in sync with the integration workspace.

One thing to keep in mind during the integration cycle—you need to make sure that everyone is checking in their changes in a timely fashion. If you have team members who don't check in changes for days or weeks after they have been made, the integration work is never caught up, since by the time you find problems in the integration cycle, the sources might be very different.

Building Your Software

Building your software is the act of constructing or coalescing the components into the completed deliverable program. You will probably be doing two types of builds while developing your software—intermediate builds that you do as you are working on changes, and release builds that you use to create the releases of your software. Team members usually do their intermediate builds in their own local workspaces, and may do several intermediate builds in a day. Release builds are likely done in the integration workspace, and you usually end up doing more than one release build per release (because someone finds that last-minute error that just has to be fixed before you really release your program).

Most people these days use some sort of mechanism to help with their build process, rather than just typing commands one at a time to complete the build. Many systems (like Visual C++) try to insulate the users from the build process as much as possible—you create files to be used in the build, and the system takes care of building the project for you. Also, *makefiles* are used quite frequently to help with builds. Makefiles are files that contain rules for building a program—then a make program (several of which exist) is run using the makefile.

RCS and most of the more inexpensive, lower-end configuration management systems don't provide much additional help in the build process. You can take advantage of the system to help execute and keep track of your builds, though.

> *Team members are responsible for their own intermediate builds. They use a make program and a makefile that Elaine created in their local workspaces, and can build as often as they find necessary.*

Elaine is in charge of the integration workspace for the team. She has an automated script that checks out (read-only) the latest version of each file from RCS into the integration workspace, and then stores the revision number of each file in another file she has named buildinfo. Then the script executes a make program (using the makefile Elaine has created). Finally, the script checks in the new copy of the buildinfo file, to keep the history of what went into the build.

Most people are more concerned with capturing information about release builds than they are about capturing information about intermediate builds. By using configuration management functions in a batch file or script, you can be quite flexible about what you do and the information you capture. One of the ways you can use a configuration management system to help with release builds is by setting up a script to check out the latest versions of each of the files you need to create the build. Then, if you keep track of what each of those versions is, you can check to make sure you have included everything you expected, and you can re-create the build later, if necessary. We talk in Chapter 3-6 about grouping files, which helps make some of the capture of all of this information easier.

If you are using a makefile or another type of build script to help with your build process, you want to make sure that you check that file into your configuration management system, and keep track of its version number as well. If you are using a system like Visual C++ to help with the builds, you want to keep track of which version of the system you are using, as well as any other attributes of the system that might change. You may also have environment settings that affect the results of your build. If so, you want to make sure these are set correctly when you create the build, and that the settings are captured. Any information that you capture should be stored in the configuration management system, so that it can be retrieved later.

If you have bigger build problems, at some point you may choose to look at one of the higher-end configuration management systems.

Group Activities— Getting Something out the Door

U sually, the goal of working on your software is to eventually make it available to your customers (sometimes even for pay). Thus, you created the software, made changes to it, checked files in and out of the configuration management system, and finally integrated your work with the work of the other team members. Two important activities that are typical parts of release operations are marking all of the files used to create the release, and writing release notes, which talk about what has changed since the last release. Configuration management helps with both of these activities.

While some team members are busy releasing a version of the product, other team members may be ready to start working on the next version of the software. You don't want these people messing with the files you need for this release, but you do want them to be able to get their work done. Again, configuration management can help with this sticky problem.

Grouping Files

When you create a release, you want to keep track of the version of each file that went into the release. You do this by marking the appropriate version of each file with a symbolic name that is specific to the release you are creating. Once you have marked a version of a file with a symbolic name, you can use that symbolic name in other configuration management operations, such as checking in and out files, so you don't have to remember the specific version number of each file you need to access.

You can mark a version of a file with a symbolic name when you create the version (by checking it in) or you can do it after the version has already been created and stored in the configuration management system.

*The Stuff I Need team has been working hard on their product and George is anxiously awaiting the release. He comes in one day and tells them that they need to have a release ready to go to the operators by the end of the week. Cosmo suggests that they use the name **bogus1** for this release (because he doesn't feel it is ready for use). After some discussion, they settle on **b1** (just in case George gets a look at the symbolic name). They are going to use **b1** as the symbolic name to mark all of the versions of the files that go into the release. The day before the release, they have all of their changes checked in by noon. Then Cosmo marks the last checked-in version of each file with the symbolic name, **b1** (see Figure 3-6-1):*

```
cd g:/sources

rcs -nb1: *.*
RCS file: RCS/stuff.c,v
done
RCS file: RCS/promo.c,v
done
RCS file: RCS/cust.c,v
done
```

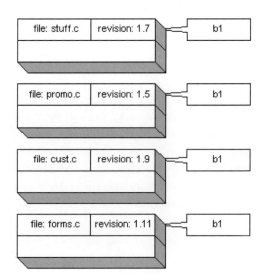

Figure 3-6-1　Files tagged with **b1** symbolic name

As soon as he is done with the changes, however, Elaine comes rushing into his office to let him know that she needed to make one more change to the file forms.c. Cosmo has already marked this file, so he tells Elaine to move the symbolic name on forms.c to the new version when she checks it in. Elaine starts by checking out the file forms.c.

```
co -l forms.c
```

```
g:/sources/RCS/forms.c --> forms.c
revision 1.11 (locked)
done
```

Elaine makes the necessary change to the forms.c file and then checks it back into RCS, moving the tag so that the version with her changes is marked b1 (see Figure 3-6-2).

```
ci -u -Nb1 forms.c
```

```
g:/sources/RCS/forms.c <-- forms.c
new revision 1.12; previous revision: 1.11
enter log message, terminated with single '.' or end of file:
>> Spelled Address wrong on form!
>> .
done
```

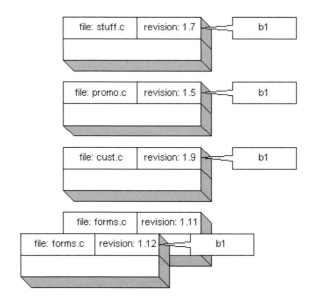

Figure 3-6-2   New **forms.c** tagged with **b1** symbolic name by Elaine

Symbolic names can really make your life easier if you have to deal with groups of files for any reason. When you first check in files, they all have the same version number (e.g., version 1.1). But as you and your team members change files over time, you usually end up with different version numbers of each file. (Rarely does every file have to be changed exactly the same number of times.) If not for symbolic names, you would have to remember the version number for each file that you need to group together. With symbolic names, all you have to remember is the symbolic name that stands for the release of the software you need to access.

When grouping your files to mark a release: remember that your software often depends on other things on your system. Usually, you are using someone else's tools (e.g., Visual C++) to build your software or to create some of the artifacts that you use. Also, you may depend on some configuration files or variables set on your machine. As your machine environment changes over time, reproducing a release may become very hard, even if you have marked all of your software files with a symbolic name. An easy way to capture and save the information about the tools you are using is to create a file in which you manually enter the data you need. Then you check this file in (and mark it with the symbolic name), along with your software. Another way you can capture information about configuration files is to put those files under configuration management (again, making sure to mark them with appropriate symbolic names).

Writing Release Notes

Often one of the things you want to include with a second (or third or fourth or . . .) release of a software program is a description of what has changed since the last release. Customers are interested in what is new with this release (i.e., why should they buy it?), what problems have been fixed, and any other changes that have been made. In a team environment, with several people making changes, one person won't likely remember (or even know about) all of the changes that have been made since the last release. One way to help keep track of all the changes that have been made is to be diligent about using check-in comments to describe how a file has changed since it was last checked into the system. The person responsible for compiling all of the changes can start by taking a look at the check-in comments of the files to create a first draft of the release notes. Getting the release notes reviewed by the team members is a good idea before giving it to the customers, to make sure that you really understand what is said in the release notes.

> *Jerry, Elaine, and Cosmo were really rushed to get the first release (remember **b1**?) out to their customers. It did have some problems, so they worked almost nonstop for a month to get the second release (**b2**) ready to go. Because they have been working so hard at*

*it, they decide that George should be the one to write the release notes while they take a day off. George examines all of the check-in comments for the files since the first (and only) release that they created and builds release notes from those. In this case, he uses the full pathname to the RCS archive directory in order to use the *.* wildcard:*

rlog g:\sources\RCS.**

```
rlog g:\sources\RCS\cust.c
RCS file: g:/sources/RCS/cust.c
Working file: g:/sources/RCS/cust.c
head: 1.6
branch:
locks: strict
access list:
symbolic names:
rev1: 1.4
rev2: 1.6
keyword substitution: kv
total revisions: 6;selected revisions: 3
description:
---------------------------
revision 1.6
date: 1996/10/10 11:38:13; author:jerry; state: Exp;
lines: +4-1
changed the background color for the form again
---------------------------
revision 1.5
date: 1996/10/09 08:18:19; author:jerry; state: Exp;
lines: +10-20
changed the background color for the form
---------------------------
revision 1.4
date: 1996/10/08 12:18:19; author:jerry; state: Exp;
lines: +10-20
made the display flash when overdue balance
---------------------------
 .  .  .
```

Of course, you could take a look at the files themselves, to see exactly what has changed in them. Usually, though, you don't want to pore over source code, line by line, trying to determine from your customers' point of view what has changed in this release of your program—especially in those files that you never touched (because some other team member worked on them). If you and your team members have written good check-in comments, you won't have to pore over the source code!

Working Ahead (Branching)

Often, while some of the team members are working on the final touches to get a release out to the customers, other team members have finished all they need to do on the current release. Rather than having them all take vacation while the release is finished up, you want them to still be productive. But, of course, you don't want them to screw up the current release while they are being productive.

The use of symbolic names helps keep the changes made for the current release separate from those made for the future release. If a team member makes a change to a file that should not be included in the current release, he or she should not move the symbolic name to the new revision.

A more complicated case occurs when you make a future change to a file and then notice it has a defect that needs to be fixed in the current release. Usually, you don't want to include the future changes (because they aren't tested or many times even completed), but you do need to include the fix. Thus, you start with the version of the file that is currently marked with the symbolic name for the release. You make changes to this file and then check it back into the configuration management system. This action creates a branch in the version tree of the file (because you already created a version after the version marked with the symbolic name for the release). You want to make sure you move the symbolic name to this new version when you check it in.

At some point after the release, you also want to make sure that you include this fix in the current development stream. Thus, you need to merge the branch back into the main development line, using the same merging techniques we described in Chapter 3-4.

Group Activities — Getting Something out the Door Again

U nfortunately, we don't know of any programs that are perfect the first time out. Unless you start over from scratch each time you work on a program, you spend time finding and fixing defects after you have released a version of your software.[18] Many times you can fix defects as part of your work for the next release of your software. Thus, you just incorporate the fix in with the other changes you are making to your source files. Other times, however, you need to fix a defect before your next scheduled release. If you are in the middle of a huge change to your software and an important customer calls in with a really big problem, you don't want to have to wait for a month or more before you can get the customer back up and running.

Finding a Defect

The first step in fixing a defect is to find it. Usually, the first thing to do to find the defect is to try out your latest version of the program to see if you can reproduce the defect. If you can, the next step is to start hunting through the code to figure out where it went wrong. If you can't, you want to go back to the version of the program that was being used when the defect was found, to track down the problem. In Chapter 3-6, we talked about how to group files. If you created a symbolic name that represents all of the files that created your release, you can easily re-cre-

---

18.   Unless you con some other unfortunate team member to take over the maintenance tasks from you.

ate that release and start hunting for the defect. The integration workspace is often a good workspace to use to re-create the release and hunt for the defect.

> *After the team created the **b2** release, they started working on making some of the database access calls faster—many of the operators (their customers) have been complaining that they have to slow their customers down while the system looks for data. A couple of weeks after they have immersed themselves in this latest project, George calls in a panic. Apparently many customers have been getting angry because they have been accused of having unpaid bills when, in fact, they are paid up in full. The problem is that Cosmo left in a diagnostic by mistake that indicates that any customer named George is delinquent. Elaine and Jerry tell him that he has to fix the problem.*

> *Cosmo uses the integration workspace to work on the change. He checks out the **b2** versions of all of the files:*

```
co -rb2 *
```

> *Once he has all of the files that went into making **b2** of his program, Cosmo has to find and fix the defect (sorry, we can help, but we can't do it all).*

Rebuilding a Fixed Release

Once you have fixed the defect, you want to be able to give your customers a new version of the software (otherwise, why would you have bothered?). Just like any release of your software, you want to keep track of what went into the release (so that if you find another problem the customer really needs fixed right away, you can add that fix to this version, instead of starting over with the original one). Thus, you want to re-group the files and add information to your release notes. We recommend that you mark the files with a symbolic name that gives you some information about why you created this release. For instance, you might want to name it *b2_1* if the original release was named *b2* and this is the first bug fix you have made to that release.

> *After Cosmo has found and fixed his defect, he rebuilds the software and rushes a new copy up to the operators. He also marks each of the files he used in this release b2george, to help him remember that he created this version to fix the George problem.*

Merging Your Fix with Your Current Version

Many times, if you make a change in an old version of your software, you also want that change incorporated into the current version. Each file you changed as part of your defect fix needs to be updated in the current work you are doing to include the defect fix information. Just as in the case where some team members are working ahead of the current release, you can't just check in the changed files in place of the current ones, or you lose any of the changes that you made since your last release. Instead, you need to *merge* the two versions of the files, to come up with a version that includes the defect fix, as well as any later changes you have made. In RCS, you can use the **rcsmerge** command to combine the versions.

Beyond the Basics

W e thought a few topics would be impor-
tant to mention, without going into great depth. These are topics that will not be of
interest to everyone—you can do a lot with a configuration management system
without addressing any of these topics. These are some of the areas in which the various systems can be most differentiated. The topics we discuss here are security,
projects, change management, the copy-merge configuration management model
and distributed development.

Security

If you are in an environment where others can potentially have access to the files
stored on your computer systems, security can be a very important topic. If you
are working alone, you can isolate the files from others and usually don't need to
worry about additional security that can be provided by a configuration management system (although you may want to make doing destructive things hard, like
deleting the files from the configuration management system, so that you don't
destroy things by mistake).

If you are working in a team, two levels of security are important. The first
level is the basic security provided by your operating system. This level allows you
to give read-only, read-write, or no access to your files to various other people. This
granularity of security is fine for some files, but for configuration management files,
you often want to give people permission to perform some operations on the files but
not other operations. For example, you need to give all members of your team per-

147

mission to check in and check out files. You might not want to give everyone permission to delete files.

In addition to limiting access to operations, you sometimes want to limit access to certain modifications of the files' attributes. Once you have assigned a symbolic name to a given version of a file (because it was used in a particular release, for example), you often don't want just anyone to reassign that symbolic name to a different version. You do want the team to be able to move a symbolic name that is dealing with the current release, however.

The security capabilities provided by configuration management systems vary from system to system. If they are an issue for you, RCS is probably not the best choice for a configuration management system, since it is very limited in its security capabilities.

Projects

We have discussed how to group files to better manage releases of products, or other events of interest. Some configuration management systems go even farther in grouping files. Many systems have the concept of a *"project."* With projects, you don't just check a file into the configuration management system; rather, you *add it to the project*. Adding a file to a project stores the file in the configuration management system, and it also associates it with a particular project. The project model is useful if you are dealing with a large number of files across several directories, or if you are creating more than one program or product.

Systems that support the project model usually have commands that allow you to work with projects, in addition to working with individual files. For example, in many systems you can "check out a project," creating copies of all of the files contained in that project in your local workspace. Projects usually have revisions (just like files). So usually, each time you make any change to the project (e.g., check in a file, create a new file, etc.), the project revision changes. You can also tag the project when you are ready for a release, rather than tagging each individual file. This setup effectively captures the current revision of each file used in the project. Then, if you ever need to get back, you just check out that particular revision of the project, and you get the correct version of each file used in the project.

For systems that don't have project support, you can mimic some of the ideas by storing all of the files for a project in one location. Although you won't have built-in capabilities for project support, you can use commands on groups of files to get a similar result. In general, though, if you are interested in project capabilities, your best bet is to use a system that supports them directly.

Change Management

Something that is important to many software development individuals and teams is the ability to track defects in their software and to easily know when and in which version a particular defect has been fixed. Given a defect, you want to know:

- Is it fixed?
- If it is fixed, what files were modified to fix it (and what revisions were created as part of the fix)?
- If it is fixed, what release of your product contains the fix (or is it waiting to be released)?
- If it is not fixed, have you done anything yet to start fixing it (e.g., have any files been modified)?

Some configuration management systems now provide defect tracking support along with configuration management, which can help keep track of the information necessary to answer these types of questions. In some systems, if you check out a file as part of the work to fix a defect, that filename and revision are added to the information stored about the defect. Sometimes, the defect number or identity is also added to the check-in comments when the file is checked in, so that reason for the change is kept with the file.

If you are very disciplined in your use of any configuration management system, you can annotate the check-in comments of files with this information, and you can store filenames and versions with the defect information that you manage. This approach can get to be a big pain quickly, however. Thus, if this is something that you would find useful, you might want to find a configuration management system that has the built-in capabilities already.

The Copy-Merge Configuration Management Model

The configuration management model that we have used in this book is the "check-out/check-in" model. In this model, if you want to make a change to a file, you lock the file, creating a modifiable version of the file for you to change. When you are completed with your change, you check in the file, creating a new revision in the configuration management system. While you have the file locked, other team members can access read-only versions of the file, but cannot lock the same revision as you. Thus, two people cannot easily make changes to the same revision of a file at the same time. This model is used by RCS and by many other configuration management systems.

Another configuration management model used by some systems is the *copy-merge* model. In this model, you don't lock files to make modifications to them. Rather, you can make modifications whenever you want. When you want to save a modification, you check in the file. If the file has not changed in the system since you checked it out, your changes are stored to the system and a new revision for the file created, much like before. If the file has changed in the system (e.g., a new revision has been created), a merge must take place before you can check in your changes. In this model, two people can make changes to the same revision of a file at the same time. The first person who checks in changes does not have any extra work, beyond the check-in. The second person, however, has to do a merge since the file has been changed in the system.

Good and bad things exist in both models. In the check-out/check-in model, when you get ready to create a release, you can easily see who has files checked out and locked. You can make sure all files have been checked in before creating the release, and thus know you have everyone's latest changes. In the copy-merge model, however, you would have to talk to each team member to make sure they had checked in their changes, since no easy way exists to determine who has un-checked-in changes.

In the check-out/check-in model, if you want to make a change to a file that someone has locked, you either have to wait until it gets checked in, or you have to go around the system to create a modifiable version of the file and then do a merge when you check in your changes. In the copy-merge model, you can always make changes and check them in, regardless of who else is making changes at the same time. You will have to make nontrivial merge decisions when the changes are not disjoint. Note that this situation can be extremely difficult if you are working with nontext files. For instance, if you store Microsoft Word or spreadsheet files in your configuration management system and need to do a merge of two versions of those files, it is not simply a matter of merging text. Some systems (such as Microsoft Word) provide a merge capability within them that you can use. If no merge capability is provided, however, merging two revisions can be almost impossible. In this case, you should probably stay away from systems using the copy-merge model.

We don't have the "right" answer as to which model is better. If you are interested in the second model, the CVS system is a good system to examine, since it uses this model (and it's free!).

Distributed Development

If you are working on a distributed team, your configuration management situation gets a little trickier. RCS isn't very friendly when sharing files among different computers in the same room, and gets even less friendly if you are trying to share files across states, or even continents. Some of the best systems for distributed teams are client-server systems. These systems have a server, on which all of the configuration management files are kept. Then each team member executes the client portion of the system on his or her own system. The client uses some communications mechanism to gain access to the files. When a file is checked out of the system, a copy is transferred to the user's (client) machine, and the user can modify it at will. When the file is checked in, it is transferred back to the server system, where it is checked back into the system. You really want someone to "own" the server in these cases, to make sure that it gets backed up regularly. Also, note that security in these situations is even more critical than when you are all physically located together.

Choosing a Tool for Your Team

By now, you may be ready to choose your configuration management tool. First of all, don't be afraid of moving off or staying on RCS. What you have been going through is just a warmup. Let your needs and the characteristics of the tools determine which is the appropriate tool.

You have many options for a configuration management tool. Think about what are your real needs and boundary conditions. In Section 1, we offered a series of questions for you to look at and consider. It's time to come back to that and rethink some of your answers.

- From an overall point of view, what are the major problems, issues, or events that you have encountered doing your software development?
- What problems, issues, or events have you had with the various parts of your development environment?
  - ❑ System hardware
  - ❑ Operating system
  - ❑ System configuration
  - ❑ Development tools
  - ❑ Applications
  - ❑ Libraries
- What problems, issues, or events have the people working on the project caused during development process?

- What problems, issues, or events have you had with the various development artifacts in your software development?
  - ❑ Source files
  - ❑ Binary files
  - ❑ Data files
  - ❑ Graphics
  - ❑ Icon bitmaps
  - ❑ User documents
  - ❑ Help files
  - ❑ Tests
  - ❑ Design Documents
  - ❑ Other . . .

Now, having reconsidered some of the issues you are dealing with, what are the characteristics of your environment and what are the boundary conditions within which you need to stay?

- How much do you want to spend?
  - ❑ Nothing   ($0)
  - ❑ A small amount   (<$100)
  - ❑ A moderate amount   ($100–$500)
  - ❑ A great deal   ($1000 and up)
  - ❑ Whatever it takes   (give us a call . . .)
- How technically competent is the team?
  - ❑ Beginning
  - ❑ Mixed   (this is probably the toughest)
  - ❑ Moderate
  - ❑ Advanced
- How easy should the tool be to use?
  - ❑ Very easy   (need a graphical interface)
  - ❑ Moderately easy   (would like a graphical interface)
  - ❑ Not an issue   (command line/guru)
- How complex are the team's configuration management needs?
  - ❑ Very simple   (simple versioning)
  - ❑ Moderate   (like branching)
  - ❑ Very complex   (like multiple projects)
- What is your hardware computing environment?
  - ❑ Single type of computer (e.g., all PCs)
  - ❑ Mixed types   (e.g., PCs and workstations)

- What is your operating system environment?
    - ❏ Single type of OS   (e.g., all Windows95)
    - ❏ Similar mixed types   (e.g., Windows95 and NT)
    - ❏ Widely mixed types   (e.g., Windows and UNIX)
- What is the smallest hardware configuration that a team member will be working on?
    - ❏ CPU: _____
    - ❏ RAM size: _____
    - ❏ Hard drive size: _____
    - ❏ Operating system: _____ver___
- What is the team's software development environment?
    - ❏ Language: _____
    - ❏ Development tools: _____
- How critical is support to your team's software development process?
    - ❏ Not critical   (you can deal with problems yourself or can get along without solutions)
    - ❏ Moderate   (want or need some help from time to time)
    - ❏ Critical   (you need solutions, probably in a timely fashion)

Given the answers to these key questions, you can now go to Section 4 of the book and compare your characteristics with the tools' characteristics.

Characteristic	Heading found under
How much do you want to spend?	Tool comparisons: *General or Cost*
What is your HW configuration?	Tool comparisons: *Platforms*
How critical is support?	Tool comparisons: *Support*
What is your SW environment?	Tool comparisons: *Bindings*
How technically competent are you?	Tool overviews: *Best suited for*
How easy should the tool be to use?	Tool overviews: *Best suited for*
How complex are your CM needs?	Tool overviews: *Best suited for*

The recommended approach is to presort the choices (and any other tools that you may find) based on price, hardware, and support needs. Note software bindings are a nice feature, but just because a tool does not have your development environment as a binding is not a good reason to remove it from the list. However, for two otherwise similar configuration management tools, having bindings can be a deciding factor. Next go through the set of tools and look at the *Best suited for* portion of the specific tool overview and see if the tool is reasonable for you based on your technical skills, ease of use, and problem complexity.

After you have gotten to this point, look at the tool specific information and make sure that it is a reasonable match to your needs.

After You Have Narrowed Your Choices . . .

If possible, get an evaluation copy and use the tool or tools that interest you. We have made every attempt at providing useful and correct information. However, tools change and you should check the vendors' current releases. Also, these tools have a lot of features—more than we can cover in this book. Nothing can substitute for actually looking at and using the real tool.

After You Have Made Your Choice . . .

As you start using a tool, be sure to pay attention to terminology differences. Most tools use similar terminology—but some of them can be fairly subtle—like version versus revision.

Recommendations for Teams and Team Projects

When you work alone, you get to determine the structure for your projects and the "rules" you use to work with it. Generally, you won't write down rules and probably don't even think about them much; you just do them. On a team, however, everyone must understand and buy into the project structure and rules. Thus, formalizing the rules at least a little makes sense. How much *"a little"* is depends quite a bit on the makeup of the team and the projects you are creating.

In this chapter, we give a set of recommendations for both projects and team rules for dealing with the projects. Also we address some of the potential problems you may encounter. This chapter is really a set of recommendations—not requirements. We know that every project and team are different and not all of the recommendations are applicable. So use the ones you like and don't worry about the rest.

How Do You Structure Your Projects?

In a team environment, usually more than one machine is involved. Generally, each team member has his or her own machine. In the better situations, one or more centralized machines are also used to store the project files, and are often used for building and/or testing the project.

Each team member's machine is used to store a local version of the software for the project, as well as some or all of the supporting materials that go along with it (like readme files, bug reports, user lists, etc.). The shared machines store information similar to the team members' machines. In addition, the versioned copies of the project files are usually stored on a shared machine. Here you create the structure for your project.

Most configuration management systems do not have a detailed set of requirements regarding how you structure your projects or name the files and directories that are part of those projects. Most of this section discusses things that you should consider about the structure of your projects regardless of whether or not you use a configuration management system. Some of them you have probably already thought about, and your team most likely already has a structure in place for your projects. Putting a configuration management system in place causes you to make some changes, however, and is an ideal time to reconsider what you have already done and make changes as appropriate.

Following are some of our recommendations:

- *Create a root directory for all of your projects, with a subdirectory for each project below it.* Generally, you want to keep all of your files associated with a project separate from everything else you store on your computer. If you are working on more than one project, backing up and sharing files across projects is easier if you have a shared root directory for all of them. Even if you only have one project now, you might consider making a root directory in case you expand what you are doing in the future. Once you have created a shared root directory for all of your projects, you usually want to create a separate subdirectory under that for each project. This subdirectory will be the root directory for that project.
- *Use a hierarchical directory structure for each of your projects.* Once you have created a root directory for a project, you probably want several subdirectories under *that* root, in which you logically group all of the files that belong to your project. For instance, if you are building one executable and a couple of libraries, you might want to put the source for each library in its own directory, and the source for the executable in a separate directory. You might find separating the documentation files from the source files easier as well. That way, when you are working on documentation, you only have to browse through the documentation files, and when you are working on source, you only have to browse through the source files. A good rule is: "When in doubt, add another level in the hierarchy." Many people start out putting too much in the top-level directory, and over time end up with unnecessary top-level clutter. Adding another level in the hierarchy can help alleviate this overload.
- *Make sure each subdirectory contains a manageable set of files.* For instance, don't store 100 files in one directory!
- *If you share source or libraries among projects, create a subdirectory for the shared code directly under the root directory, rather than under one project.*

Also, if you are creating something (a library, for instance) that you currently use only in one project, but think you may use several places in the future, create a separate location for its files now. This will make reuse of that code easier—it will be easier to find (since you won't have to remember which project you stored it with), and it should be easier to merge with all of your projects that need it.

- *Use names and a structure that are meaningful to you and your team so that everyone can find things easily.* The separation into subdirectories causes confusion if you find yourself hunting through all of the subdirectories to find the one file you need!

How about Personal Files?

In this section, we have been talking about team projects and how to use a configuration management system in a team environment. Even if you are a member of a team, you have personal files that you care about but the rest of the team does not. You probably don't want to store the versioned copies of these files with the team files, since they might cause confusion for the other team members, and you might lose control over them.

Nothing precludes you from storing versioned copies of your personal files in a location on your own machine. If you have a large amount of personal files and personal projects, you might want to browse through Section 2, which talked about configuration management for the individual. Otherwise, you can just create a project as we have suggested for a team; but store it on your local machine rather than a centralized machine.

How Often Do You Check In Your Files?

In a team environment, the process of checking in a file accomplishes two different goals:

- It saves a new version of the file in the configuration management system
- It allows other team members to access that version of the file more easily (i.e., it "publicizes" the new version to other team members)

So you might have different reasons to check in files—any of which can influence how often you and other team members check in files. Dictating to a team of (hopefully) intelligent people how often files should be checked in would be hard. Rather, we suggest that you implement a set of guidelines, and keep the absolute rules to a minimum. Here are some potentially useful suggestions:

- *Use symbolic names and a promotion scheme to make sure that what you publish to team members won't stop their work.* In a team environment, the files you check in are often used by other team members in their work. So you don't want to check in "garbage" for other team members to use. You also don't want to be stopped from checking in changes until you get everything right. Using symbolic names to promote files allows you to do both.
- *If you are going to experiment with your files, check in everything first, so you can keep track of where you are.* Often, you are involved in a change and realize that you aren't sure exactly how to proceed. So you start trying a little of this and a little of that, and pretty soon you realize that you have no idea what you are doing and you just want to go back to something you had before you started experimenting. If you had checked in the files, going back would be easy.
- *Check in meaningful chunks together, so that you generally have something that works together.* Most changes involve more than one file. If you are working on several changes over the course of a night, check in all files involved with the first change before you jump into the second change—even if you are modifying some of the same files in the second change. Then, even if you screw up completely while working on the second change, you at least have the first change completed and saved.
- *Check in before backing up.* We talk about backup strategies later in this chapter, but in general, you want to check in your changes before you do backups, in order to make sure the changes are included in your backup.
- *If you are going to be gone for three weeks, check in and back up!* This one is an obligatory "good sense" recommendation. Just like you wouldn't leave your editor open with five hours of work unsaved for a long period of time, don't leave your modified files unprotected (i.e., not checked in). Also, some other team member may need to modify some of "your" files in your absence, and keeping them locked while you are gone would be rude.
- *Checking in never hurts.* This one is another obligatory "good sense" recommendation. Even if you aren't sure if the changes you made are entirely correct or even complete, saving them by checking them in won't hurt. One of the beauties of the configuration management systems, as we have seen, is that you can get back to any previous version of your files easily. Most systems even allow you to "obsolete" specific versions if you really want to get rid of them forever (although in most cases, the disk space you save is not really worth the effort). Thus, checking in is even less destructive than saving in your editor—you can always go back![19]

---

19.   Of course, we realize that this recommendation contradicts the second recommendation (check in meaningful chunks . . .). Which you use depends on the circumstances. If you take weeks to create a meaningful chunk, don't wait to check in the pieces! Make sure the other team members aren't trying to build with the new stuff, though, or it might get really frustrating for all of you. This scenario is a perfect reason for using symbolic names and a promotion scheme.

Check-in Comments

In a team environment, check-in comments can be very useful if members on the team use them consistently. The configuration management system automatically stores information about who made a change, when the change was made, the new version number of the file, and differences between versions. Good check-in comments can provide additional information to help you determine why files were changed, where specific changes were made, and what other files were changed as part of a system modification. Some suggestions for check-in comments:

- *As part of the check-in comment include the reason the file was changed.* If a file was modified to fix a defect, you should include some mechanism to identify which defect was fixed (e.g., a defect number or short explanation of the defect). If a file was modified to add new functionality, a short explanation of the functionality should be given.
- *Include information about other files that were changed as part of this modification.* Most changes you make to your system involve changing more than one file. By including a list of all files that have changed in the check-in comment, you make tracking down all of the changes that were made as part of a particular modification easier.
- *Give any known information about the state of the file.* Often, you check in a file with incomplete changes—you may be working on implementing some new functionality that is going to take weeks and this check-in is intermediate. In these cases, you want to give some indication in the check-in comment that you aren't finished. Once you have the complete functionality implemented, you want the check-in comment to reflect the new state.

What Files to Store

We have mainly focused on how to manage your source files in the configuration management system. Remember that you do need other information besides the source to re-create old versions of your projects. Also, for most people, source files aren't the only type of information that you create and need to manage. Once you get comfortable with a configuration management system, consider *all* types of information you may want to store there—not just source files. Although this list isn't comprehensive, it may help trigger your memory about something else you should store in the system:

- Tool versions (or the tools themselves), even if you didn't create them
- Accounting information
- Customer data
- Documentation

- System configuration files
- Makefiles or other batch files or scripts

Team Dynamics

When working on a team, you need to have established team rules (either formal or informal) in order to work well together. Some common team problems with configuration management and suggestions for solutions include:

- *A team member keeps files locked for extended periods of time.* Besides the immediate desire to do something nasty to the person or their computer, you have a couple of different options. The first option is diplomacy. Explain to the individual the importance of checking in changes and making things accessible to other team members. If this doesn't work, you can do a *break lock* operation in most tools. However, you don't know in what state the individual has left things.
- *Someone on the team doesn't lock files.* This problem is really as bad as someone keeping file locks for a long time. Again, the appropriate first step is to talk with the person.
- *Someone on the team mucks around with the archive files.* This problem could include something as catastrophic as deleting the files or as foolish as editing the files. A key step is to keep backups. As stated earlier, configuration management is not a replacement for backup strategies and processes. Other reasonable steps involve protecting the archive, possibly meaning putting the archives on a server that is more difficult for accidental or malicious modifications. Many configuration management systems have better security mechanisms than RCS. If you are using one of these systems, you should utilize their security mechanisms as fully as reasonable for your team.

Backup Strategies

We really can't stress enough that a configuration management system is *not* a backup system. No matter how many times you check in a working file, if the shared disk crashes and you lose the configuration management file associated with it, your information will be gone. You hopefully already have some sort of backup strategy (you do backups, right?). But having a configuration management system changes that strategy somewhat.

We recommend that you just back up your configuration management files, and not the working files. If you check in before backing up, your configuration management files contain all of the information found in the working files. If you lose your disk, you can re-create both the configuration management files and the working files from your backups, and yet you have managed to keep your backups as small as possible.[20]

Because the configuration management files include all of the historical information directly in the files, you don't need to keep several different versions of your backups (because from today's backup you can not only re-create what you had today, but you can also re-create what you had last week). Thus, although we do recommend that you keep a few of your last backups, you don't need to keep every single backup since the beginning of time. And, since you can recycle your backup disks or tapes more often, you should consider doing backups more often than before.

One caveat is that we do recommend keeping a backup of each real release you create. That way, if you need to get to it quickly, you don't have to rebuild everything from the master backups. Rather, you can just copy it off and you are ready to go. If you fix a bug in a release, make sure you create a backup of the fixed release. Then use that backup instead of the original one if you have to re-create the release.

System Errors

Most of the available configuration management systems are fairly good. Like all software, unfortunately, these tools have defects that can cause you trouble. If you are just getting started with a system and it doesn't seem to work well, you may have something misconfigured. Some common problems include:

- The PATH variable is not set correctly.
- Other environment variables have not been set correctly.
- Another tool installed on your system is causing the new tool to function incorrectly. Many of the configuration management systems use RCS as a base. These systems sometimes have utilities named with the same name as RCS utilities (e.g., co, ci, etc.). If you have installed RCS and the new system, you need to make sure the correct utility is in your PATH first. If it is not, an incorrect version of each utility might be called mistakenly, causing the system to malfunction.

If you have been using the system without problems for a while, it has probably been installed correctly. If you run into a problem in these cases, troubleshooting

---

20. This recommendation does assume that you check in as frequently as you back up. If this assumption is not the case, backing up just the configuration management files does not always get the latest changes. We do recommend that you check in all files before doing a backup, or at least back up very frequently so the amount you lose in a catastrophe is small.

might be harder. If you are using a graphical user interface, you might try using the command line function to see if the error message is more informative. Sometimes, you might want to even check out the available documentation or online help! Also, news forums are dedicated to configuration management (see Section 4 in the tool information chapters, 4-3 and 4-4, under "Information Sources" for more information), in which you can pose questions.

Next Steps for a Team

Hopefully we have given you enough information about configuration management to help you understand how you can use it in your environment. You have several ways to proceed from here: You might want to learn more about RCS; you might want to review some of the other tools available; or you might want to just jump in and get started.

If you are interested in learning more about RCS, we have included some sample RCS files on the CD to help you. You can use these files to play around with RCS and the commands that we have described. They will give you a feel for how the system really works, and allow you to watch files changing over time. These files have different versions, check-in comments, branches, etc. The structure of the files is similar to files that have been stored in RCS for a while and have undergone various changes in that time. The instructions on how to install the sample files are in Section 5: Appendix A.

Once you have installed the files on your disk, you can practice with any of the commands we have described. For example, try doing some (or all) of the following:

- Show the history of a file
- Show the differences between two revisions of a file
- Take a look at the symbolic names that are defined on a file
- Check out the default version of a file
- Check out a particular version of a file, given by a revision number
- Check out a particular version of a file, given by a symbolic name
- Check in a file

165

We realize, however, that RCS is not the ideal system for everyone. One of its drawbacks is that it is a command line system, without a user-friendly interface. Another is that it isn't the most friendly team-based configuration management system around. Earlier in this section, we discussed what to consider when choosing a tool. In Section 4, we describe some of the tools (both public domain and for sale) that are available to use. We have not done complete reviews of any of the tools, but do provide information on what they can and cannot do for you. We have also included directions on how to get information on each of the tools.

Regardless of the tool and methods you choose, we wish you good luck in using configuration management in your team development situation!

Tools

"A tool so powerful, it can only be used for good or evil . . ."

What Software Is Available for Configuration Management

$\mathbf{T}$he point of this section is **not** to make a specific recommendation about which tool to use. The point is to provide you with enough information to help you decide what tools to consider. If at all possible, you should "try before you buy," by using an evaluation copy of the package(s) you are considering.

As with almost all software these days, you can get commercial, public domain, and shareware configuration management tools. The commercial tools fall into every price range, with the least expensive being a few hundred dollars and the most expensive being several thousands of dollars. If you are reading this book, you are probably most interested in the lower-end tools. Therefore, the commercial tools we discuss here are the lower-priced packages.

Public Domain

Public domain software is "free"—at least in purchase price. If you are excessively analytical, you may think about the line charges to download public domain software. But it is inexpensive in the relative scale of things. Some public domain software that you find is of poor quality. In many cases, however, you get more than you pay for with public domain configuration management software. Often, the quality can be very good to excellent.

The challenge with public domain configuration management software is not the quality, availability, or usability, but it is often installation, documentation, and support. Sometimes, you have to build the system from scratch once you have down-loaded it (this requirement tends not to be as much of a problem with PCs as with other systems). Public domain tool documentation may be limited or brief. A common approach for support is to try posting questions on the Internet Newsgroups (which are described in the tool descriptions in Chapters 4-3 and 4-4).

You should be aware that most public domain tools are intended for use, but not for resale. The normal disclaimer that most contain says "for noncommercial use only." This generally means you can use it—even within your corporation if you work at one—but you can't include it as part of a product that you sell or for which you get some compensation.

Note that we say *public domain* in this discussion and that captures the sense and use of free software, but much of the current free software is covered under the GNU[21] General Public License. It is still freely available for most uses, but it is legally protected. Be sure to review the license.

Shareware

Shareware is the step between public domain and commercial. Generally, the author(s) expect some form of payment (ranging from money through postcards all the way to donating blood). Ethically, you should send in the money, blood, or whatever. The software tends to be better than public domain software and usually has at least a better installation process and documentation. The requested monetary amounts tend to be in the $10-$60 range. For this payment, the authors often send the official or full release and the full documentation.

Commercial

If you have the money, review the available commercial packages. Some very good packages are available and the support should be better. In the process of analyzing the tools that are available, we found that two major classes of commercial tools exist— *moderate complexity* and *big science* configuration management. We focus on the *moderate complexity* class of tools here, not to say that the *big science* tools are not worth considering. We feel that these tend to be too complex for the problems faced by most individual and small teams. These *big science* tools do excel at helping large teams with many difficult problems, but they are normally out of the price range of most individuals and small teams. However, your time is still well spent checking out the Internet home pages as well as Newsgroups for the various vendors.

A note about pricing: the prices listed in this section were the current list price when this book was printed. Many vendors offer competitive upgrade or introductory price offers. And with competitive pressures, prices change.

---

21.   For those not familiar with GNU—it is a collection of free software associated with the Free Software Foundation started by Richard Stallman. GNU is a recursive acronym that stands for "GNU's Not UNIX."

Tool
Comparisons

T his chapter provides a high-level description and comparison of many, but not all, configuration management tools available. The tools that we discuss were chosen because they run on PC hardware (DOS, Windows, Win95, or WinNT), are relatively mainstream, are accessible, and are moderately priced. Note that these comparisons are not product reviews but are, as stated earlier, high-level and feature comparisons. Note also that we are not including all of the features of all of the tools.

The public domain and shareware tools examined here are:

CVS	by Brian Berliner (and others)
QVCS	by Jim Voris
RCS	by Walter Tichy (and others)

The commercial tools examined here are:

PVCS	from Intersolv
Source Integrity	from Mortice Kern Systems
SourceSafe	from Microsoft Corporation
StarTeam	from StarBase Corporation
TLIB	from Burton Systems

Since we don't discuss all configuration management tools here, take the time to look on the Internet for additional information. One site that is worth checking out is David Eaton's excellent *Configuration Management Tools Summary* site located at: **http://www.iac.honeywell.com/Pub/Tech/CM/CMTools.html**

The tables that follow in this chapter are intended to be self-explanatory in nature. In the remaining chapters in this section, there are a standard set of more detailed information about each tool. Again the intention is that this information is self-explanatory.

		CVS	QVCS	RCS
General	**Price** (on April 13, 1996)	$ 0	$ 25 & $20/ yr	$ 0
	Source code	Yes	No	Yes
	Evaluation copy	N/A	full version	N/A
Platforms	**PC - DOS**	No	Yes	Yes
	PC - Windows 3.1	No	Yes	(via DOS)
	PC - Windows 95	Yes	Yes	(via DOS)
	PC - Windows NT	Yes	Yes	(via DOS)
	UNIX	Yes	No	Yes
	Linux	Yes	No	Yes
	Other	OS/2,VMS,...	No	OS/2,others...
Interface	**Command line**	Yes	Yes	Yes
	GUI	Add-on	Yes	No
Features	**Change logging**	Yes	Yes	Yes
	File locking	No	Yes	Yes
	Branching	Yes	Yes	Yes
	Merge	Yes	Yes	Yes
	Symbolic tags	Yes	Yes	Yes
	Comments	Yes	No	Yes
	State info	Yes	No	Yes
	Embedded info	Yes	Yes	Yes
	Conversions	RCS, SCCS	No	SCCS
Support	**Online help**	No	Yes	No
	Tutorial	Yes	Partial	Yes
	Online manuals	Yes	Yes	Yes
	Printed manuals	No	No	No
	Web page(s)	Yes	Yes	No
	News or BBS	No	No	No
	Phone support	Commercial	No	No
	E-mail support	Commercial	Yes	Some
Bindings	**File Manager**	No	No	No
	Microsoft VC++	No	No	No
	Microsoft VBasic	No	No	No
	Borland C++	No	No	No

		PVCS	TLIB
General	Price (on April 13, 1996)	$499 ($599 UNIX)	$139/$225
	Source code	No	No
	Evaluation copy	Yes	No
Platforms	PC - DOS	Yes	Yes
	PC - Windows 3.1	Yes	Yes
	PC - Windows 95	Yes	Yes
	PC - Windows NT	Yes	Yes
	UNIX	Yes	No
	Linux	No	No
	Other	OS/2, VMS	OS/2
Interface	Command line	Yes	Yes
	GUI	Yes	Yes
Features	Change logging	Yes	Yes
	File locking	Yes	Yes
	Branching	Yes	Yes
	Merge	Yes	Yes
	Symbolic tags	Yes	Somewhat
	Comments	Yes	Yes
	State info	Yes	Yes
	Embedded info	Yes	Yes
	Conversions	RCS, SCCS	PVCS, RCS, Delta, ...
Support	Online help	Yes	Yes
	Tutorial	Yes	No
	Online manuals	Yes	No
	Printed manuals	Yes	Yes
	Web page(s)	Yes	Yes
	News or BBS	CompuServe	BBS
	Phone support	Yes	Yes
	E-mail support	Yes	Yes
Bindings	File Manager	No	No
	Microsoft VC++	Yes	No
	Microsoft VBasic	Yes	Yes
	Borland C++	Yes	Yes

		Source Integrity	SourceSafe	StarTeam
General	Price (on April 13, 1996)	$599	$499/$449	$99/$199/$549
	Source code	No	No	No
	Evaluation copy	Yes	Yes	Yes
Platforms	PC - DOS	Yes	Some	No
	PC - Windows 3.1	Yes	Some	No
	PC - Windows 95	Yes	Yes	Yes
	PC - Windows NT	Yes	Yes	Yes
	UNIX	Yes	via Mainsoft	No
	Linux	No	No	No
	Other	OS/2	Macintosh	No
Interface	Command line	Yes	Yes	Some
	GUI	Yes	Yes	Yes
Features	Change logging	Yes	Yes	Yes
	File locking	Yes	Yes	Yes
	Branching	Yes	Yes (project model)	Yes
	Merge	Yes	Yes	Yes
	Symbolic tags	Yes	Yes	Yes
	Comments	Yes	Yes	Yes
	State info	Yes	No	Somewhat
	Embedded info	Yes	Yes	Yes
	Conversions	RCS, SCCS, PVCS	PVCS, Delta	PVCS
Support	Online help	Yes	Yes	Yes
	Tutorial	Yes	No	Yes
	Online manuals	Yes	Yes	Yes
	Printed manuals	Yes	Yes	Yes
	Web page(s)	Yes	Yes	Yes
	News or BBS	BBS	AOL, BBS, ...	CompuServe
	Phone support	Yes	Yes	Yes
	E-mail support	Yes	Yes	Yes
Bindings	File Manager	Yes	Somewhat	No
	Microsoft VC++	Yes	Yes	Yes
	Microsoft VBasic	Yes	Yes	Yes
	Borland C++	Yes	Yes	No

Free, Public Domain, and Shareware Tools

CVS—Concurrent Versions System

CVS Overview	
Type of package	GNU General Public License
Cost	free
Author	Brian Berliner (and others)
Official source	GNU distribution
Platforms	PC - Windows 95 PC - Windows NT UNIX (binaries for SunOS, Solaris) Linux OS/2 (client only) VAX/VMS (client only) NeXTStep
Available from	A good source for the current CVS release is Cyclic Software at **ftp://ftp.cyclic.com/pub/cvs/** Pascal Molli has a good source of international ftp sites for CVS at **http://www.loria.fr/~molli/cvs-ftp.html** From this list, the US ftp sites for CVS are: **ftp://prep.ai.mit.edu/pub/gnu** **ftp://labrea.stanford.edu** **ftp://uiarchive.cso.uiuc.edu/pub/gnu** **ftp://gatekeeper.dec.com/pub/GNU**
Source code	Yes—via the above GNU distribution sites
Evaluation copy	Yes—because the full system is in the public domain
Version	Version 1.9 (October 1996)
General comments	CVS is a collection of extensions on top of RCS (which is required for CVS to run). It can do a great deal, is oriented towards the upper end of functionality, and has a number of useful facilities for team and networked development. One specific feature of CVS is its ability to import ongoing source code drops (i.e., new releases from another organization or company). A fair amount of configuration is necessary to get things set up properly for path defaults, system defaults, and configuration. The standard CVS release is a command line system. However, several Tcl/Tk based extensions provide a graphical interface: GIC, RadCVS, and tkCVS. Also, light-weight GNU Emacs extensions are available for CVS: Light CVS and pcl-cvs.
Best suited for	Number of users: one to many, focused on many Type of users: technically competent Complexity level: moderate to complex needs Platforms supported: very wide range

CVS Information sources		Comments
Online help	No	CVS is a command line tool so it does not have a GUI online help system. However, you can type **cvs -H** or **cvs -H** *command* to get some command help.
Online manuals	Reference ~110 pages	<u>Version Management with CVS</u> This reference is for CVS 1.9 written by Per Cederqvist, et al. This is available as a series of HTML Web pages from **http://www.loria.fr/~molli/cvs/doc/cvs_toc.html** It is also available as a postscript document from **http://www.loria.fr/~molli/cvs/doc/cvs.ps**
Tutorial	Yes ~13 pages	<u>CVS Tutorial</u> This is a limited tutorial written by Gray Watson for CVS. It is available as a series of HTML Web pages from **http://www.loria.fr/~molli/cvs/cvs-tut/cvs_tutorial.html** It is also available as a postscript document from **http://www.loria.fr/~molli/cvs/cvs-tut/cvs.ps**
Printed manuals	No	None
Web page(s)	Yes	Several Web pages are dedicated to the CVS software. One of these is associated with Cyclic Software at **http://www.cyclic.com/** Another Web site is Pascal Molli's site, with CVS specific information pages at **http://www.loria.fr/~molli/cvs-index.html**
News or BBS	Newsgroups	Often "good Samaritan" (i.e., you ask and hope some kind person answers) support is available from the general configuration management newsgroup **comp.software.config-mgmt**
Phone support	Commercial	Cyclic Software is in the business of selling support for CVS. Cyclic Software can be found at **http://www.cyclic.com/**
E-mail support	Commercial	Cyclic Software is in the business of selling support for CVS. Cyclic Software can be found at **http://www.cyclic.com/**

CVS Features	
Storage	Versioned files are stored in the normal file system but as a repository (both locally and also remotely over a network). This repository is built on top of RCS, and the files in it are RCS-style with a **,v** suffix. You can have multiple repositories.
Locking	Checked-out files are NOT locked, but an automatic merge occurs if the areas of modification are different. A manual merge is triggered if not.
Version identifiers	The initial version of a file is always 1.1. The naming of a normal revision number is *release.level*.
Branching	Branching is of the form *release.level.branch.sequence*. If you are at revision 1.3, you will get branch 1.3.2. The first revision of 1.3.2 is revision 1.3.2.1, the next would be 1.3.2.2, and so on. Note that there can be branches off branches as well (like 1.3.2.2.2.8.6.2), but things may get rather hard to manage.
Embedded information	Information can be optionally embedded in the versioned file using the standard RCS keyword substitution strings of the form *$keyword$*:

$Author$	becomes $Author: *author*$
$Date$	becomes $Date: *date-and-time*$
$Header$	becomes $Header: *path+file rev date time author state*$
Id	becomes $Id: *file rev date time author state*$
$Locker$	becomes $Locker: *name*$
Log	becomes $Log: *log-message*$
$RCSfile$	becomes $RCSfile: *file*$
$Revision$	becomes $Revision: *rev-number*$
$Source$	becomes $Source: *path+file*$
$State$	becomes $State: *state*$

CVS Operations	Operation	Command	Comments
Version	Create	**cvs add**	To create an initial version, you add the directory and/or file of interest.
	Check out	**cvs checkout**	
	Check in	**cvs commit**	
	Cancel check-out	**cvs release**	Not exactly necessary since CVS doesn't lock files, but a good idea.
	Update	**cvs update**	Brings a file up to date from the repository and if necessary will merge in your current changes.
Comparison	File difference		Not applicable.
	Version difference	**cvs diff**	Compares different CVS versions without changing any files.
Merge	File merge	**cvs update -j**	Incorporates changes from the working file and a revision.
	Version merge	**cvs update -j**	Incorporates changes of two versions. This command has two **-j** parameters.
Control	Change log	**cvs log**	Shows change log.
Build	Make		Not applicable.
Branches	Create branch	**cvs rtag -b**	
Grouping	Tagging	**cvs tag**	
	Set state	**cvs admin -s**	User definable.
Project	Project		Done via tagging.
Utility	Configuration	**cvs admin**	An RCS front end. Some options don't work with CVS.
	Identify file		None
	Clean up	**cvs release**	Cleans up and deletes working files—can throw away changes.
	Conversion	**sccs2rcs**	Imports SCCS files.

CVS Single developer	Command line Use scenario
Set up project	cvs add *mydir* cd *mydir*
Create initial version	cvs add *myfile*
Check out file	cvs checkout *mydir*
Check in file	cvs commit *myfile*
Tag with symbolic name	cvs tag *name myfile*
Create a branch	cvs rtag -b -r *name myfile*
Show file history	cvs log *myfile*

CVS Team of developers	Command line Use scenario
Set up project	cvs add *mydir* cd *mydir*
Create initial version	cvs add *myfile*
User attached to project	cvs watch add -a all *
Check out file	cvs checkout *mydir*
Check in file	cvs commit *myfile*
Identify user	cvs watch on *myfile* cvs editors *myfile*
Break lock	Not available.
Show file changes	cvs diff -r *name myfile*
Merge	cvs update -j *name myfile*

QVCS—Quma Version Control System

QVCS Overview	
Type of package	Shareware
Cost	$25 per year for the first year license $20 per year thereafter
Author	Jim Voris
Official source	Jim Voris 20 Warren Manor Court Cockeysville, MD 21030
Platforms	PC - DOS PC - Windows 3.1 PC - Windows 95 PC - Windows NT
Available from	**ftp://ftp.clark.net/pub/jimv/**
Source code	No
Evaluation copy	Yes, because the full version is available as shareware. If, after 60 days, you are still using it, you are expected to pay the license fee.
Version	2.2 (November 1996)
General comments	QVCS is an inexpensive general-purpose system intended for general use on PC platforms. It provides Command line and windows-based interfaces. QVCS also supports an activity log facility (called journals). This logs all QVCS activities to a log file for individual files or globally.
Best suited for	Number of users: one to several, focused on fewer Type of users: beginner to advanced Complexity level: simple to moderate needs Platforms supported: PCs running DOS or Windows

QVCS Information sources		Comments
Online help	Yes	QVCS has a Windows online help system. It includes general information as well as help on both the Command line interface and the Windows interface.
Online manuals	No	An HTML-based reference used to be available. This has now been folded into the online help system.
Tutorial	Partial	A pair of tutorials are mentioned in the Online help system. The introductory tutorial exists in the Online help system. It's enough to get you started, but it remains incomplete. The second is an advanced topics section for branching and merging that does not yet exist.
Printed manuals	No	Not applicable.
Web page(s)	Yes	Web pages dedicated to the QVCS software are available at **http://www.clark.net/pub/jimv/qvcsman.htm**
News or BBS	Newsgroups	Often "good Samaritan" (i.e., you ask and hope some kind person answers) support is available from the general configuration management newsgroup **comp.software.config-mgmt**
Phone support	No	Not applicable.
E-mail support	Some	Jim Voris, the author, states in the reference material that he wants satisfied customers and provides an e-mail address for questions, requests, and defects at **jimv@clark.net**

QVCS Features	
Storage	The workfiles (normal and accessible) and logfiles (containing the versioning information) are stored in the normal file system (with the logfiles put in a user defined location).
Locking	Checked-out files are not locked (by default), but this option is configurable.
Version identifiers	The initial version of a file is always 1.0. The naming of a normal revision number is *release.level*.
Branching	Branching is of the form *release.level.branch.sequence*. If you are at revision 1.0, you will get branch 1.0.1. The first revision of 1.0.1 is revision 1.0.1.1, the next would be 1.0.1.2, and so on. QVCS does an automatic branch when you try to check in and lock a file that is not the newest file revision.
Embedded information	Information can be optionally embedded in the versioned file using the standard keyword substitution strings of the form $*keyword*$:

$Author$	becomes $Author: *author*$
$Comment$	gets added to the revision comment
$Copyright$	becomes $Copyright: *copyright-message*$
$Date$	becomes $Date: *date-and-time*$
$Endlog$	used internally by QVCS
$Filename$	becomes $Filename: *filename*$
$Header$	becomes $Header: *path+file rev date time author state*$
Log	becomes $Log: *path log-message*$
$Log*X*$	becomes $Logx: *path last-X-log-messages*$
$Logfile$	becomes $Logfile: *path*$
$Owner$	becomes $Owner: *owner*$
$Revision$	becomes $Revision: *rev-number*$
$Version$	becomes $Version: *version-tag*$
VER	becomes $Ver: *file version-tag*$

QVCS Operations	Operation	Command	Comments
Version	Create	**qput**	To create an initial version, do a **qput -create** *file* and QVCS creates the initial logfile associated with *file*.
	Check out	**qget**	
	Check in	**qput**	
	Lock	**qlock**	Locks the file.
	Unlock	**qunlock**	Unlocks the file. This does not break a lock.
Comparison	File difference	**qdiff**	Done via **qdiff** *file1 file2*.
	Version difference	**qdiff -r**	
Merge	File merge	**qmerge**	Used by doing a **qmerge** *base file1 file2 out*.
	Version merge	**qmerge**	
Control	Change log	**qlog**	
Build	Make		Not applicable.
Branches	Create branch	**qget**	Do a checkout with a lock on a previous revision with **qget -l -r** *rev file*.
Grouping	Tagging	**qstamp**	Adds a label to a revision.
	Untagging	**qunstamp**	Removes just the label from a revision.
	Set state		Not applicable.
Project	Project		Done via tagging.
Utility	Configuration		Done via Command line options or environment variables.
	Identify file	**qident**	Displays any expanded QVCS keywords.
	Delete rev info	**qdelrev**	Permanently deletes information associated with specific revisions from a logfile.
	Modify logfile	**qmodhdr**	Modifies logfile information and attributes.
	Modify logfile revision	**qmodrev**	Modifies the logfile information and attributes for a specific revision.
	Conversion		None

QVCS Single developer	Command line Use scenario
Set up project	qstamp -v *'mylabel-for-myproject'* *
Create initial version	qput -create *myfile*
Check out file	qget -l *myfile*
Check in file	qput *myfile*
Tag with symbolic name	qstamp -v *'mylabel'* *myfile*
Create a branch	qget -r *revision* -l *myfile*
Show file history	qlog *myfile*

QVCS Team of developers	Command line Use scenario
Set up project	qstamp -v *'mylabel-for-myproject'* *
Create initial version	qput -create *myfile*
User attached to project	qmodhdr <*access-list-file* -mm * qmodhdr <*access-list-file* -ma *
Check out file	qget -l *myfile*
Check in file	qput *myfile*
Update files	Not available.
Identify user with lock	qlog -l *
Break lock	Not available.
Show file changes	qdiff -r *rev myfile myfile*
Merge	qmerge *mybasefile myfile1 myfile2 outputfile*

QVCS GUI	Main application window

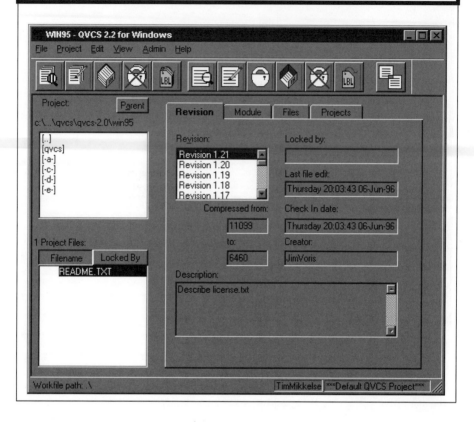

QVCS GUI	Main application window menu items	
File	**Project**	**Edit**
Get	Get	Undo Ctrl+Z
Check Out	Check Out	Cut Ctrl+X
Lock	Lock	Copy Ctrl+Y
Check In	Check In	Paste Ctrl+V
Unlock	Unlock	
Label	Label	
Remove Label	Remove Label	
Compare	Settings . . .	
Modify >	Refresh Files	
Exit		
View	**Admin**	**Help**
Revision Tab	Maintain Users . . .	QVCS Help Contents
Module Tab	Register QVCS . . .	Using Help
Files Tab		About QVCS
Projects Tab		
Toolbar		
Status Bar		

RCS—Revision Control System

RCS Overview	
Type of package	GNU General Public License
Cost	Free
Author	Walter Tichy (and others)
Official source	GNU distribution
Platforms	PC - DOS PC - Windows 3.1 (via DOS) PC - Windows 95 (via DOS) PC - Windows NT (via DOS) UNIX Linux OS/2 VAX/VMS Atari Amiga
Available from	Original sources are available from **ftp://ftp.cs.purdue.edu/pub/RCS** PC/DOS versions are available from **http://rfs63.Berkeley.edu/users/elf/rcsdos/**
Source code	Yes—via GNU distribution
Evaluation copy	Yes—because the full system is in the public domain
Version	Version 5.7 (June 1995) (Be careful on PCs with versions prior to 5.7 because they did not allow for binary/nontext files.)
General comments	By far the most popular of the public domain systems. It has been broadly ported and is very functional and small. It does not include a GUI interface. Commercial versions and variants are available. In particular, RCE was developed by Walter Tichy. MKS Source Integrity is also based on RCS.
Best suited for	Number of users: one to many Type of users: technically competent Complexity level: simple to moderate Platforms supported: very wide range

RCS Information sources		Comments
Online help	No	Not applicable.
Online manuals	Reference ~50 pages	A collection of UNIX-style "man" (i.e., manual) pages for each individual command is available (ranging in size from 1 to 10 pages each).
Tutorial	Overview ~20 pages	RCS - A System for Version Control This is an introduction written by Walter Tichy in 1991 available from **ftp://ftp.cs.purdue.edu/pub/RCS/rcs.ps**
Printed manuals	No	There are none since this is a public domain offering. However, there are books available.
Web page(s)	No	Not applicable.
News or BBS	Newsgroups	Often "good Samaritan" (i.e., you ask and hope some kind person answers) support is available from the general configuration management newsgroup. **comp.software.config-mgmt**
Phone support	No	Not applicable.
E-mail support	Some	Limited email support is available in that you can mail defects to **rcs-bugs@cs.purdue.edu**

RCS Features	
Storage	Versioned files are stored in the normal file system with a configurable extension indicating a versioned file. The default is normally *file-name*,**v**.
Locking	Checked-out files are locked, but this option is configurable.
Version identifiers	The naming of a normal revision number is *release.level*. The initial version of a file is always 1.1.
Branching	Branching is of the form *release.level.branch.sequence*. If you are at revision 1.3, you get branch 1.3.1. The first revision of 1.3.1 is revision 1.3.1.1, the next would be 1.3.1.2, and so on. Note that there can be branches off branches as well (like 1.3.1.2.2.8.6.2), but things may get rather hard to manage.
Embedded information	Information can be optionally embedded in the versioned file in a number of ways via special keyword substitution strings. Some caution needs to be taken with binary files to turn off keyword substitution, or corrupted files can occur. The keywords look like $*keyword*$: **$Author$** becomes $Author: *author*$ **$Date$** becomes $Date: *date-and-time*$ **$Header$** becomes $Header: *path+file rev date time author state*$ **Id** becomes $Id: *file rev date time author state*$ **$Locker$** becomes $Locker: *name*$ **Log** becomes $Log: *log-message*$ **$RCSfile$** becomes $RCSfile: *file*$ **$Revision$** becomes $Revision: *rev-number*$ **$Source$** becomes $Source: *path+file*$ **$State$** becomes $State: *state*$

RCS Operations	Operation	Command	Comments
Version	Create	**ci**	To create an initial version, do a **ci** *file* and RCS creates the initial version 1.1.
	Check out	**co**	
	Check in	**ci**	
	Cancel check-out	**rcs -u**	
Comparison	File difference	**diff**	Does a difference on two files.
	Version difference	**rcsdiff**	Compares different RCS versions.
Merge	File merge	**merge**	Incorporates changes (to the display or to a file) of two files.
	Version merge	**rcsmerge**	Incorporates changes (to the display or to a file) of two versions.
Control	Change log	**rlog**	Shows change log.
Build	Make		Not applicable.
Branches	Create branch	**ci -r***branch*	If the branch is off *x.y*, then *branch* should be *x.y*.1 in the command.
Grouping	Tagging	**ci -n***name*	
	Set state	**ci -s***state*	User definable.
Project	Project		Done via tagging.
Utility	Configuration	**rcs**	Changes archive attributes.
	Identify file	**ident**	Finds files using keywords.
	Cleanup	**rcsclean**	Unlocks and deletes unchanged working files.
	Conversion		Not applicable.

RCS Single developer	Command line Use scenario
Set up project	**mkdir** *myproj* **cd** *myproj*
Create initial version	**ci** *myfile*
Check out file	**co** *myfile*
Check in file	**ci** *myfile*
Tag with symbolic name	**ci -n***name myfile*
Create a branch	**co -l -r***previous-rev myfile* **ci** *myfile*
Show file history	**rlog** *myfile*

RCS Team of developers	Command line Use scenario
Set up project	**mkdir** *myproj* **cd** *myproj*
Create initial version	**ci** *myfile*
User attached to project	Not available.
Check out file	**co** *myfile*
Check in file	**ci** *myfile*
Update files	Not available.
Identify user with lock	**rlog** *myfile*
Break lock	**rcs -u** *myfile*
Show file changes	**rcsdiff -r***rev1* **-r***rev2 myfile*
Merge	**rcsmerge -r***rev1* **-r***rev2 myfile*

Commercial Tools

INTERSOLV PVCS

PVCS Overview	
Type of package	Commercial
Cost	$499 $599 (for the UNIX versions)
Author	INTERSOLV, Inc.
Official source	INTERSOLV, Inc.
Platforms	PC - DOS PC - Windows 3.1 PC - Windows 95 PC - Windows NT (both Intel and Alpha) UNIX (including HP-UX, IBM AIX, Sun and SCO) OS/2 VMS
Available from	INTERSOLV, Inc. 9420 Key West Avenue Rockville, Maryland 20850 Phone:(301)838-5000 Fax:(301) 838-5432
Source code	No
Evaluation copy	No
Version	5.2.20
General comments	There are a variety of other bindings including Borland's Delphi, PowerSoft PowerBuilder, and Oracle's Developer 2000.
Best suited for	Number of users: one to many, focused on team Type of users: beginner to advanced Complexity level: moderate to complex Platforms supported: wide range

PVCS Information sources		Comments
Online help	Yes	
Online manuals	Yes	The CD-ROM includes FrameViewer files of product manuals so that you can browse them online.
Tutorial	Yes	PVCS Guided Tour There is an online guided tour that includes information on navigation, basic and advanced features, and administration.
Printed manuals	Installation ~50 pages	PVCS Version Manager Installation Guide This is the administrator's manual and reference for installing PVCS.
	Licensing Reference ~8 pages	License Configuration Facility Reference Card This is the administrator's quick reference for the licensing mechanism.
	Licensing User Guide ~12 pages	Development Suite License Installer User Guide This is the administrator's manual and reference for the installing licenses.
	Licensing Admin. Ref. ~30 pages	Development Suite License Administration Facility Reference Guide This is the administrator's manual and reference for the licensing mechanism.
	Introduction ~35 pages	PVCS Version Manager Quick Start This is a simple introduction that includes setup, version control, the GUI, and the Command line.
	User Guide ~350 pages	PVCS Version Manager User Guide and Reference This is the general user and administration manual.
	Reference ~35 pages	PVCS Version Manager Command-Line Reference Guide This is the user's quick reference for the command-line interface.
Web page(s)	Yes	INTERSOLV has a general home page at **http://www.intersolv.com** Specific PVCS Version Manager information is at **http://www.intersolv.com/Products/scm.htm** Users with an access code can access a knowledge base via INTERSOLV's Web site.

PVCS Information sources		Comments
News or BBS	CompuServe	On CompuServe, at any ! prompt, type GO INTERSOLV to access the INTERSOLV forums.
	Newsgroups	Even though PVCS is a commercial product, you can often get help from other configuration management users in the general configuration management news-group **comp.software.config-mgmt**
Phone support	Yes	(800)-443-1601 5:30am–6:00pm Pacific Mon–Fri
	Yes	INTERSOLV also has some fax support. The regular fax technical support number is Fax: (503)-645-6260 A marketing and technical information fax number (Fax Plus) is also available at Fax Plus: (301)-230-3230
Email support	Yes	The general support e-mail address is **pvcs_answerline@intersolv.com**

PVCS Features	
Storage	Versioned files are stored in the normal file system, but in a separate library directory with a configurable extension indicating a versioned file. The library directory path is configurable as well (allowing you to put the versioned files in the same directory as the source files). The default extension takes the filename extension and replaces the last character of the extension with a "v." (So *file-name*.**txt** would become *filename*.**txv** .)
Locking	Checked-out files can be locked through a check-out option. The default is to lock files, but an option can be set by the PVCS administrator to allow for *multilocking*, which only warns a user who is accessing a file marked as locked.
Version identifiers	The naming of a normal revision number is *release.level*. The initial version of a file is always 1.0.
Branching	Branching is of the form *release.level.branch.sequence*. If you are at revision 1.3, you get branch 1.3.1. The first revision of 1.3.1 is revision 1.3.1.0, the next would be 1.3.1.1, and so on.
Embedded information	Information can be optionally embedded in the versioned file in a number of ways via special keyword substitution strings: **$Archive$** becomes $Archive: *path+file*$ **$Author$** becomes $Author: *author*$ **$Date$** becomes $Date: *date*$ **$Header$** becomes $Header: *name rev date author*$ **Log** becomes $Log: *log-message*$ **$Modtime$** becomes $Modtime: *time*$ **$Revision$** becomes $Revision: *rev-number*$ **$Workfile$** becomes $Workfile: *workfile-name*$

PVCS Operations	Operation	Command	Comments
Version	Create	**put**	PVCS will create an archive the first time you check a file in.
	Check out	**get**	
	Check in	**put**	
Comparison	File difference	**vdiff**	
Merge	File merge	**vmrg**	
	Version merge	**vmrg**	
Control	Change log	**vlog**	
Build	Make		Done via PVCS Configuration Builder product.
Branches	Create branch	**put -fb**	
Grouping	Tagging	**vcs -v**	Files can also be tagged by doing a **put -v** at check in.
	Set state	**vpromote** **vcs -G**	
Project	Add to project		Done through other PVCS mechanisms.
Utility	Configuration	**vcs** **vconfig**	Both are used for configuration. Also done via environment variables.
	Purge	**vdel**	
	Regenerate	**vregen**	
	Compress	**vcompres**	
	Change description	**vcs**	
	Identify file	**ident**	
	Show journal	**vjournal**	
	Export data	**vsql**	
	Conversion		Not applicable.

PVCS Single developer	Command line Use scenario
Set up project	Done via the GUI.
Create initial version	**put** *myfile*
Check out file	**get** *myfile*
Check in file	**put** *myfile*
Tag with symbolic name	**vcs -v** *tag myfile*
Create a branch	**put -fb** *branch myfile*
Show file history	**vlog** *myfile*

PVCS Team of developers	Command line Use scenario
Set up project	Done via the GUI.
Create initial version	**put** *myfile*
User attached to project	**vcs -a** *user-id* *
Check out file	**get** *myfile*
Check in file	**put** *myfile*
Update files	**regen** *
Identify user with lock	**vjournal -xl**
Break lock	**vcs -u** *myfile*
Show file changes	**vdiff** *referencefile myfile*
Merge	**vmrg -r***rev1* **-r***rev2 myfile*

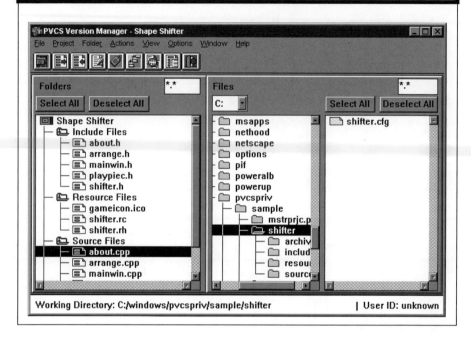

**PVCS
GUI** .... **Main application window**

PVCS GUI	PVCS application window menu items	
File	**Project**	**Folder**
Move/Rename...	Open Project... Ctrl+O	New Folder...
Copy...	Close Project	Change Folder...
Delete...	New Project...	Delete Folder...
Create Directory...	Configure Project... Ctrl+G	Change Folder Members...Ctrl+B
Exit	Copy Project...	Copy Folder Members...
	Delete Project...	Change Workfile Directory...
	Lock Project	Update Project Folder
	Unlock Project	
Actions	**View**	**Options**
Check Out... Ctrl+T	Folder Details	Preferences...
Check In... Ctrl+N	File Details	Toolbar...
Edit Ctrl+E	Locked Files	Editor...
Version Label... Ctrl+L	Modified Files	Difference Display...
Merge... Ctrl+M	Sort By...	Data File Locations...
Promotion Group... Ctrl+P	Refresh Ctrl+F	Log In...
Archive Report... Ctrl+A		Security
Difference Report... Ctrl+D		
Journal Report... Ctrl+J		
SQL Export...		
Lock... Ctrl+K		
Unlock... Ctrl+U		
Create Archive...		
Change Attributes		
Delete Revision		
Window	**Help**	
New Window	Contents	
	Search for Help on...	
	How to Use Help	
	What's New in 5.2	
	Guided Tour	
	Run Sample Project	
	About PVCS Version Manager...	

MKS Source Integrity

Source Integrity Overview	
Type of package	Commercial
Cost	$599
Author	Mortice Kern Systems, Inc.
Official source	Mortice Kern Systems, Inc.
Platforms	PC - DOS PC - Windows 3.1 PC - Windows 95 PC - Windows NT UNIX OS/2 2.1, Warp, Warp Connect
Available from	Mortice Kern Systems, Inc. 185 Columbia Street Waterloo, Ontario Canada N2L 5Z5 Phone: (519)-884-2251 Fax: (519)-884-8861 US: (800)-265-2797
Source code	No
Evaluation copy	Yes
Version	7.2 (July 1996)
General comments	Source Integrity is a very broad product supporting single first-time users through larger teams with more complex needs. Source Integrity includes a security administration facility for larger team needs. It includes integration with Borland Delphi, PowerBuilder, and Watcom's C++. It also has archive compatibility with MKS's Web Integrity product. Although never mentioned in the product documentation, the MKS Source Integrity product is based on, but is a clear superset of, the RCS system. Clear enhancements over RCS include the GUI, project management, administration, build management, and a "sandbox" concept.
Best suited for	Number of users: one to many Type of users: beginner to advanced Complexity level: simple to complex Platforms supported: wide range

Source Integrity Information sources		Comments
Online help	Yes	
Online manuals	No	Not applicable.
Tutorial	Yes	A self-paced online tutorial is available. This will start automatically when you run Source Integrity for the first time.
Printed manuals	Introduction ~35 pages	Getting Started with Source Integrity This is a brief introduction to configuration management concepts and the guide to installing Source Integrity.
	Quick Reference ~30 pages	Source Integrity Quick Reference This is a small format quick reference for the Command line interface operations and options, as well as the graphical user interface.
	Tutorial ~70 pages	Understanding Configuration Management This is a general introduction to configuration management concepts and the specific features in Source Integrity.
	Command Reference ~180 pages	Command Line Interface Reference Manual This is a general reference that includes information on managing projects and archives, configuration, and commands.
	Administration ~170 pages	Security and Administration Module Administrator's Guide This is the administrators' guide, which includes security.
	Build ~80 pages	MKS Make User's Guide This manual describes the **make** facility associated with Source Integrity.
Web page(s)	Yes	MKS has a general home page at **http://www.mks.com** Specific Source Integrity information is at **http://www.mks.com/solution/si/**
News or BBS	BBS	MKS has its own Bulletin Board System available at (519)-884-2861 (with the modem characteristics of v.34, no parity, 1 stop bit).
	Newsgroups	Even though Source Integrity is a commercial product, you can often get help from other configuration management users in the general configuration management newsgroup **comp.software.config-mgmt**

Source Integrity Information sources		Comments
Phone support	Yes	(519)-884-2270 8:30am–6:00pm Eastern Mon–Fri
E-mail support	Yes	The sales contact address is **sales@mks.com** and the general support e-mail address is **support@mks.com**

Source Integrity Features	
Storage	Versioned files are stored in the normal file system in an **rcs** directory.
Locking	Checked-out files are locked, but this option is configurable.
Version identifiers	The initial version of a file is always 1.1. The naming of a normal revision number is *release.level*.
Branching	Branching is of the form *release.level.branch.sequence*. If you are at revision 1.3, you get branch 1.3.1. The first revision of 1.3.1 is revision 1.3.1.1, the next would be 1.3.1.2, and so on. Note that there can be branches off branches as well (like 1.3.1.2.2.8.6.2), but things may get rather hard to manage.
Embedded information	Information can be optionally embedded in the versioned file in a number of ways via special keyword substitution strings:

$Author$	becomes $Author: *author*$
$Date$	becomes $Date: *date-and-time*$
$Header$	becomes $Header: *path+file rev date time author state*$
Id	becomes $Id: *file rev date time author state*$
$Locker$	becomes $Locker: *name*$
Log	becomes $Log: *log-message*$
$Name$	becomes $Name: *revision-labels*$
$RCSfile$	becomes $RCSfile: *file*$
$Revision$	becomes $Revision: *rev-number*$
$Source$	becomes $Source: *path+file*$
$State$	becomes $State: *state*$

Source Integrity Operations	Operation	Command	Comments
Version	Create	**ci**	To create an initial version, do a **ci** *file*.
	Check out	**co**	
	Check in	**ci**	
	Cancel check out	**unlock**	A configuration option enables anyone to break other locks.
	Update	**pj refresh**	Also, a GUI function resynchronizes.
Comparison	File difference	**diff**	Compares two files.
	Version difference	**rcsdiff**	Compares different RCS versions.
	File difference	**diffb**	Compares two binary files.
	File difference	**diff3**	Compares three files.
Merge	File merge	**merge**	Incorporates changes (to the display or to a file) of two files.
	Version merge	**rcsmerge**	Incorporates changes of two versions.
Control	Change log	**rlog**	Shows change log.
Build	Make	**make**	Builds the system.
	Create a make file	**mkmf**	Makes a makefile for building.
	Show dependencies	**pj finddep**	Shows makefile dependencies.
Branches	Create branch	**co -l -r***branch*	To branch, check out a version, locked, that is not at the head of the revision tree and then check it in.
Grouping	Tagging	**pj label**	Labels members.
	Set state	**ci -s***state*	Source Integrity refers to changing state as promotion.
Project	Add to project	**pj add**	Adds files to a project.
	Remove member	**pj drop**	Removes files from a project.
	Set attribute	**pj addrule**	Sets member attribute.
	Clear attribute	**pj droprule**	Clears member attribute.
	Build a release	**pj build**	
	Checkpoint	**pj checkpoint**	New project revision.
	Check out	**pj co**	Checks out the project or a file.
	Check in	**pj ci**	Checks in the project or a file.

Source Integrity Operations	Operation	Command	Comments
Project (continued)	Difference	**pj diff**	Compares the project or a file.
	Lock	**pj lock**	Locks the project or a file.
	Unlock	**pj unlock**	Unlocks the project or a file.
	Show history	**pj rlog**	Shows the history of the project or a file.
	Clean up	**pj clean**	Removes unchanged files.
	Create	**pj create**	Creates a project.
	Show changes	**pj mods**	Shows changes to project members since last checkpoint.
	Show changes	**pj log**	Shows change history.
	Print info	**pj print**	
	Set state	**pj state**	
	Update name	**pj update**	
	Show attributes	**pj vars**	
	Show changes	**pj what**	
	Create sandbox	**pj sandbox**	
Utility	Configuration	**rcs**	Changes archive attributes.
	Configuration	**pj set** **pj unset**	Also done through configuration files, environment variables, and commands.
	Events	**pj set** **pj unset** **pj dropblock** **pj editblock**	Source Integrity has several commands that allow for event-based triggers to make various configuration changes.
	Identify file	**ident**	Finds files using keywords.
	Clean up	**rcsclean**	Unlocks and deletes unchanged working files.
	Conversion	**pvcs2rcs**	Imports PVCS files.
	Conversion	**sccs2rcs**	Imports SCCS files.

Source Integrity Single developer	Command line Use scenario
Set up project	mkdir *myproj* cd *myproj*
Create initial version	ci *myfile*
Check out file	co *myfile*
Check in file	ci *myfile*
Tag with symbolic name	ci -n*name myfile*
Create a branch	co -l -r*previous-rev myfile* ci *myfile*
Show file history	rlog *myfile*

Source Integrity Team of developers	Command line Use scenario
Set up project	pj create *myproj* pj add *myfile*
Create initial version	ci *myfile*
User attached to project	Not available.
Check out file	co *myfile*
Check in file	ci *myfile*
Update files	pj refresh
Identify user with lock	rlog *myfile*
Break lock	unlock *myfile*
Show file changes	rcsdiff -r*rev1* -r*rev2 myfile*
Merge	rcsmerge -r*rev1* -r*rev2 myfile*

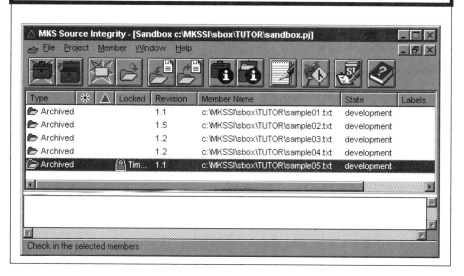

Source Integrity
GUI   Main application window

Source Integrity GUI	Main application window menu items	
File	**Project**	**Members**
Create Project...	Open Project Archive	Check In...
Create Sandbox...	Check In Project ...	Check Out...
Open Project/Sandbox...	Project Information...	Resynchronize F6
Create Archive...	Promote Project...	Select... F4
Open Archive...	Demote Project...	Label...
Import Archive...	Freeze Project	Differences...
Compare Files...	Thaw Project	Open Member Archive Alt+Enter
Configuration...	Reports...	Member Information...
Close	Build... F9	View Working File
Exit	View Log	Promote...
	Add Members... Ins	Demote...
	Remove Members... Del	Freeze
		Thaw
		Lock
		Unlock
		Remove Unused Locks
		Dependencies...
		Update to Head Rev F7
Window		**Help**
Cascade Shift+F5		Contents F1
Tile Horizontally		Technical Support
Tile Vertically Shift+F4		Tutorial
Arrange Icons		About Source Integrity
Refresh F5		

Source Integrity
GUI   Create Project dialog box

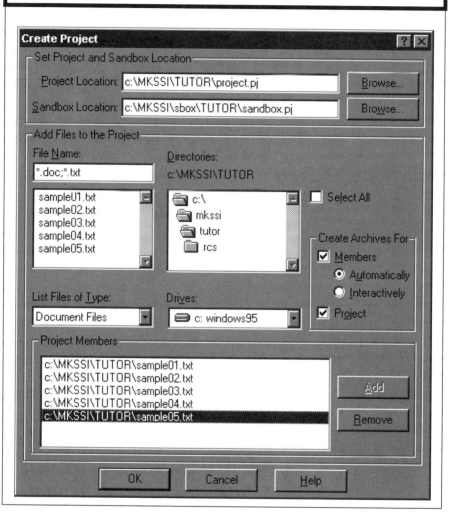

Microsoft SourceSafe

SourceSafe Overview	
Type of package	Commercial
Cost	Full Retail Version $499.00
	Single User License Pack $449.00
Author	Microsoft Corporation
Official source	Microsoft Corporation
Platforms	(PC - DOS is supported via the 4.0 version)
	(PC - Windows 3.1 is supported via the 4.0 version)
	PC - Windows 95
	PC - Windows NT
	Macintosh (available from MetroWerks)
	UNIX (available from Mainsoft)
Available from	Microsoft Corporation
	1 Microsoft Way
	Redmond, Washington 98052
Source code	No
Evaluation copy	Yes
Version	5.0 (October 1996)
General comments	SourceSafe is an easy-to-use tool for people doing software development. It is also designed for other uses including development of Web pages, documentation, databases, etc.
	SourceSafe also has an OLE automation API that allows it to be integrated into other packages. A Visual Basic integration is available and is a good example of this facility. There are also 3rd party defect tracking packages that integrate with SourceSafe.
	Note that the 4.0 version of Source Safe is shipped with the 5.0 version. This has been included specifically to support the 16bit OS users (DOS and Windows 3.1). The databases are compatible between 4.0 and 5.0 but 4.0 users do not get several of the new 5.0 features (like the Web facilities and the visual difference and merge).
Best suited for	Number of users: one to many, focused on teams
	Type of users: beginner to moderate
	Complexity level: simple to moderate
	Platforms supported: wide range

SourceSafe Information sources		Comments
Online help	Client help	Microsoft Visual SourceSafe Help The online help includes sections on using SourceSafe, commands, Command line reference, general reference material, a glossary, pointers to technical support.
	Server help	Microsoft Visual SourceSafe Administrator Help The online help includes sections on performing SourceSafe administration, commands, configuration, utilities, reference material, pointers to technical support.
Online manuals	User's Guide	Visual SourceSafe User's Guide This is a general introductory document that includes sections on features, installation, user interface and commands, integration, project concepts, customization, and administration.
Tutorial	No	Not applicable.
Printed manuals	User's Guide ~250 pages	Visual SourceSafe User's Guide This is a printed version of the online user's guide.
Web page(s)	Yes	Microsoft has a general home page at **http://www.microsoft.com** Specific SourceSafe information is at **http://www.microsoft.com/ssafe/**
News or BBS	BBS	Microsoft Download Service (206) 936-6735 (U.S.) (905) 507-3022 (Canada) Contact with 1200, 2400, or 9600 baud; no parity; 8 data bits; 1 stop bit.
	CompuServe	On CompuServe, at any ! prompt, type GO MSKB to access the Microsoft Knowledge Base, GO MSL to access the Microsoft Software Library, and GO MICROSOFT to access the Microsoft forums.
	America Online	To access the Microsoft Knowledge Base on America Online, type GOTO MICROSOFT in the America Online client application.
	Newsgroups	Even though SourceSafe is a commercial product, you can often get help from other configuration management users in the general configuration management newsgroup **comp.software.config-mgmt**

SourceSafe Information sources		Comments
Phone support	Free	(206) 635-7014 (U.S.) 6:00am–6:00pm Pacific Mon–Fri (905) 568-3503 (Canada) 8:00am–8:00pm Eastern Mon–Fri Excludes holidays. This support is available for the first two support calls.
	Priority (cost)	*Microsoft Support Network* Microsoft offers a priority telephone support line (which does cost and will be billed to your phone or to a credit card). This operates 24 hours a day, 7 days a week, excluding holidays. (900) 555-2300 (U.S. billed to phone) (800) 936-5800 (U.S. billed to credit card) (800) 668-7975 (Canada)
	Automated	Microsoft FastTips (800) 936-4300
E-mail support	No	Not applicable.

SourceSafe Features	
Storage	Versioned files are stored in the file system in an archive directory under the control of the SourceSafe server, which is a separate program from the SourceSafe client.
Locking	Checked-out files are locked; no option prevents locking.
Version identifiers	The initial version of a file is always 1. Each additional version is incremented by one.
Branching	Branching has a different model in SourceSafe from many other tools. In SourceSafe, a file can be shared by different projects. A branch is said to have occurred when a change is made to the shared file in only one of the projects. In this sense, a SourceSafe branch breaks the sharing linkage between the two projects. You can bring them back together with the Merge Branches command.
Embedded information	Information can be optionally embedded in the versioned file in a number of ways via special keyword substitution strings:

$Archive:$	becomes $Archive: *archive-location*$
$Author:$	becomes $Author: *author*$
$Date:$	becomes $Date: *date-and-time*$
$Header:$	becomes $Header: *logfile rev date author*$
$History:$	becomes $History: *file-history*$
$Log:$	becomes $Log: *rcs-file-history*$
$Logfile:$	becomes $Logfile: *archive-location*$
$Modtime:$	becomes $Modtime: *time-of-last-revision*$
$Revision:$	becomes $Revision: *rev-number*$
$Workfile:$	becomes $Workfile: *file*$
$Nokeywords:$	disables expansion below it in the file
$JustDate:$	becomes $JustDate: *date*$

Use of double colons in the keyword (like *$Author:: $*) will cause a consistent column format for the information.

SourceSafe Operations	Operation	Command	Comments
Version	Create	ss **Add**	Done by adding a file to a project.
	Check out	ss **Checkout**	
	Check in	ss **Checkin**	
	Cancel check out	ss **Undocheckout**	
	Update	ss **Get**	Gets read-only copies of files.
Comparison	File difference	ss **Diff**	Also works on projects. There is also a visual difference GUI.
Merge	File merge		Via the GUI.
	Version merge	ss **Merge**	There is also a visual merge GUI.
Control	Change log	ss **History**	
Build	Make		Not applicable.
Branches	Create branch	ss **Branch**	
Grouping	Tagging	ss **Label**	
	Set state		Not applicable.
Project	Add to project	ss **Add**	Adds member.
	Move project	ss **Move**	
	Remove member	ss **Delete**	Recoverable.
	Remove member	ss **Destroy**	Not recoverable.
	Show attributes	ss **Status**	
	Create project	ss **Create**	
	Delete project	ss **Delete**	Recoverable.
	Delete project	ss **Destroy**	Not recoverable.
	Update name	ss **Rename**	Renames member.
	Show attributes	ss **Properties**	
	Difference		Via the GUI.
Utility	Configuration	.	Via the GUI.
	Security	ss **Password**	Sets user passwords.
	Purge	ss **Purge**	Destroys previously deleted files or projects.
	Recover	ss **Recover**	Brings back previously deleted files or projects.
	Identify file	ss **findinfiles**	Looks for a string in one or more files.
	Find file	ss **Locate**	

SourceSafe Operations	Operation	Command	Comments
Utility (cont.)	Find sharing	**ss Links**	Shows the projects sharing a file.
	Clean up	**analyze**	Checks and optionally repairs the database.
	Clean up	**ss Rollback**	Undoes all changes back to a specific version.
	Archive	**ssarc**	Archives parts of a SourceSafe database.
	Archive	**ssrestor**	Restores a previous archive of a SourceSafe database.
	Unlock	**unlock**	Frees database locks.
	Conversion	**pvcs_ss**	Converts from PVCS.
	Conversion	**delta_ss**	Converts from Delta.
	Conversion	**ddconv**	Updates a SourceSafe database from an older format.

SourceSafe Single developer	Command line Use scenario
Set up project	ss **Create** *myproj*
Create initial version	ss **Add** *myfile*
Check out file	ss **Checkout** *myfile*
Check in file	ss **Checkin** *myfile*
Tag with symbolic name	ss **Label** *myfile* **-L***tag*
Create a branch	ss **Branch** *myfile*
Show file history	ss **History** *myfile*

SourceSafe Team of developers	Command line Use scenario
Set up project	ss **Create** *myproj*
Create initial version	ss **Add** *myfile*
User attached to project	Done via Add User command in the GUI.
Check out file	ss **Checkout** *myfile*
Check in file	ss **Checkin** *myfile*
Update files	ss **Get**
Identify user with lock	ss **Status** *myfile*
Break lock	ss **Undocheckout** *myfile* **-Y** *user*
Show file changes	ss **Diff** *myfile* **-V***revision*
Merge	ss **Merge** *myfile*

SourceSafe client
        GUI   Main application window

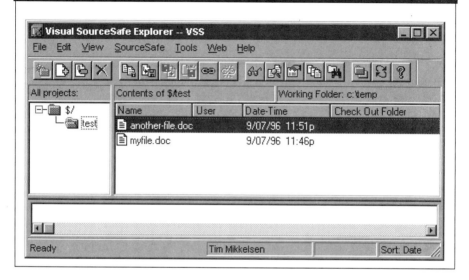

SourceSafe client GUI	SourceSafe application window menu items	
File	**Edit**	**View**
Open SourceSafe Database...Ctrl+P	View File...	Sort >
Add Files... Ctrl+A	Edit File...	Search >
Create Project...	Select... Ctrl+L	Cancel Search Ctrl+Q
Delete... <Del>	Select All Ctrl+Shift+L	Refresh File List F5
Rename...	Invert Selection	
Properties...		
Set Working Directory... Ctrl+D		
Label...		
Move Project...		
Exit		
SourceSafe	**Tools**	**Web**
Get Latest Version Ctrl+G	Show History... Ctrl+H	Deploy...
Check Out Ctrl+K	Show Differences... Ctrl+F	Check Hyperlinks...
Check In... Ctrl+U	Find in Files...	Create Site Map...
Undo Check Out	Files Report...	
Share...	Options...	
Branch...	Font...	
Merge Branches...	Customize Toolbar...	
	Change Password...	
Help		
Contents		
Search for Help on...		
Technical Support		
Books Online		
Microsoft on the Web>		
About Visual SourceSafe...		

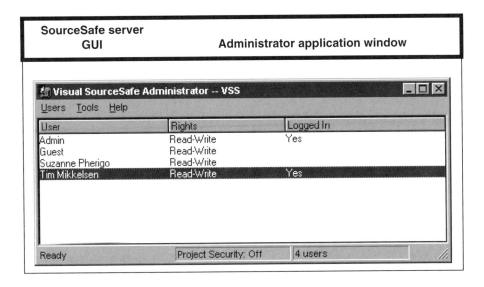

SourceSafe server GUI	Administrator application window menu items	
Users	**Tools**	**Help**
Open SourceSafe Database... Ctrl+O	Rights by Project...	Contents
Add User... Ctrl+A	Rights Assignments for User...	Search for Help on...
Delete User... Ctrl+D	Copy User Rights...	Technical Support
Edit User... Ctrl+E	Lock SourceSafe database...	Books Online
Change Password...	Options...	About Administrator...
Exit	Font...	

StarBase StarTeam

StarTeam Overview	
Type of package	Commercial
Cost	StarBase Versions $ 99 StarBase StarTeam Standalone $199 StarBase StarTeam Workstation $549
Author	StarBase Corporation
Official source	StarBase Corporation
Platforms	PC - Windows 95 PC - Windows NT
Available from	StarBase Corporation 18872 MacArthur Blvd. Suite 300 Irvine, CA 92612 Phone: 714-442-4400 Sales: 888-STAR700 Fax: 714-442-4404
Source code	No
Evaluation copy	Yes An evaluation CD-ROM contains both Win95 and WinNT full versions of StarTeam Workstation (as well as their Web product and a StarTeam network server product). The evaluation copy functions for 60 days without a license key.
Version	StarTeam Workstation Release 2.0 (July 1996)
General comments	StarTeam is quite a bit more than just a configuration management or versioning tool. It also includes facilities for build, test, defect tracking, reporting, and team communication. The StarBase Versions product is the versioning portion.
Best suited for	Number of users: one to many, focused on teams Type of users: beginner to advanced Complexity level: moderate to advanced Platforms supported: PCs running Windows only

StarTeam Information sources		Comments
Online help	Yes	
Online manuals	Yes	The CD-ROM includes Adobe Acrobat files of the product manuals so that you can browse them online.
Tutorial	Yes	The evaluation CD-ROM contains an audio/visual tutorial.
Printed manuals	Installation ~20 pages	Installation Guide This is a general installation manual for three of StarTeam's products (Workstation, Server, and Web Connect).
	Tutorial ~45 pages	Software Configuration Management Overview This is a general introduction and overview of StarTeam's products.
	User's Guide ~235 pages	StarTeam User's Guide This is a general user and administration guide.
Web page(s)	Yes	StarBase has a general home page at **http://www.starbase.com**
News or BBS	CompuServe	On CompuServe, at any ! prompt, type Go Star-Base to access the StarBase forums.
	Newsgroups	Even though StarTeam is a commercial product, you can often get help from other configuration management users in the general configuration management newsgroup **comp.software.config-mgmt**
Phone support	Yes	(714) 442-4460 9:00am–5:00pm Pacific, Mon–Fri
E-mail support	Yes	The general support e-mail address is **support@starbase.com**

StarTeam Features	
Storage	Versioned files are stored in the file system in an archive directory. The archive directory can be local or remote. Some project and file information is also stored in the project database (making some operations much faster).
Locking	StarTeam supports locking, but the default is no locking.
Version identifiers	StarTeam Workstation uses integer version numbers, such as 1, 2, and 3.
Branching	StarTeam supports the concept of branching off subprojects from the main project. As such, files are not branched. (However, you can do some parallel development by merging a file modified without a lock with a more recently checked-in revision of the same file. Internally, StarTeam tracks the files leading to this merge condition so that the system can perform a 3-way merge.)
Embedded information	Information can be optionally embedded in the versioned file in a number of ways via special keyword substitution strings:

$Archive:$ becomes $Archive: *archive-location*$
$Author:$ becomes $Author: *author*$
$Date:$ becomes $Date: *date-and-time*$
$Header:$ becomes $Header: *logfile rev date author*$
$Locker:$ becomes $Locker: *locking-user*$
$Log:$ becomes $Log: *file-history*$
$Project:$ becomes $Project: *project-name* $
$Revision:$ becomes $Revision: *rev-number* $
$Subproject:$ becomes $Subproject: *subproject-name*$
$Workfile:$ becomes $Workfile: *file*$
$Nokeywords:$ disables expansion below it in the file

StarTeam Operations	Operation	Command	Comments
Version	Create	**stcmd add**	
	Check out	**stcmd co**	
	Check in	**stcmd ci**	
	Lock/Unlock	**stcmd lck**	
Comparison	File difference	**visdiff.exe**	This is a GUI for visual compares.
Merge	File merge		Not applicable.
	Version merge	**stcmd mrg**	Merges branched subprojects.
Control	Change log		Via the GUI.
Build	Make	**stcmd dbd**	StarTeam refers to this as designating a build.
Branches	Create branch		Via the GUI.
Grouping	Tagging		Via the GUI.
	Set state	**stcmd dms**	A project (but not a subproject) can be marked with a label via the GUI interface.
Project	Delete version	**stcmd dvr**	
	Add to project	**stcmd add**	
Utility	Configuration		Via the GUI.
	Purge	**stcmd prg**	Purges "nonpermanent" versions.
	Compress	**stcmd cmp**	Compresses or decompresses files.
	Change description	**stcmd dsc**	
	Identify file		Not applicable.
	Conversion	**maintenance**	GUI to import StarTeam 1.0 files.
	Conversion	**pvcsimp**	GUI to import PVCS.

StarTeam Single developer	Command line Use scenario
Set up project	Done via the GUI.
Create initial version	**stcmd add** *myfile*
Check out file	**stcmd co** *myfile*
Check in file ·	**stcmd ci** *myfile*
Tag with symbolic name	**stcmd dms** */p "myproj" /nl "label"*
Create a branch	Done via the GUI.
Show file history	Done via the GUI.

StarTeam Team of developers	Command line Use scenario
Set up project	Done via the GUI.
Create initial version	**stcmd add** *myfile*
User attached to project	Done via the GUI.
Check out file	**stcmd co** *myfile*
Check in file	**stcmd ci** *myfile*
Update files	Not available.
Identify user with lock	Done via the GUI.
Break lock	Not available.
Show file changes	Done via the GUI.
Merge	**stcmd co** */p "myproj" /s "subproj" myfile*

StarTeam GUI	Main application window

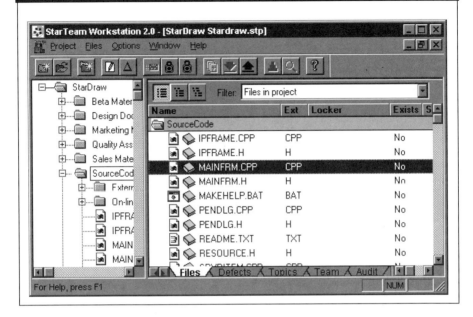

StarTeam GUI	StarTeam application window menu items	
Project	**Files** *(but menu varies w/tab)*	**Options**
New... Ctrl+N	Open	Workstation...
Open... Ctrl+O	Edit	
Open Remote...	Send To...	
Close	Add Files...	
Delete...	Check In...	
Send Note To...	Check Out...	
Properties...	Lock	
Subproject >	Unlock	
Expand	Maximum Versions...	
Collapse	Purge	
Build	Compare	
Test	Merge	
Designate Build...	Compress Vault File	
Designate Milestone...	Decompress Vault File	
Recent Remote Project	Delete Del	
Exit	Charts...	
	Reports...	
	Select All	
	Properties...	
Windows	**Help**	
Cascade	Help Topics	
Tile Horizontally	How to Use Help	
Tile Vertically	Tip of the Day...	
Arrange Icons	About StarTeam Workstation...	
Close All Charts		
Close All Reports		
Refresh F5		

Burton Systems TLIB

TLIB Overview	
Type of package	Commercial
Cost	Windows & DOS version $225.00 additional user license $175.00 per user DOS version $139.00 additional user license $100.00 per user
Author	David A. Burton W. Mike Hare
Official source	Burton Systems Software
Platforms	PC - DOS PC - Windows 3.1 PC - Windows 95 PC - Windows NT OS/2
Available from	Burton Systems Software P.O. Box 4157 Cary, North Carolina 27519-4157 Phone: (919) 233-8128 Fax: (919) 233-0716
Source code	No
Evaluation copy	No
Version	5.04
General comments	TLIB is able to run very well on very small PCs (limited memory and disk space).
Best suited for	Number of users: one to many Type of users: technically competent Complexity level: moderate to advanced Platforms supported: PCs with DOS, Windows, OS/2

TLIB Information sources		Comments
Online help	Yes	
Online manuals	No	Not applicable.
Tutorial	No	Not applicable.
Printed manuals	User's Guide ~325 pages	<u>TLIB Version Control User's Guide and Reference Manual</u> This is the general user's guide.
Web page(s)	Yes	Burton Systems has a home page at **http://www.burtonsys.com/**
News or BBS	Discussion	You can join an e-mail discussion group by sending the message body **subscribe tlib-l** *your-email-address* to **majordomo@burtonsys.com**
	BBS	Burton Systems Software BBS (919)-481-3787 (try first) (919)-481-4792 (try next) (919)-481-0149 (try last) Contact with up to 14400 baud. The lines do not rollover automatically.
	Newsgroups	Even though TLIB is a commercial product, you can often get help from other configuration management users in the general configuration management newsgroup **comp.software.config-mgmt**
Phone support	Free	(919)-233-8128 9:00am–5:00pm Eastern, Mon–Fri
Email support	Yes	The general support e-mail address is **support@burtonsys.com**

TLIB Features	
Storage	Versioned files are stored in the normal file system, but in a separate library directory with a configurable extension indicating a versioned file. The library directory path is configurable as well (allowing you to put the versioned files in the same directory as the source files). The default extension takes the filename extension and replaces the second character of the extension with a "$." (So *filename*.**txt** would become *filename*.**t$t**.)
Locking	Checked-out files can be locked through a configurable option. The default is set at an initial configuration step.
Version identifiers	The initial version of a file is 1. The versions are simple integers (except when a branch occurs). TLIB also supports an optional *major:minor* scheme using the ":" delimiter. (So 1 and 1:0 are equivalent.)
Branching	Branching is of the form *release.branch*. If you are at revision 3, you get a branch with revision 3.1. The next revision of 3.1 is revision 3.2, and so on. An optional mechanism supports N-way branching and branches off branches.
Embedded information	Information can be optionally embedded in the versioned file in a number of ways via special keyword substitution strings. This capability is supported only in nonbinary files. The keywords look like *%keyword*: %**d**　　becomes *file-date* %**f**　　becomes *file-date+time* %**l**　　becomes *lock-status* %**n**　　becomes *file-name* %**t**　　becomes *file-time* %**v**　　becomes *version* %**w**　　becomes *user-id* %**%**　　becomes *%* There are some settings that need to be configured to embed information in **tlib.cfg**. To use embedded information, one line contains a flag indicating a substitution. The next line contains the source line that contains the segment to substitute. A separate mechanism allows placement of full revision histories within comment blocks in the source files.

TLIB Operations	Operation	Command	Comments
Version	Create	**tlib n**	Creates new library.
	Check out	**tlib e**	Extracts a version.
	Check in	**tlib u**	Updates a library.
	Cancel check out	**tlib ud**	Discards changes.
	Update	**tlib ebf**	Update out of date files.
Comparison	File difference	**cmpr**	
	File difference	**tlib comp**	
	File difference	**compare**	
	File difference	**compar**	
Merge	File merge	**diff3**	
	Version merge	**tlib m**	Migrates changes.
Control	Change log	**tlib l**	Lists versions.
Build	Make	**make**	
Branches	Create branch	**tlib us**	
Grouping	Tagging	**tlib s**	Snapshots files (done by creating a named file that points to the appropriate files).
	Set state		Done via project promotion
Project	Add to project	**tlib a**	Adds to project level.
	Delete version	**tlib ad**	Deletes from project level.
	Promote	**tlib ap**	Promotes to next level.
Utility	Configuration	**tlib c**	Also done through the configuration files and commands.
	Storage path	**tlib cp**	Sets library path.
	Conversion		Via automated conversion from RCS, PVCS, Delta, and Sorcerer's Apprentice.

TLIB Single developer	Command line Use scenario
Set up project	Not available.
Create initial version	tlib n *myfile*
Check out file	tlib e *myfile*
Check in file	tlib u *myfile*
Tag with symbolic name	tlib s *snapshot-file file-list*
Create a branch	tlib us *myfile version.branch*
Show file history	tlib l *myfile*

TLIB Team of developers	Command line Use scenario
Set up project	Not available.
Create initial version	tlib n *myfile*
User attached to project	Not available.
Check out file	tlib e *myfile*
Check in file	tlib u *myfile*
Update files	tlib ebf *
Identify user with lock	tlib t *myfile*
Break lock	tlib ud *myfile*
Show file changes	cmpr *myfile1 myfile2*
Merge	tlib ms *myfile version-num1 version-num2*

TLIB
GUI   Main application window

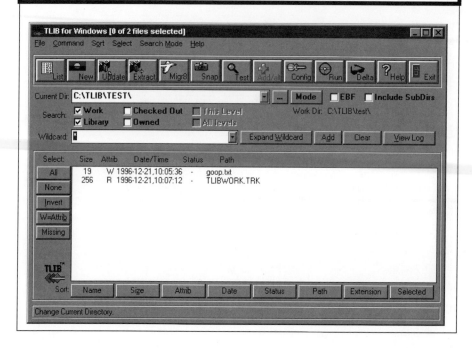

TLIB GUI	TLIB application window menu items	
File	**Command**	**Sort**
Expand Wildcard F5	Edit	Name
Clear	List	Size
Change Directory	Test	Attrib
Run Manual Command	Update	Date
Configuration Options	Extract	Status
Change User ID	Delta Compare	Path
Edit Configuration File (TLIB.CFG)	Migrate	Extension
Config Wizard (creates TLIB.CFG)	Snapshot	Selected
View Log	Add/Alter Project Level	
Exit Ctrl+X	Create New Library	
Select	**Search Mode**	**Help**
All	Work	Contents
None	Library	About
W-Attribute	Checked Out	
Missing	Owned	
Invert Selection	This Level	
	All levels	
	Include Subdirs	

Appendices

"Don't touch that! You don't know what it's connected to . . ."

What's on the CD-ROM?

Introduction

The CD-ROM included with this book includes RCS, CVS, QVCS, and some RCS examples. For each of the tools, the CD-ROM includes the actual tool executables, documentation, and source code (for RCS and CVS). The CD is readable on most computers and operating systems (DOS, Windows 3.1, Windows 95, Windows NT, and UNIX).

The general organization of the CD is a collection of directories for the various tools. Within each tool directory, several directories exist—for sources and for precompiled executables. The following table shows the contents of the CD.

Cvs	**cvs-1.9**	Directory with sources and utilities to build CVS on the various platforms (including gunzip).
	winnt	Directory with the Windows NT executable, which also works with Windows 95.
	cvs_tut.ps	Postscript file of the CVS tutorial and overview.
	cvs_paper.ps	Postscript file of the article by Brian Berliner, "CVS II: Parallelizing Software Development."
	cvs.ps	Postscript file of the CVS 1.8 reference manual.
Qvcs	**qvcs-2.2**	Directory with the compressed zip files for QVCS 2.2 for DOS/Win3.1 and Win95/NT.
	win3_1	Directory with the DOS and Windows 3.1 executables for QVCS 2.2.
	win95	Directory with the Windows 95 and NT executables for QVCS 2.2.

Rcs	**dos**	Directory with the DOS executables and documentation. Also included are compressed files (zip files and tar files).
	rcs-5.7	Directory with sources and utilities to build RCS on UNIX and PCs.
	readme	ASCII file that includes the copyright information and a discussion of new features and defect fixes of RCS 5.7.
	readme.txt	ASCII file that includes the specific DOS port information and a discussion of new features, suggestions, additional installation information, and defects.
Examples	**Dennis**	Directory with the "hello world" example from Section 1 of this book.
	literature	Directory with an example of bad writing, but at least it is under configuration management so that you can see the improvements.

CVS

Follow these instructions to install the PC versions of CVS on your PC running either Windows 95 or Windows NT. Note that you need to have installed RCS first—since CVS is based on RCS. The appropriate version of RCS is included in the CVS directories, but you do have to unpack them and install them properly. Remember that CVS is not for the faint of heart; you need to be willing to deal with its technical complexities in order to get its additional power.

1	Insert the CD-ROM into your CD drive.
2	If you are using MS-DOS or Windows 3.1: Assuming that the CD-ROM drive is the **D:** drive, use the following DOS commands or use the File Manager to examine the QVCS directory: ``` CD D:\CVS DIR D: ``` If you are using Windows 95 or Windows NT: Use the Windows Explorer to locate the CD and the CVS directory (at the top directory level on the CD).
3	Read the **cvs\cvs-1.9\copying** file on the CD, which contains the copyright information (the GNU general public license).
4	Read the **cvs\cvs-1.9\cvs-1.9\readme** file on the CD (written by Brian Berliner and Jeff Polk). This file contains the general information about CVS.
5	Read the **cvs\cvs-1.9\cvs-1.9\install** file on the CD. This file contains the detailed installation information.
6	Create a directory on your hard drive. I would recommend (assuming **C:** as your drive letter) **C:\cvs**. You can use something other than this, but be sure you set the appropriate path information (as described later).

7	Copy all the files on the CD from the directory d:**cvs\winnt** on the CD into the directory on your hard drive.
8	Follow the instructions in **cvs\cvs-1.9\cvs-1.9\install** file.
9	Edit your autoexec.bat file and add the CVS directory to your path by adding the following line to the file: `SET PATH=%PATH%;C:\CVS`
10	Reboot to allow the changes to take effect.

QVCS

Follow these instructions to install the PC versions of QVCS on your PC running MS-DOS, Windows 3.1, Windows 95, or Windows NT.

1	Insert the CD-ROM into your CD drive.

2	If you are using MS-DOS or Windows 3.1: Assuming that the CD-ROM drive is the **D:** drive, use the following DOS commands or use the File Manager to examine the QVCS directory:
	
	`CD D:\QVCS`
	`DIR D:`
	`CD D:\QVCS\WIN3_1`
	`DIR D:`
	
	If you are using Windows 95 or Windows NT: Use the Windows Explorer to locate the CD and the QVCS directory (at the top directory level on the CD). Look inside the **qvcs\win95** directory.

3	Read the **Readme.txt** file (in either **qvcs\win95** or **qvcs\win3_1**) on the CD. This file contains the copyright information and installation instructions. The following information is drawn from the QVCS installation instructions.
4	Read the **License.txt** file (in either **qvcs\win95** or **qvcs\win3_1**) on the CD. This file contains the legal copyright information.
5	Create a directory on your hard drive. I would recommend (assuming **C:** as your drive letter) **C:\qvcs**. You can use something other than this, but be sure you set the appropriate path information (as described later). If you are using MS-DOS, execute the following command: `MKDIR C:\QVCS`

6	Copy all the files on the CD from the appropriate directory (either d:\qvcs\win95 or d:\qvcs\win3_1) on the CD into the directory on your hard drive. If you are using MS-DOS, execute the following command: `COPY D:\QVCS\WIN3_1\* C:\QVCS`

7	Edit your `autoexec.bat` file and add the following lines:
	
	`SET QVCS_BIN=C:\QVCS`
	`SET QVCS_ID=YourLoginName`
	`SET QVCS_ACCESSLIST=YourLoginName,AnotherName`
	`SET TZ=YourTimeZone`
	
	If your system already has a TZ environment variable set, you do not need to add it here.

8	Edit your autoexec.bat file and add the QVCS directory to your path by adding the following line to the file: `SET PATH=%PATH%;C:\QVCS`
9	Reboot to allow the changes to take effect.

RCS

These directions are equivalent to those earlier in the book. Follow these instructions to install the DOS version of RCS on your PC running MS-DOS, Windows 3.1, Windows 95, or Windows NT.

1	Insert the CD-ROM into your CD drive.

2	If you are using MS-DOS: Assuming that the CD-ROM drive is the **D:** drive, do the following DOS commands to examine the RCS directory:
	
	`CD D:\RCS`
	`DIR D:`
	
	If you are using Windows: Use File Manager or Windows Explorer to locate the CD and the RCS directory (at the top directory level on the CD).

3	Read the **rcs\readme** file on the CD, which contains the copyright information and a discussion of new features and defect fixes.

4	Read the **rcs\readme.txt** file on the CD (written by Marc Singer, the person who did this port to DOS). This file contains the specific DOS port information and a discussion of new features, suggestions, additional installation information, and defects.
5	Read the **rcs\rcs-5.7\rcs-5.7\man\Copying** file on the CD, which contains the "GNU General Public License," the legal copyright information.
6	Create a directory on your hard drive. I would recommend (assuming **C:** as your drive letter) **C:\rcs**. You can use something other than this, but be sure you set the appropriate path information (as described later). If you are using MS-DOS, execute the following command: MKDIR **C:\RCS**
7	Copy all the files on the CD under **rcs\dos\bin** into the directory on your hard drive. If you are using MS-DOS, execute the following command: COPY D:\RCS\DOS\BIN* **C:\RCS**
8	Copy all the files on the CD under **rcs\dos\util** into the same directory on your hard drive. If you are using MS-DOS, execute the following command: COPY D:\RCS\DOS\UTIL* **C:\RCS**
9	Edit your autoexec.bat file and add the following lines: SET RCSBINPATH=**C:\RCS** SET RCSBIN=**C:\RCS** SET USER=*YourLoginName* SET TZ=*YourTimeZone* If your system already has a USER and a TZ environment variable set, you do not need to add those here. MS-DOS (not running from Windows 95 or Windows NT) requires that files be of the *XXXXXXXX.yyy* form (filename and file type extension). This causes problems in RCS because of the addition of a **,v** suffix to file names. So if you are using MS-DOS, you should turn this name extension feature off by adding the following line to your autoexec.bat file: SET RCSINIT=-x

10	Edit your `autoexec.bat` file and add the RCS directory to your path by adding the following line to the file:
	`SET PATH=%PATH%;C:\RCS`
11	Reboot to allow the changes to take effect.

Be careful with RCS when it is installed with some other configuration management tools, because they may be based on RCS technology and commands. Similar commands may conflict and you end up using whichever command is found first in the path search.

Examples

The CD-ROM also includes a few example files for use with RCS (and also with some of the other tools that are compatible with or based on RCS).

The intention is to use RCS to examine the examples, look at the history, and check out various previous versions. To put the examples on your system:

1	Insert the CD-ROM into your CD drive.
2	If you are using MS-DOS: Assuming that the CD-ROM drive is the **D:** drive, do the following DOS commands to examine the Examples directory:
	`CD D:\EXAMPLES`
	`DIR D:`
	If you are using Windows: Use File Manager or Windows Explorer to locate the CD and the Examples directory (at the top CD directory level).
3	Create a directory on your hard drive. I would recommend (assuming **C:** as your drive letter) **C:\examples**. You can use something other than this, but be sure you set the appropriate path information (as described later).
	If you are using MS-DOS, execute the following commands:
	`MKDIR C:\examples`
	`MKDIR C:\examples\Dennis`
	`MKDIR C:\examples\literature`

4   Copy all the directories and files on the CD under **Examples** into the directory on your hard drive.

If you are using MS-DOS, execute the following commands:

```
CD D:\Examples\Dennis
COPY D:* C:\examples\Dennis
COPY D:rcs\* C:\examples\Dennis\rcs
CD D:\Examples\literature
COPY D:* C:\examples\literature
COPY D:rcs\* C:\examples\literature\rcs
```

The "Dennis" example you just copied has the structure you see in Figures 5-A-1 and 5-A-2:

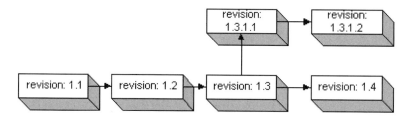

Figure 5-A-1   Dennis example revision structure

```
Archive file: C:/Examples/Dennis\rcs\hello.c;Working file: C:/Exam-
ples/Dennis/hello.c
head:          1.4
branch:
locks:
access list:
symbolic names:
comment leader:
total revisions: 6; branches: 1; branch revisions: 2
file format: text
description:
This is the classic 'hello world' program.

---------------------------
revision 1.4
date: 1996/10/11 17:39:05; author: mks; state: Exp; lines: +3 -1
Putting the message in 3 different printf statements.
---------------------------
revision 1.3.1.2
date: 1996/10/11 17:52:32; author: mks; state: Exp; lines: +3 -1
Split up the lines in the capitalized branch.
---------------------------
```

```
revision 1.3.1.1
date: 1996/10/11 17:44:44; author: mks; state: Exp; lines: +1 -1
Doing a branch with capitalization changes in the message.
--------------------------
revision 1.3
date: 1996/10/11 17:37:48; author: mks; state: Exp; lines: +1 -2
branches: 1.3.1;
Fixing the introduced error.
--------------------------
revision 1.2
date: 1996/10/11 17:36:31; author: mks; state: Exp; lines: +2 -1
Introducing an error by putting the quote on the next line.
--------------------------
revision 1.1
date: 1996/10/11 17:35:15; author: mks; state: Exp;
Initial revision
--------------------------
selected revisions: 6
=====================================================================
```

Figure 5-A-2 Dennis example rlog contents

The literature example you just copied has the structure you see in Figures 5-A-3 and 5-A-4.

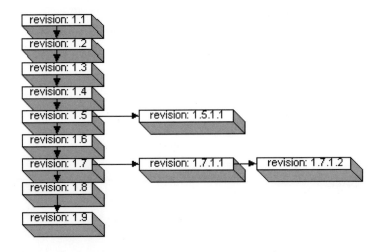

Figure 5-A-3 Literature example revision structure

Archive file: C:/Examples/literature\rcs\story.txt;Working file: C:/
Examples/literature/story.txt
head: 1.9
branch:
locks:
access list:
symbolic names:
comment leader:
total revisions: 12; branches: 2; branch revisions: 3
file format: text
description:
This is my story!

----
revision 1.9
date: 1996/09/30 05:09:19; author: mks; state: Exp; lines: +0 -0
I am checking in with no changes.
----
revision 1.8
date: 1996/09/30 05:05:05; author: mks; state: Exp; lines: +12 -1
Get my punctuation and formatting better (relatively).
----
revision 1.7.1.2
date: 1996/09/30 05:15:22; author: mks; state: Exp; lines: +3 -1
I wanted to put in the separator at the end of
my encheferized story.
----
revision 1.7.1.1
date: 1996/09/30 05:11:39; author: mks; state: Exp; lines: +29 -17
You know I like the swedish chef from the
muppets.

So, I did an encheferized branch.
Bork, bork, bork!
----
revision 1.7
date: 1996/09/30 05:03:22; author: mks; state: Exp; lines: +5 -0
branches: 1.7.1;
Add some action
----
revision 1.6
date: 1996/09/30 04:58:19; author: mks; state: Exp; lines: +7 -1
Add some more characters - and swiftly too.
----
revision 1.5.1.1
date: 1996/09/30 05:00:47; author: mks; state: Exp; lines: +2 -1
Do a branch for the animal rights activists
They don't like sheep, apparently.
----
revision 1.5
date: 1996/09/30 04:55:44; author: mks; state: Exp; lines: +3 -1
branches: 1.5.1;
I parenthesized my apology - it looks nicer.

```
---------------------------
revision 1.4
date: 1996/09/30 04:53:25; author: mks; state: Exp; lines: +6 -0
Add some dialog - dialog is always nice.
Oh, yes - and add some more physical interest (the 2nd thud).

You know, I took some community college english classes once.
I hope to actually take an entire term someday.
---------------------------
revision 1.3
date: 1996/09/30 04:51:15; author: mks; state: Exp; lines: +2 -0
Give it a 'shot' at being more descriptive.
---------------------------
revision 1.2
date: 1996/09/30 04:49:44; author: mks; state: Exp; lines: +1 -0
be sure to say your sorry for writing this.
---------------------------
revision 1.1
date: 1996/09/30 04:48:24; author: mks; state: Exp;
Initial revision
---------------------------
selected revisions: 12
======================================================================
```

Figure 5-A-4   Literature example rlog contents

RCS Manual Pages

Introduction

This appendix contains the command "man" pages for RCS. Additional "man" pages and other introductory documents are included on the CD-ROM.

RCSINTRO   Introduction to RCS

NAME

    rcsintro—introduction to RCS commands

DESCRIPTION

    The Revision Control System (RCS) manages multiple revisions of files. RCS automates the storing, retrieval, logging, identification, and merging of revisions. RCS is useful for text that is revised frequently, for example programs, documentation, graphics, papers, and form letters.

    The basic user interface is extremely simple. The novice only needs to learn two commands: ci(1) and co(1). ci, short for "check-in," deposits the contents of a file into an archival file called an RCS file. An RCS file contains all revisions of a particular file. co, short for "check-out," retrieves revisions from an RCS file.

Functions of RCS

- Store-and-retrieve multiple revisions of text. RCS saves all old revisions in a space-efficient way. Changes no longer destroy the original, because the previous revisions remain accessible. Revisions can be retrieved according to ranges of revision numbers, symbolic names, dates, authors, and states.
- Maintain a complete history of changes. RCS logs all changes automatically. Besides the text of each revision, RCS stores the author, the date, and time of check-in, and a log message summarizing the change. The logging makes finding out what happened to a module easy, without having to compare source listings or having to track down colleagues.
- Resolve access conflicts. When two or more programmers wish to modify the same revision, RCS alerts the programmers and prevents one modification from corrupting the other.
- Maintain a tree of revisions. RCS can maintain separate lines of development for each module. It stores a tree structure that represents the ancestral relationships among revisions.
- Merge revisions and resolve conflicts. Two separate lines of development of a module can be coalesced by merging. If the revisions to be merged affect the same sections of code, RCS alerts the user about the overlapping changes.
- Control releases and configurations. Revisions can be assigned symbolic names and marked as released, stable, experimental, etc. With these facilities, configurations of modules can be described simply and directly.

- Automatically identify each revision with name, revision number, creation time, author, etc. The identification is like a stamp that can be embedded at an appropriate place in the text of a revision. The identification makes simple determining which revisions of which modules make up a given configuration.
- Minimize secondary storage. RCS needs little extra space for the revisions (only the differences). If intermediate revisions are deleted, the corresponding deltas are compressed accordingly.

Getting Started with RCS

Suppose you have a file f.c that you wish to put under control of RCS. If you have not already done so, make an RCS directory with the command

```
mkdir RCS
```

Then invoke the check-in command

```
ci f.c
```

This command creates an RCS file in the RCS directory, stores f.c into it as revision 1.1, and deletes f.c. It also asks you for a description. The description should be a synopsis of the contents of the file. All later check-in commands ask you for a log entry, which should summarize the changes that you made.

Files in the RCS directory are called RCS files; the others are called working files. To get back the working file f.c in the previous example, use the check-out command

```
co f.c
```

This command extracts the latest revision from the RCS file and writes it into f.c. If you want to edit f.c, you must lock it as you check it out, with the command

```
co -l f.c
```

You can now edit f.c.

Suppose after some editing you want to know what changes you have made. The command

```
rcsdiff f.c
```

tells you the difference between the most recently checked-in version and the working file. You can check the file back in by invoking

```
ci f.c
```

This increments the revision number properly.
If ci complains with the message

```
ci error: no lock set by your name
```

then you have tried to check in a file even though you did not lock it when you checked it out. Of course, it is too late now to do the check-out with locking, because another check-out would overwrite your modifications. Instead, invoke

```
rcs -l f.c
```

This command locks the latest revision for you, unless somebody else got ahead of you already. In this case, you'll have to negotiate with that person.

Locking assures that you, and only you, can check in the next update, and avoids nasty problems if several people work on the same file. Even if a revision is locked, it can still be checked out for reading, compiling, etc. All that locking prevents is a check-in by anybody but the locker.

If your RCS file is private, i.e., if you are the only person who is going to deposit revisions into it, strict locking is not needed and you can turn it off. If strict locking is turned off, the owner of the RCS file need not have a lock for check-in; all others still do. You can turn strict locking off and on with the commands

```
rcs -U f.c and rcs -L f.c
```

If you don't want to clutter your working directory with RCS files, create a subdirectory called RCS in your working directory, and move all your RCS files there. RCS commands look first into that directory to find needed files. All the commands discussed above still work, without any modification. (Actually, pairs of RCS and working files can be specified in three ways: (a) both are given, (b) only the working file is given, (c) only the RCS file is given. Both RCS and working files may have arbitrary path prefixes; RCS commands pair them up intelligently.)

To avoid deletion of the working file during check-in (in case you want to continue editing or compiling), invoke

```
ci -l f.c or ci -u f.c
```

These commands check in f.c as usual, but perform an implicit check-out. The first form also locks the checked-in revision, the second one doesn't. Thus, these options save you one check-out operation. The first form is useful if you want to continue editing, and the second one if you just want to read the file. Both update the identification markers in your working file (see below).

You can give ci the number you want assigned to a checked-in revision. Assume all your revisions were numbered 1.1, 1.2, 1.3, etc., and you would like to start release 2. The command

```
ci -r2 f.c or ci -r2.1 f.c
```

assigns the number 2.1 to the new revision. From then on, ci will number the subsequent revisions with 2.2, 2.3, etc. The corresponding co commands

```
co -r2 f.c and co -r2.1 f.c
```

retrieve the latest revision numbered 2.x and the revision 2.1, respectively. co without a revision number selects the latest revision on the trunk, i.e., the highest revision with a number consisting of two fields. Numbers with more than two fields are needed for branches. For example, to start a branch at revision 1.3, invoke

```
ci -r1.3.1 f.c
```

This command starts a branch numbered 1 at revision 1.3, and assigns the number 1.3.1.1 to the new revision. For more information about branches, see rcsfile(5).

Automatic Identification

RCS can put special strings for identification into your source and object code. To obtain such identification, place the marker

```
$Id$
```

into your text, for instance inside a comment. RCS will replace this marker with a string of the form

```
$Id: filename revision date time author state$
```

With such a marker on the first page of each module, you can always see with which revision you are working. RCS keeps the markers up-to-date automatically. To propagate the markers into your object code, simply put them into literal character strings. In C, do as follows:

```
static char rcsid[] = "$Id$";
```

The command ident extracts such markers from any file, even object code and dumps. Thus, ident lets you find out which revisions of which modules were used in a given program.

You may also find useful putting the marker Log into your text, inside a comment. This marker accumulates the log messages that are requested during check-in. Thus, you can maintain the complete history of your file directly inside it. Several additional identification markers are available; see co(1) for details.

IDENTIFICATION

    Author: Walter F. Tichy.
    Manual Page Revision: 5.3; Release Date: 1993/11/03.
    Copyright (C) 1982, 1988, 1989, Walter F. Tichy.
    Copyright (C) 1990, 1991, 1992, 1993, Paul Eggert.

SEE ALSO

    ci(1), co(1), ident(1), rcs(1), rcsdiff(1), rcsintro(1), rcsmerge(1), rlog(1)
    Walter F. Tichy, RCS—A System for Version Control, Software—Practice & Experience 15, 7 (July 1985), 637–654.

CI	check files in

NAME

ci—check in RCS revisions

SYNOPSIS

ci [options] file . . .

DESCRIPTION

ci stores new revisions into RCS files. Each pathname matching an RCS suffix is taken to be an RCS file. All others are assumed to be working files containing new revisions. ci deposits the contents of each working file into the corresponding RCS file. If only a working file is given, ci tries to find the corresponding RCS file in an RCS subdirectory and then in the working file's directory. For more details, see FILE NAMING later in this appendix.

For ci to work, the caller's login must be on the access list, except if the access list is empty or the caller is the superuser or the owner of the file. To append a new revision to an existing branch, the tip revision on that branch must be locked by the caller. Otherwise, only a new branch can be created. This restriction is not enforced for the owner of the file if nonstrict locking is used [see rcs(1)]. A lock held by someone else can be broken with the rcs command.

Unless the -f option is given, ci checks whether the revision to be deposited differs from the preceding one. If not, instead of creating a new revision, ci reverts to the preceding one. To revert, ordinary ci removes the working file and any lock; ci -l keeps and ci -u removes any lock, and then they both generate a new working file much as if co -l or co -u had been applied to the preceding revision. When reverting, any -n and -s options apply to the preceding revision.

For each revision deposited, ci prompts for a log message. The log message should summarize the change and must be terminated by end-of-file or by a line containing . by itself. If several files are checked in, ci asks whether to reuse the previous log message. If the standard input is not a terminal, ci suppresses the prompt and uses the same log message for all files. See also -m.

If the RCS file does not exist, ci creates it and deposits the contents of the working file as the initial revision (default number: 1.1). The access list is initialized to empty. Instead of the log message, ci requests descriptive text (see -t later in this appendix).

The number rev of the deposited revision can be given by any of the options -f, -i, -I, -j, -k, -l, -M, -q, -r, or -u. rev can be symbolic, numeric, or mixed. Symbolic names in rev must already be defined; see the -n and -N options for assigning names during check-in. If rev is $, ci determines the revision number from keyword values in the working file.

If rev begins with a period, then the default branch (normally the trunk) is prepended to it. If rev is a branch number followed by a period, then the latest revision on that branch is used.

If rev is a revision number, it must be higher than the latest one on the branch to which rev belongs, or it must start a new branch.

If rev is a branch rather than a revision number, the new revision is appended to that branch. The level number is obtained by incrementing the tip revision number of that branch. If rev indicates a nonexisting branch, that branch is created with the initial revision numbered rev.1.

If rev is omitted, ci tries to derive the new revision number from the caller's last lock. If the caller has locked the tip revision of a branch, the new revision is appended to that branch. The new revision number is obtained by incrementing the tip revision number. If the caller locked a nontip revision, a new branch is started at that revision by incrementing the highest branch number at that revision. The default initial branch and level numbers are 1.

If rev is omitted and the caller has no lock, but owns the file and locking is not set to strict, then the revision is appended to the default branch [normally the trunk; see the -b option of rcs(1)].

Exception: On the trunk, revisions can be appended to the end, but not inserted.

OPTIONS

-rrev
Checks in revision rev.

-r
The bare -r option (without any revision) has an unusual meaning in ci. With other RCS commands, a bare -r option specifies the most recent revision on the default branch, but with ci, a bare -r option reestablishes the default behavior of releasing a lock and removing the working file, and is used to override any default -l or -u options established by shell aliases or scripts.

-l[rev]
Works like -r, except it performs an additional co -l for the deposited revision. Thus, the deposited revision is immediately checked out again and locked. This is useful for saving a revision although one wants to continue editing it after the check-in.

-u[rev]
Works like -l, except that the deposited revision is not locked. This lets one read the working file immediately after check-in.

The -l, bare -r, and -u options are mutually exclusive and silently override each other. For example, ci -u -r is equivalent to ci -r because bare -r overrides -u.

-f[rev]
Forces a deposit; the new revision is deposited even if it is not different from the preceding one.

-k[rev]
Searches the working file for keyword values to determine its revision number, creation date, state, and author [see co(1)], and assigns these values to the deposited revision, rather than computing them locally. It also generates a default login message noting the login of the caller and the actual check-in date. This option is useful for software distribution. A revision that is sent to several sites should be checked in with the -k option at these sites to preserve the original number, date, author, and state. The extracted keyword values and the default log message can be overridden with the options -d, -m, -s, -w, and any option that carries a revision number.

-q[rev]
Quiet mode; diagnostic output is not printed. A revision that is not different from the preceding one is not deposited, unless -f is given.

-i[rev]
Initial check-in; reports an error if the RCS file already exists. This avoids race conditions in certain applications.

-j[rev]
Just checks in and does not initialize; reports an error if the RCS file does not already exist.

-I[rev]
Interactive mode; the user is prompted and questioned even if the standard input is not a terminal.

-d[date]
Uses date for the check-in date and time. The date is specified in free format as explained in co(1). This is useful for lying about the check-in date, and for -k if no date is available. If date is empty, the working file's time of last modification is used.

-M[rev]

Sets the modification time on any new working file to be the date of the retrieved revision. For example, ci -d -M -u f does not alter f's modification time, even if f's contents change due to keyword substitution. Use this option with care; it can confuse make(1).

-mmsg

Uses the string msg as the log message for all revisions checked in. By convention, log messages that start with # are comments and are ignored by programs like GNU Emacs's vc package. Also, log messages that start with {clumpname} (followed by white space) are meant to be clumped together if possible, even if they are associated with different files; the {clumpname} label is used only for clumping, and is not considered to be part of the log message itself.

-nname

Assigns the symbolic name to the number of the checked-in revision. ci prints an error message if name is already assigned to another number.

-Nname

Same as -n, except that it overrides a previous assignment of name.

-sstate

Sets the state of the checked-in revision to the identifier state. The default state is Exp.

-tfile

Writes descriptive text from the contents of the named file into the RCS file, deleting the existing text. The file cannot begin with -.

-t-string

Writes descriptive text from the string into the RCS file, deleting the existing text. The -t option, in both its forms, has effect only during an initial check-in; it is silently ignored otherwise. During the initial check-in, if -t is not given, ci obtains the text from standard input, terminated by end-of-file or by a line containing . by itself. The user is prompted for the text if interaction is possible; see -I earlier in this appendix. For backward compatibility with older versions of RCS, a bare -t option is ignored.

-T

Sets the RCS file's modification time to the new revision's time if the former precedes the latter and a new revision exists; preserves the RCS file's modification time otherwise. If you have locked a revision, ci usually updates the RCS file's modification time to the current time, because the lock is stored in the RCS file and removing the lock requires changing the RCS file. This update can create an RCS file newer than the working file in one of two ways: First, ci -M can create a working file with a date before the current time; second, when reverting to the previous revision, the RCS file can change although the working file remains unchanged. These two cases can cause excessive recompilation caused by a make(1) dependency of the working file on the RCS file. The -T option inhibits this recompilation by lying about the RCS file's date. Use this option with care; it can suppress recompilation even when a check-in of one working file should affect another working file associated with the same RCS file. For example, suppose the RCS file's time is 01:00, the (changed) working file's time is 02:00, some other copy of the working file has a time of 03:00, and the current time is 04:00. Then ci -d -T sets the RCS file's time to 02:00 instead of the usual 04:00; this difference causes make(1) to think (incorrectly) that the other copy is newer than the RCS file.

-wlogin
Uses login for the author field of the deposited revision. Useful for lying about the author, and for -k if no author is available.

-V
Prints RCS's version number.

-Vn
Emulates RCS version n. See co(1) for details.

-xsuffixes
Specifies the suffixes for RCS files. A nonempty suffix matches any pathname ending in the suffix. An empty suffix matches any pathname of the form RCS/path or path1/RCS/path2. The -x option can specify a list of suffixes separated by /. For example, -x,v/ specifies two suffixes: ,v and the empty suffix. If two or more suffixes are specified, they are tried in order when looking for an RCS file; the first one that works is used for that file. If no RCS file is found but an RCS file can be created, the suffixes are tried in order to determine the new RCS file's name. The default for suffixes is installation-dependent; normally it is ,v/ for hosts like UNIX that permit commas in filenames, and is empty (i.e., just the empty suffix) for other hosts.

-zzone
Specifies the date output format in keyword substitution, and specifies the default time zone for date in the -ddate option. The zone should be empty, a numeric UTC offset, or the special string LT for local time. The default is an empty zone, which uses the traditional RCS format of UTC without any time zone indication and with

slashes separating the parts of the date; otherwise, times are output in ISO 8601 format with time zone indication. For example, if local time is January 11, 1990, 8 P.M. Pacific Standard Time, eight hours west of UTC, then the time is output as 1990/01/11 04:00:00 with -z, as 1990-01-11 20:00:00-0800 with -zLT, and as 1990-01-11 09:30:00+0530 with -z+0530. This option does not affect dates in RCS files themselves, which are always UTC.

FILE NAMING

Pairs of RCS files and working files can be specified in three ways (see also the example section later in this appendix).

1. Both the RCS file and the working file are given. The RCS pathname is of the form path1/workfileX, and the working pathname is of the form path2/workfile, where path1/ and path2/ are (possibly different or empty) paths, workfile is a filename, and X is an RCS suffix. If X is empty, path1/ must start with RCS/ or must contain /RCS/.
2. Only the RCS file is given. Then the working file is created in the current directory and its name is derived from the name of the RCS file by removing path1/ and the suffix X.
3. Only the working file is given. Then ci considers each RCS suffix X in turn, looking for an RCS file of the form path2/RCS/workfileX or (if the former is not found and X is nonempty) path2/workfileX.

If the RCS file is specified without a path in (1) and (2), ci looks for the RCS file first in the directory ./RCS and then in the current directory.

ci reports an error if an attempt to open an RCS file fails for an unusual reason, even if the RCS file's pathname is just one of several possibilities. For example, to suppress use of RCS commands in a directory d, create a regular file named d/RCS so that casual attempts to use RCS commands in d fail because d/RCS is not a directory.

EXAMPLES

Suppose ,v is an RCS suffix and the current directory contains a subdirectory RCS with an RCS file io.c,v. Then each of the following commands checks in a copy of io.c into RCS/io.c,v as the latest revision, removing io.c.

```
ci io.c;  ci RCS/io.c,v;  ci io.c,v;
ci io.c RCS/io.c,v;  ci io.c io.c,v;
ci RCS/io.c,v io.c;  ci io.c,v io.c;
```

Suppose instead that the empty suffix is an RCS suffix and the current directory contains a subdirectory RCS with an RCS file io.c. Then each of the following commands checks in a new revision.

```
ci io.c; ci RCS/io.c;
ci io.c RCS/io.c;
ci RCS/io.c io.c;
```

FILE MODES

An RCS file created by ci inherits the read and execute permissions from the working file. If the RCS file exists already, ci preserves its read and execute permissions. ci always turns off all write permissions of RCS files.

FILES

Temporary files are created in the directory containing the working file, and also in the temporary directory (see TMPDIR under ENVIRONMENT later in this appendix). A semaphore file or files are created in the directory containing the RCS file. With a nonempty suffix, the semaphore names begin with the first character of the suffix; therefore, do not specify a suffix whose first character could be that of a working filename. With an empty suffix, the semaphore names end with _, so working filenames should not end in _.

ci never changes an RCS or working file. Normally, ci unlinks the file and creates a new one; but instead of breaking a chain of one or more symbolic links to an RCS file, it unlinks the destination file instead. Therefore, ci breaks any hard or symbolic links to any working file it changes; and hard links to RCS files are ineffective, but symbolic links to RCS files are preserved.

The effective user must be able to search and write the directory containing the RCS file. Normally, the real user must be able to read the RCS and working files, and to search and write the directory containing the working file; however, some older hosts cannot easily switch between real and effective users, so on these hosts the effective user is used for all accesses. The effective user is the same as the real user unless your copies of ci and co have setuid privileges. As described in SETUID USE later in this appendix, these privileges yield extra security if the effective user owns all RCS files and directories, and if only the effective user can write RCS directories.

Users can control access to RCS files by setting the permissions of the directory containing the files; only users with write access to the directory can use RCS commands to change its RCS files. For example, in hosts that allow a user to belong to several groups, one can make a group's RCS directories writeable to that group only. This approach suffices for informal projects, but it means that any group member can arbitrarily change the group's RCS files, and can even remove them entirely. Hence more formal projects sometimes distinguish between an RCS administrator, who can change the RCS files at will, and other project members, who can check in new revisions but cannot otherwise change the RCS files.

SETUID USE

To prevent anybody but their RCS administrator from deleting revisions, a set of users can employ setuid privileges as follows:

- Check that the host supports RCS setuid use. Consult a trustworthy expert if you have any doubts. The best result is if the setuid system call works as described in Posix 1003.1a Draft 5, because RCS can switch back and forth easily between real and effective users, even if the real user is root. If not, the second best result is if the setuid system call supports saved setuid (the {_POSIX_SAVED_IDS} behavior of Posix 1003.1-1990); this fails only if the real or effective user is root. If RCS detects any failure in setuid, it quits immediately.
- Choose a user A to serve as RCS administrator for the set of users. Only A can invoke the rcs command on the users' RCS files. A should not be root or any other user with special powers. Mutually suspicious sets of users should use different administrators.
- Choose a path name B to be a directory of files to be executed by the users.
- Have A set up B to contain copies of ci and co that are setuid to A, by copying the commands from their standard installation directory D as follows:

```
mkdir B
cp D/c[io] B
chmod go-w,u+s B/c[io]
```

- Have each user prepend B to their path as follows:

```
PATH=B:$PATH; export PATH # ordinary shell
set path=(B $path) # C shell
```

- Have A create each RCS directory R with write access only to A as follows:

```
mkdir R
chmod go-w R
```

- If you want to let only certain users read the RCS files, put the users into a group G, and have A further protect the RCS directory as follows:

```
chgrp G R
chmod g-w,o-rwx R
```

- Have A copy old RCS files (if any) into R, to ensure that A owns them.
- An RCS file's access list limits who can check in and lock revisions. The default access list is empty, which grants check-in access to anyone who can read the RCS file. If you want limit check-in access, have A invoke rcs -a on the file; see rcs(1). In particular, rcs -e -aA limits access to just A.
- Have A initialize any new RCS files with rcs -i before initial check-in, adding the -a option if you want to limit check-in access.
- Give setuid privileges only to ci, co, and rcsclean; do not give them to rcs or to any other command.
- Do not use other setuid commands to invoke RCS commands; setuid is trickier than you think!

ENVIRONMENT
RCSINIT

Options prepended to the argument list, separated by spaces. A backslash escapes spaces within an option. The RCSINIT options are prepended to the argument lists of most RCS commands. Useful RCSINIT options include -q, -V, -x, and -z.

TMPDIR

Name of the temporary directory. If not set, the environment variables TMP and TEMP are inspected instead, and the first value found is taken; if none of them are set, a host-dependent default is used, typically /tmp.

DIAGNOSTICS

For each revision, ci prints the RCS file, the working file, and the number of both the deposited and the preceding revision. The exit status is zero if and only if all operations were successful.

IDENTIFICATION

Author: Walter F. Tichy.
Manual Page Revision: 5.15; Release Date: 1994/03/17.
Copyright (C) 1982, 1988, 1989, Walter F. Tichy.
Copyright (C) 1990, 1991, 1992, 1993, 1994, Paul Eggert.

SEE ALSO

co(1), emacs(1), ident(1), make(1), rcs(1), rcsclean(1), rcsdiff(1), rcsintro(1), rcsmerge(1), rlog(1), setuid(2), rcsfile(5)
Walter F. Tichy, RCS—A System for Version Control, Software—Practice & Experience 15, 7 (July 1985), 637–654.

CO	check files out

NAME

co—checks out RCS revisions

SYNOPSIS

co [options] file . . .

DESCRIPTION

co retrieves a revision from each RCS file and stores it into the corresponding working file.

Pathnames matching an RCS suffix denote RCS files; all others denote working files. Names are paired as explained in ci(1).

Revisions of an RCS file can be checked out locked or unlocked. Locking a revision prevents overlapping updates. A revision checked out for reading or processing (e.g., compiling) need not be locked. A revision checked out for editing and later check-in must normally be locked. Checkout with locking fails if the revision to be checked out is currently locked by another user. [A lock can be broken with rcs(1).] Check-out with locking also requires the caller to be on the access list of the RCS file, unless he is the owner of the file or the superuser, or the access list is empty. Check-out without locking is not subject to access list restrictions, and is not affected by the presence of locks.

A revision is selected by options for revision or branch number, check-in date/ time, author, or state. When the selection options are applied in combination, co retrieves the latest revision that satisfies all of them. If none of the selection options is specified, co retrieves the latest revision on the default branch [normally the trunk; see the -b option of rcs(1)]. A revision or branch number can be attached to any of the options -f, -I, -l, -M, -p, -q, -r, or -u. The options -d (date), -s (state), and -w (author) retrieve from a single branch, the selected branch, which is either specified by one of -f, ..., -u, or the default branch.

A co command applied to an RCS file with no revisions creates a zero-length working file. co always performs keyword substitution (see KEYWORD SUBSTITUTION later in this appendix).

OPTIONS

-r[rev]

Retrieves the latest revision whose number is less than or equal to rev. If rev indicates a branch rather than a revision, the latest revision on that branch is retrieved. If rev is omitted, the latest revision on the default branch [see the -b option of rcs(1)] is retrieved. If rev is $, co determines the revision number from keyword values in the working file. Otherwise, a revision is composed of one or more numeric or symbolic fields separated by periods. If rev begins with a period, then the default branch (normally the trunk) is prepended to it. If rev is a branch number followed by a period, then the latest revision on that branch is used. The numeric equivalent of a symbolic field is specified with the -n option of the commands ci(1) and rcs(1).

-l[rev]
Same as -r, except that it also locks the retrieved revision for the caller.

-u[rev]
Same as -r, except that it unlocks the retrieved revision if it was locked by the caller. If rev is omitted, -u retrieves the revision locked by the caller, if one exists; otherwise, it retrieves the latest revision on the default branch.

-f[rev]
Forces the overwriting of the working file; useful in connection with -q. See also FILE MODES later in this appendix.

-kkv
Generates keyword strings using the default form, e.g., $Revision: 5.12$ for the Revision keyword. A locker's name is inserted in the value of the Header, Id, and Locker keyword strings only as a file is being locked, i.e., by ci -l and co -l. This option is the default.

-kkvl
Like -kkv, except that a locker's name is always inserted if the given revision is currently locked.

-kk
Generates only keyword names in keyword strings; omits their values. See KEYWORD SUBSTITUTION later in this appendix. For example, for the Revision keyword, it generates the string $Revision$ instead of $Revision: 5.12 $. This option is useful for ignoring differences due to keyword substitution when comparing different revisions of a file. Log messages are inserted after Log keywords even if -kk is specified, since this technique tends to be more useful when merging changes.

-ko
Generates the old keyword string, present in the working file just before it was checked in. For example, for the Revision keyword, it generates the string $Revi-

sion: 1.1$ instead of $Revision: 5.12$ if that is how the string appeared when the file
was checked in. This option can be useful for binary file formats that cannot tolerate
any changes to substrings that happen to take the form of keyword strings.

-kv

Generates only keyword values for keyword strings. For example, for the Revision
keyword, it generates the string 5.12 instead of $Revision: 5.12$. This option can
help generate files in programming languages in which stripping keyword delimiters
like $Revision:$ from a string is hard. However, further keyword substitution cannot
be performed once the keyword names are removed, so this option should be used
with care. Because of this danger of losing keywords, this option cannot be com-
bined with -l, and the owner write permission of the working file is turned off; to
edit the file later, check it out again without -kv.

-p[rev]

Prints the retrieved revision on the standard output rather than storing it in the working file. This option is useful when co is part of a pipe.

-q[rev]

Quiet mode; diagnostics are not printed.

-I[rev]

Interactive mode; the user is prompted and questioned even if the standard input is
not a terminal.

-ddate

Retrieves the latest revision on the selected branch whose check-in date/time is less
than or equal to date. The date and time can be given in free format. The time zone
LT stands for local time; other common time zone names are understood. For example, the following dates are equivalent if local time is January 11, 1990, 8 P.M.
Pacific Standard Time, eight hours west of Coordinated Universal Time (UTC):

8:00 P.M. LT	
4:00 A.M., Jan. 12, 1990	default is UTC
1990-01-12 04:00:00+0000	ISO 8601 (UTC)
1990-01-11 20:00:00-0800	ISO 8601 (local time)
1990/01/12 04:00:00	traditional RCS format
Thu Jan 11 20:00:00 1990 LT	output of ctime(3) + LT
Thu Jan 11 20:00:00 PST 1990	output of date(1)
Fri Jan 12 04:00:00 GMT 1990	
Thu, 11 Jan 1990 20:00:00 -0800	Internet RFC 822
12-January-1990, 04:00 WET	

Most fields in date and time can be defaulted. The default time zone is normally UTC, but you can override it with the -z option. The other defaults are determined in the order year, month, day, hour, minute, and second (most to least significant). At least one of these fields must be provided. For omitted fields that are of higher significance than the highest provided field, the time zone's current values are assumed. For all other omitted fields, the lowest possible values are assumed. For example, without -z, the date 20, 10:30 defaults to 10:30:00 UTC of the 20th of the UTC time zone's current month and year. The date/time must be quoted if it contains spaces.

-M[rev]
Sets the modification time on the new working file to be the date of the retrieved revision. Use this option with care; it can confuse make(1).

-sstate
Retrieves the latest revision on the selected branch whose state is set to state.

-T
Preserves the modification time on the RCS file even if the RCS file changes because a lock is added or removed. This option can suppress extensive recompilation caused by a make(1) dependency of some other copy of the working file on the RCS file. Use this option with care; it can suppress recompilation even when it is needed, i.e., when the change of lock would mean a change to keyword strings in the other working file.

-w[login]
Retrieves the latest revision on the selected branch that was checked in by the user with login name login. If the argument login is omitted, the caller's login is assumed.

-jjoinlist
Generates a new revision that is the join of the revisions on joinlist. This option is largely obsoleted by rcsmerge(1) but is retained for backward compatibility.

The joinlist is a comma-separated list of pairs of the form rev2:rev3, where rev2 and rev3 are (symbolic or numeric) revision numbers. For the initial such pair, rev1 denotes the revision selected by the above options -f, . . . -w. For all other pairs, rev1 denotes the revision generated by the previous pair. (Thus, the output of one join becomes the input to the next.)

For each pair, co joins revisions rev1 and rev3 with respect to rev2. So all changes that transform rev2 into rev1 are applied to a copy of rev3. This option is particularly useful if rev1 and rev3 are the ends of two branches that have rev2 as a common ancestor. If rev1<rev2<rev3 are on the same branch, joining generates a new revision that is like rev3, but with all changes that lead from rev1 to rev2 undone. If changes from rev2 to rev1 overlap with changes from rev2 to rev3, co reports overlaps as described in merge(1).

For the initial pair, rev2 can be omitted. The default is the common ancestor. If any of the arguments indicate branches, the latest revisions on those branches are assumed. The options -l and -u lock or unlock rev1.

-V

Prints RCS's version number.

-Vn

Emulates RCS version n, where n can be 3, 4, or 5. This option can be useful when interchanging RCS files with others who are running older versions of RCS. To see which version of RCS your correspondents are running, have them invoke rcs -V; this approach works with newer versions of RCS. If it doesn't work, have them invoke rlog on an RCS file. If none of the first few lines of output contain the string branch; it is version 3; if the dates' years have just two digits, it is version 4; otherwise, it is version 5. An RCS file generated while emulating version 3 loses its default branch. An RCS revision generated while emulating version 4 or earlier has a time stamp that is off by up to 13 hours. A revision extracted while emulating version 4 or earlier contains abbreviated dates of the form yy/mm/dd and can also contain different white space and line prefixes in the substitution for Log.

-xsuffixes

Uses suffixes to characterize RCS files. See ci(1) for details.

-zzone

Specifies the date output format in keyword substitution, and specifies the default time zone for date in the -ddate option. The zone should be empty, a numeric UTC offset, or the special string LT for local time. The default is an empty zone, which uses the traditional RCS format of UTC without any time zone indication and with slashes separating the parts of the date; otherwise, times are output in ISO 8601 format with time zone indication. For example, if local time is January 11, 1990, 8 P.M. Pacific Standard Time, eight hours west of UTC, then the time is output as follows:

option	time output	
-z	1990/01/11 04:00:00	(default)
-zLT	1990-01-11 20:00:00-0800	
-z+0530	1990-01-11 09:30:00+0530	

The -z option does not affect dates stored in RCS files, which are always UTC.

KEYWORD SUBSTITUTION

Strings of the form $keyword$ and $keyword:...$ embedded in the text are replaced with strings of the form $keyword:value$, where keyword and value are pairs listed below. Keywords can be embedded in literal strings or comments to identify a revision.

Initially, the user enters strings of the form $keyword$. On checkout, co replaces these strings with strings of the form $keyword:value$. If a revision containing strings of the latter form is checked back in, the value fields will be replaced during the next check-out. Thus, the keyword values are automatically updated on check-out. This automatic substitution can be modified by the -k options.

Keywords and their corresponding values:

$Author$
The login name of the user who checked in the revision.

$Date$
The date and time the revision was checked in. With -zzone a numeric time zone offset is appended; otherwise, the date is UTC.

$Header$
A standard header containing the full pathname of the RCS file, the revision number, the date and time, the author, the state, and the locker (if locked). With -zzone a numeric time zone offset is appended to the date; otherwise, the date is UTC.

Id
Same as $Header$, except that the RCS filename is without a path.

$Locker$
The login name of the user who locked the revision (empty if not locked).

Log
The log message supplied during check-in, preceded by a header containing the RCS filename, the revision number, the author, and the date and time. With -zzone a numeric time zone offset is appended; otherwise, the date is UTC. Existing log messages are not replaced. Instead, the new log message is inserted after $Log:...$. This option is useful for accumulating a complete change log in a source file. Each inserted line is prefixed by the string that prefixes the Log line. For example, if the Log line is "// $Log: tan.cc $," RCS prefixes each line of the log with "//." This is useful for programming languages without multiline comments.

$Name$
The symbolic name used to check out the revision, if any. For example, co -rJoe generates $Name: Joe$. Plain co generates just $Name: $.

$RCSfile$
The name of the RCS file without a path.

$Revision$
The revision number assigned to the revision.

$Source$
The full pathname of the RCS file.

$State$
The state assigned to the revision with the -s option of rcs(1) or ci(1).

The following characters in keyword values are represented by escape sequences to keep keyword strings wellformed.

char	escape sequence
tab	\t
newline	\n
space	\040
$	\044
\	\\

FILE MODES

The working file inherits the read and execute permissions from the RCS file. In addition, the owner write permission is turned on, unless -kv is set or the file is checked out unlocked and locking is set to strict [see rcs(1)].

If a file with the name of the working file exists already and has write permission, co aborts the check-out, asking beforehand if possible. If the existing working file is not writeable or -f is given, the working file is deleted without asking.

FILES

co accesses files mucha as ci(1) does, except that it does not need to read the working file unless a revision number of $ is specified.

ENVIRONMENT—RCSINIT

Options prepended to the argument list, separated by spaces. See ci(1) for details.

DIAGNOSTICS

The RCS pathname, the working pathname, and the revision number retrieved are written to the diagnostic output. The exit status is zero if and only if all operations were successful.

IDENTIFICATION

Author: Walter F. Tichy.
Manual Page Revision: 5.12; Release Date: 1994/03/17.
Copyright (C) 1982, 1988, 1989, Walter F. Tichy.
Copyright (C) 1990, 1991, 1992, 1993, 1994, Paul Eggert.

SEE ALSO

rcsintro(1), ci(1), ctime(3), date(1), ident(1), make(1), rcs(1), rcsclean(1), rcsdiff(1), rcsmerge(1), rlog(1), rcsfile(5)
Walter F. Tichy, RCS—A System for Version Control, Software—Practice & Experience 15, 7 (July 1985), 637–654.

LIMITS

Links to the RCS and working files are not preserved.

No way exists to selectively suppress the expansion of keywords, except by writing them differently. In nroff and troff, do this by embedding the null-character \& into the keyword.

IDENT	find embedded keyword strings

NAME

ident—identify RCS keyword strings in files

SYNOPSIS

ident [-q] [-V] [file ...]

DESCRIPTION

ident searches for all instances of the pattern $keyword: text$ in the named files or, if no files are named, the standard input.

These patterns are normally inserted automatically by the RCS command co(1), but can also be inserted manually. The option -q suppresses the warning given if patterns occur in a file. The option -V prints ident's version number.

ident works on text files as well as object files and dumps. For example, if the C program in f.c contains

```
#include <stdio.h>
static char const rcsid[] =
"$Id: f.c,v 5.4 1993/11/09 17:40:15 eggert Exp$";
int main() { return printf("%s\n", rcsid) == EOF; }
```

and f.c is compiled into f.o, then the command

```
ident f.c f.o
```

outputs

```
f.c:
   $Id: f.c,v 5.4 1993/11/09 17:40:15 eggert Exp $
f.o:
   $Id: f.c,v 5.4 1993/11/09 17:40:15 eggert Exp $
```

If a C program defines a string like rcsid above but does not use it, lint(1) may complain, and some C compilers optimize away the string. The most reliable solution is to have the program use the rcsid string, as shown in the example above.

ident finds all instances of the $keyword: text$ pattern, even if keyword is not actually an RCS-supported keyword. This option gives you information about non-standard keywords like $XConsortium$.

KEYWORDS

Here is the list of keywords currently maintained by co(1). All times are given in Coordinated Universal Time (UTC, sometimes called GMT) by default, but if the files were checked out with co's -zzone option, times are given with a numeric time zone indication appended.

$Author$
The login name of the user who checked in the revision.

$Date$
The date and time the revision was checked in.

$Header$
A standard header containing the full pathname of the RCS file, the revision number, the date and time, the author, the state, and the locker (if locked).

Id
Same as $Header$, except that the RCS filename is without a path.

$Locker$
The login name of the user who locked the revision (empty if not locked).

Log
The log message supplied during check-in. For ident's purposes, this is equivalent to $RCSfile$.

$Name$
The symbolic name used to check out the revision, if any.

$RCSfile$
The name of the RCS file without a path.

$Revision$
The revision number assigned to the revision.

$Source$
The full pathname of the RCS file.

$State$
The state assigned to the revision with the -s option of rcs(1) or ci(1).

co(1) represents the following characters in keyword values by escape sequences to keep keyword strings wellformed.

char	escape sequence
tab	\t
newline	\n
space	\040
$	\044
\	\\

IDENTIFICATION

Author: Walter F. Tichy.
Manual Page Revision: 5.4; Release Date: 1993/11/09.
Copyright (C) 1982, 1988, 1989, Walter F. Tichy.
Copyright (C) 1990, 1992, 1993, Paul Eggert.

SEE ALSO

ci(1), co(1), rcs(1), rcsdiff(1), rcsintro(1), rcsmerge(1), rlog(1), rcsfile(5)
Walter F. Tichy, RCS—A System for Version Control, Software—Practice & Experience 15, 7 (July 1985), 637–654.

MERGE	merge files

NAME

merge—three-way file merge

SYNOPSIS

merge [options] file1 file2 file3

DESCRIPTION

merge incorporates all changes that lead from file2 to file3 into file1. The result ordinarily goes into file1. merge is useful for combining separate changes to an original. Suppose file2 is the original, and both file1 and file3 are modifications of file2. Then merge combines both changes.

A conflict occurs if both file1 and file3 have changes in a common segment of lines. If a conflict is found, merge normally outputs a warning and brackets the conflict with <<<<<<< and >>>>>>> lines. A typical conflict will look like this:

    <<<<<<< file A
    lines in file A
    =======
    lines in file B
    >>>>>>> file B

If conflicts occur, the user should edit the result and delete one of the alternatives.

OPTIONS

-A

Output conflicts using the -A style of diff3(1), if supported by diff3. This merges all changes leading from file2 to file3 into file1, and is usually the best choice for merging. This option is the default if diff3 supports it.

-E, -e

These options specify conflict styles that generate less information than -A. See diff3(1) for details. If diff3 does not support -A, then -E is the default if it is supported, and -e is otherwise. With -e, merge does not warn about conflicts.

-L label

This option may be given up to three times, and specifies labels to be used in place of the corresponding filenames in conflict reports. That is, merge -L x -L y -L z a b c generates output that looks like it came from files x, y, and z instead of from files a, b, and c.

-p

Sends results to standard output instead of overwriting file1.

-q

Quiet; does not warn about conflicts. -V Prints version number.

DIAGNOSTICS

Exit status is 0 for no conflicts, 1 for some conflicts, 2 for trouble.

IDENTIFICATION

Author: Walter F. Tichy.
Manual Page Revision: 5.6; Release Date: 1993/11/09.
Copyright (C) 1982, 1988, 1989, Walter F. Tichy.
Copyright (C) 1990, 1991, 1992, 1993, Paul Eggert.

SEE ALSO

diff3(1), diff(1), rcsmerge(1), co(1).

RCS	change RCS file attributes

NAME

rcs—change RCS file attributes

SYNOPSIS

rcs [options] file ...

DESCRIPTION

rcs creates new RCS files or changes attributes of existing ones. An RCS file contains multiple revisions of text, an access list, a change log, descriptive text, and some control attributes. For rcs to work, the caller's login name must be on the access list, except if the access list is empty, the caller is the owner of the file or the superuser, or the -i option is present.

Pathnames matching an RCS suffix denote RCS files; all others denote working files. Names are paired as explained in ci(1). Revision numbers use the syntax described in ci(1).

OPTIONS

-i

Creates and initializes a new RCS file, but does not deposit any revision. If the RCS file has no path prefix, it tries to place it first into the subdirectory ./RCS, and then into the current directory. If the RCS file already exists, it prints an error message.

-alogins

Appends the login names appearing in the comma- separated list logins to the access list of the RCS file.

-Aoldfile

Appends the access list of oldfile to the access list of the RCS file.

-e[logins]

Erases the login names appearing in the comma-separated list logins from the access list of the RCS file. If logins is omitted, it erases the entire access list.

-b[rev]

Sets the default branch to rev. If rev is omitted, the default branch is reset to the (dynamically) highest branch on the trunk.

-cstring

Sets the comment leader to string. This option is obsolescent, since RCS normally uses the preceding Log line's prefix when inserting log lines during check-out [see co(1)]. However, older versions of RCS use the comment leader instead of the Log line's prefix. An initial ci, or an rcs -i without -c, guesses the comment leader from the suffix of the working filename.

-ksubst

Sets the default keyword substitution to subst. The effect of keyword substitution is described in co(1). Giving an explicit -k option to co, rcsdiff, and rcsmerge overrides this default. Beware of rcs -kv, because -kv is incompatible with co -l. Use rcs -kkv to restore the normal default keyword substitution.

-l[rev]

Locks the revision with number rev. If a branch is given, it locks the latest revision on that branch. If rev is omitted, it locks the latest revision on the default branch. Locking prevents overlapping changes. If someone else already holds the lock, the lock is broken as with rcs -u (see below).

-u[rev]

Unlocks the revision with number rev. If a branch is given, it unlocks the latest revision on that branch. If rev is omitted, it removes the latest lock held by the caller. Normally, only the locker of a revision can unlock it. Somebody else unlocking a revision breaks the lock. This action causes a mail message to be sent to the original locker. The message contains a commentary solicited from the breaker. The commentary is terminated by end-of-file or by a line containing . by itself.

-L

Sets locking to strict. Strict locking means that the owner of an RCS file is not exempt from locking for check-in. This option should be used for files that are shared.

-U

Sets locking to nonstrict. Nonstrict locking means that the owner of a file need not lock a revision for check-in. This option should not be used for files that are shared. Whether default locking is strict is determined by your system administrator, but it is normally strict.

-mrev:msg

Replaces revision rev's log message with msg.

-M
Does not send mail when breaking somebody else's lock. This option is not meant for casual use; it is meant for programs that warn users by other means, and invokes rcs -u only as a low-level lock-breaking operation.

-nname[:[rev]]
Associates the symbolic name with the branch or revision rev. Deletes the symbolic name if both : and rev are omitted; otherwise, prints an error message if name is already associated with another number. If rev is symbolic, it is expanded before association. A rev consisting of a branch number followed by a . stands for the current latest revision in the branch. A : with an empty rev stands for the current latest revision on the default branch, normally the trunk. For example, rcs -nname: RCS/* associates name with the current latest revision of all the named RCS files; this command contrasts with rcs -nname:$ RCS/*, which associates name with the revision numbers extracted from keyword strings in the corresponding working files.

-Nname[:[rev]]
Acts like -n, except it overrides any previous assignment of name.

-orange
Deletes ("outdates") the revisions given by range. A range consisting of a single revision number means that revision. A range consisting of a branch number means the latest revision on that branch. A range of the form rev1:rev2 means revisions rev1 to rev2 on the same branch; :rev means from the beginning of the branch containing rev up to and including rev; and rev: means from revision rev to the end of the branch containing rev. None of the outdated revisions can have branches or locks.

-q
Runs quietly; does not print diagnostics.

-I
Runs interactively, even if the standard input is not a terminal.

-sstate[:rev]
Sets the state attribute of the revision rev to state. If rev is a branch number, it assumes the latest revision on that branch. If rev is omitted, it assumes the latest revision on the default branch. Any identifier is acceptable for state. A useful set of states is Exp (for experimental), Stab (for stable), and Rel (for released). By default, ci(1) sets the state of a revision to Exp.

-t[file]

Writes descriptive text from the contents of the named file into the RCS file, deleting the existing text. The file pathname cannot begin with -. If file is omitted, it obtains the text from standard input, terminated by end-of-file or by a line containing . by itself. The option prompts for the text if interaction is possible; see -I above. With -i, descriptive text is obtained even if -t is not given.

-t-string

Writes descriptive text from the string into the RCS file, deleting the existing text.

-T

Preserves the modification time on the RCS file unless a revision is removed. This option can suppress extensive recompilation caused by a make(1) dependency of some copy of the working file on the RCS file. Use this option with care; it can suppress recompilation even when it is needed, i.e., when a change to the RCS file would mean a change to keyword strings in the working file.

-V

Prints RCS's version number.

-Vn

Emulates RCS version n. See co(1) for details.

-xsuffixes

Uses suffixes to characterize RCS files. See ci(1) for details.

-zzone

Uses zone as the default time zone. This option has no effect; it is present for compatibility with other RCS commands.

COMPATIBILITY

The -brev option generates an RCS file that cannot be parsed by RCS version 3 or earlier. The -ksubst options (except -kkv) generate an RCS file that cannot be parsed by RCS version 4 or earlier. Use rcs -Vn to make an RCS file acceptable to RCS version n by discarding information that would confuse version n. RCS versions 5.5 and earlier do not support the -x option, and require a ,v suffix on an RCS pathname.

FILES

rcs accesses files much as ci(1) does, except that it uses the effective user for all accesses, it does not write the working file or its directory, and it does not even read the working file unless a revision number of $ is specified.

ENVIRONMENT—RCSINIT

Options prepended to the argument list, separated by spaces. See ci(1) for details.

DIAGNOSTICS

The RCS pathname and the revisions outdated are written to the diagnostic output. The exit status is zero if and only if all operations were successful.

IDENTIFICATION

Author: Walter F. Tichy.
Manual Page Revision: 5.11; Release Date: 1994/03/17.
Copyright (C) 1982, 1988, 1989, Walter F. Tichy.
Copyright (C) 1990, 1991, 1992, 1993, 1994, Paul Eggert.

SEE ALSO

rcsintro(1), co(1), ci(1), ident(1), rcsclean(1), rcsd- iff(1), rcsmerge(1), rlog(1), rcs-file(5)
Walter F. Tichy, RCS—A System for Version Control, Software—Practice & Experience 15, 7 (July 1985), 637–654.

BUGS

A catastrophe (e.g., a system crash) can cause RCS to leave behind a semaphore file that causes later invocations of RCS to claim that the RCS file is in use. To fix this, remove the semaphore file. A semaphore file's name typically begins with , or ends with _.

The separator for revision ranges in the -o option used to be - instead of :, but this leads to confusion when symbolic names contain -. For backward compatibility, rcs -o still supports the old - separator, but it warns about this obsolete use.

Symbolic names need not refer to existing revisions or branches. For example, the -o option does not remove symbolic names for the outdated revisions; you must use -n to remove the names.

RCSCLEAN	clean up working files

NAME

rcsclean—cleans up working files

SYNOPSIS

rcsclean [options] [file ...]

DESCRIPTION

rcsclean removes files that are not being worked on. rcsclean -u also unlocks and removes files that are being worked on but have not changed.

For each file given, rcsclean compares the working file and a revision in the corresponding RCS file. If it finds a difference, it does nothing. Otherwise, it first unlocks the revision if the -u option is given, and then removes the working file, unless the working file is writeable and the revision is locked. It logs its actions by outputting the corresponding rcs -u and rm -f commands on the standard output.

Files are paired as explained in ci(1). If no file is given, all working files in the current directory are cleaned. Pathnames matching an RCS suffix denote RCS files; all others denote working files.

The number of the revision to which the working file is compared may be attached to any of the options -n, -q, -r, or -u. If no revision number is specified, then if the -u option is given and the caller has one revision locked, rcsclean uses that revision; otherwise rcsclean uses the latest revision on the default branch, normally the root.

rcsclean is useful for clean targets in makefiles. See also rcsdiff(1), which prints out the differences, and ci(1), which normally reverts to the previous revision if a file was not changed.

OPTIONS

-ksubst

Uses subst style keyword substitution when retrieving the revision for comparison. See co(1) for details.

-n[rev]

Does not actually remove any files or unlock any revisions. Using this option tells you what rcsclean would do without actually doing it.

-q[rev]
Does not log the actions taken on standard output.

-r[rev]
This option has no effect other than specifying the revision for comparison.

-T
Preserves the modification time on the RCS file even if the RCS file changes because a lock is removed. This option can suppress extensive recompilation caused by a make(1) dependency of some other copy of the working file on the RCS file. Use this option with care; it can suppress recompilation even when it is needed, i.e., when the lock removal would mean a change to keyword strings in the other working file.

-u[rev]
Unlocks the revision if it is locked and no difference is found.

-V
Prints RCS's version number.

-Vn
Emulates RCS version n. See co(1) for details.

-xsuffixes
Uses suffixes to characterize RCS files. See ci(1) for details.

-zzone
Uses zone as the time zone for keyword substitution; see co(1) for details.

EXAMPLES

rcsclean *.c *.h
Removes all working files ending in .c or .h that were not changed since their check-out.

rcsclean
Removes all working files in the current directory that were not changed since their check-out.

FILES

rcsclean accesses files much as ci(1) does.

ENVIRONMENT—RCSINIT

Options prepended to the argument list, separated by spaces. A backslash escapes spaces within an option. The RCSINIT options are prepended to the argument lists of most RCS commands. Useful RCSINIT options include -q, -V, -x, and -z.

DIAGNOSTICS

The exit status is zero if and only if all operations were successful. Missing working files and RCS files are silently ignored.

IDENTIFICATION

Author: Walter F. Tichy.
Manual Page Revision: 1.12; Release Date: 1993/11/03.
Copyright (C) 1982, 1988, 1989, Walter F. Tichy.
Copyright (C) 1990, 1991, 1992, 1993, Paul Eggert.

SEE ALSO

ci(1), co(1), ident(1), rcs(1), rcsdiff(1), rcsintro(1), rcsmerge(1), rlog(1), rcsfile(5)
Walter F. Tichy, RCS—A System for Version Control, Software—Practice & Experience 15, 7 (July 1985), 637–654.

BUGS

At least one file must be given in older UNIX versions that do not provide the needed directory scanning operations.

| RCSDIFF | compare RCS revisions |

NAME

rcsdiff—compares RCS revisions

SYNOPSIS

rcsdiff [-ksubst] [-q] [-rrev1 [-rrev2]] [-T] [-V[n]] [-xsuffixes] [-zzone] [diff options] file ...

DESCRIPTION

rcsdiff runs diff(1) to compare two revisions of each RCS file given.

Pathnames matching an RCS suffix denote RCS files; all others denote working files. Names are paired as explained in ci(1).

The option -q suppresses diagnostic output. Zero, one, or two revisions may be specified with -r. The option -ksubst affects keyword substitution when extracting revisions, as described in co(1); for example, -kk -r1.1 -r1.2 ignores differences in keyword values when comparing revisions 1.1 and 1.2. To avoid excess output from locker name substitution, -kkvl is assumed if (1) at most one revision option is given, (2) no -k option is given, (3) -kkv is the default keyword substitution, and (4) the working file's mode would be produced by co -l. See co(1) for details about -T, -V, -x, and -z. Otherwise, all options of diff(1) that apply to regular files are accepted, with the same meaning as for diff.

If both rev1 and rev2 are omitted, rcsdiff compares the latest revision on the default branch (by default the trunk) with the contents of the corresponding working file. This option is useful for determining what you changed since the last check-in.

If rev1 is given but rev2 is omitted, rcsdiff compares revision rev1 of the RCS file with the contents of the corresponding working file.

If both rev1 and rev2 are given, rcsdiff compares revisions rev1 and rev2 of the RCS file.

Both rev1 and rev2 may be given numerically or symbolically.

EXAMPLE

The command

```
rcsdiff f.c
```

compares the latest revision on the default branch of the RCS file to the contents of the working file f.c.

ENVIRONMENT—RCSINIT

Options prepended to the argument list, separated by spaces. See ci(1) for details.

DIAGNOSTICS

Exit status is 0 for no differences during any comparison, 1 for some differences, and 2 for trouble.

IDENTIFICATION

Author: Walter F. Tichy.
Manual Page Revision: 5.5; Release Date: 1993/11/03.
Copyright (C) 1982, 1988, 1989, Walter F. Tichy.
Copyright (C) 1990, 1991, 1992, 1993, Paul Eggert.

SEE ALSO

ci(1), co(1), diff(1), ident(1), rcs(1), rcsintro(1), rcsmerge(1), rlog(1)
Walter F. Tichy, RCS—A System for Version Control, Software—Practice & Experience 15, 7 (July 1985), 637–654.

RCSFREEZE	**tag a release**

NAME

rcsfreeze—freezes a configuration of sources checked in under RCS

SYNOPSIS

rcsfreeze [name]

DESCRIPTION

rcsfreeze assigns a symbolic revision number to a set of RCS files that form a valid configuration.

The idea is to run rcsfreeze each time a new version is checked in. A unique symbolic name (C_number, where number is increased each time rcsfreeze is run) is then assigned to the most recent revision of each RCS file of the main trunk.

An optional name argument to rcsfreeze gives a symbolic name to the configuration. The unique identifier is still generated and is listed in the log file but it does not appear as part of the symbolic revision name in the actual RCS files.

A log message is requested from the user for future reference.

The shell script works only on all RCS files at one time. All changed files must be checked in already. Run rcsclean(1) first and see whether any sources remain in the current directory.

FILES

RCS/.rcsfreeze.ver
    version number

RCS/.rcsfreeze.log
    log messages, most recent first

AUTHOR

Stephan V. Bechtolsheim

SEE ALSO

co(1), rcs(1), rcsclean(1), rlog(1)

BUGS

rcsfreeze does not check whether any sources are checked out and modified.

Although both source filenames and RCS filenames are accepted, they are not paired as usual with RCS commands.

Error checking is rudimentary.

rcsfreeze is just an optional example shell script, and should not be taken too seriously. See CVS for a more complete solution.

RCSMERGE	**merge RCS revisions**

NAME

rcsmerge—merges RCS revisions

SYNOPSIS

rcsmerge [options] file

DESCRIPTION

rcsmerge incorporates the changes between two revisions of an RCS file into the corresponding working file.

Pathnames matching an RCS suffix denote RCS files; all others denote working files. Names are paired as explained in ci(1).

At least one revision must be specified with one of the options described below, usually -r. At most two revisions may be specified. If only one revision is specified, the latest revision on the default branch (normally the highest branch on the trunk) is assumed for the second revision. Revisions may be specified numerically or symbolically.

rcsmerge prints a warning if overlaps occur, and delimits the overlapping regions as explained in merge(1). The command is useful for incorporating changes into a checked-out revision.

OPTIONS

-A
Outputs conflicts using the -A style of diff3(1), if supported by diff3. This merges all changes leading from file2 to file3 into file1, and is usually the best choice for merging. This option is the default if diff3 supports it.

-E, -e
These options specify conflict styles that generate less information than -A. See diff3(1) for details. If diff3 does not support -A, then -E is the default if it is supported, and -e is otherwise.

-ksubst
Uses subst style keyword substitution. See co(1) for details. For example, -kk -r1.1 -r1.2 ignores differences in keyword values when merging the changes from 1.1 to 1.2.

-p[rev]
Sends the result to standard output instead of overwriting the working file.

-q[rev]
Runs quietly; does not print diagnostics.

-r[rev]
Merges with respect to revision rev. Here an empty rev stands for the latest revision on the default branch, normally the head.

-T
This option has no effect; it is present for compatibility with other RCS commands.

-V
Prints RCS's version number.

-Vn
Emulates RCS version n. See co(1) for details.

-xsuffixes
Uses suffixes to characterize RCS files. See ci(1) for details.

-zzone
Uses zone as the time zone for keyword substitution. See co(1) for details.

EXAMPLES

Suppose you have released revision 2.8 of f.c. Assume furthermore that after you complete an unreleased revision 3.4, you receive updates to release 2.8 from someone else. To combine the updates to 2.8 and your changes between 2.8 and 3.4, put the updates to 2.8 into file f.c and execute

```
rcsmerge -p -r2.8 -r3.4 f.c >f.merged.c
```

Then examine f.merged.c. Alternatively, if you want to save the updates to 2.8 in the RCS file, check them in as revision 2.8.1.1 and execute co -j:

```
ci -r2.8.1.1 f.c
co -r3.4 -j2.8:2.8.1.1 f.c
```

As another example, the following command undoes the changes between revision 2.4 and 2.8 in your currently checked-out revision in f.c.

```
rcsmerge -r2.8 -r2.4 f.c
```

Note the order of the arguments, and that f.c will be overwritten.

ENVIRONMENT—RCSINIT

Options prepended to the argument list, separated by spaces. See ci(1) for details.

DIAGNOSTICS

Exit status is 0 for no overlaps, 1 for some overlaps, and 2 for trouble.

IDENTIFICATION

Author: Walter F. Tichy.
Manual Page Revision: 5.5; Release Date: 1993/11/03.
Copyright (C) 1982, 1988, 1989, Walter F. Tichy.
Copyright (C) 1990, 1991, 1992, 1993, Paul Eggert.

SEE ALSO

ci(1), co(1), ident(1), merge(1), rcs(1), rcsdiff(1), rcsintro(1), rlog(1), rcsfile(5)
Walter F. Tichy, RCS—A System for Version Control, Software—Practice & Experience 15, 7 (July 1985), 637–654.

RLOG   **show the file history**

NAME

rlog—prints log messages and other information about RCS files

SYNOPSIS

rlog [options] file ...

DESCRIPTION

rlog prints information about RCS files.

Path names matching an RCS suffix denote RCS files; all others denote working files. Names are paired as explained in ci(1).

rlog prints the following information for each RCS file: RCS pathname, working path name, head (i.e., the number of the latest revision on the trunk), default branch, access list, locks, symbolic names, suffix, total number of revisions, number of revisions selected for printing, and descriptive text. This is followed by entries for the selected revisions in reverse chronological order for each branch. For each revision, rlog prints revision number, author, date/time, state, number of lines added/deleted (with respect to the previous revision), locker of the revision (if any), and log message. All times are displayed in Coordinated Universal Time (UTC) by default; this option can be overridden with -z. Without options, rlog prints complete information. The options below restrict this output.

-L

Ignores RCS files that have no locks set. This is convenient in combination with -h, -l, and -R.

-R

Prints only the name of the RCS file. This is convenient for translating a working pathname into an RCS pathname.

-h

Prints only the RCS pathname, working pathname, head, default branch, access list, locks, symbolic names, and suffix.

-t

Prints the same as -h, plus the descriptive text.

-N
Does not print the symbolic names.

-b
Prints information about the revisions on the default branch, normally the highest branch on the trunk.

-ddates
Prints information about revisions with a check-in date/time in the ranges given by the semicolon-separated list of dates. A range of the form d1<d2 or d2>d1 selects the revisions that were deposited between d1 and d2 exclusive. A range of the form <d or d> selects all revisions earlier than d. A range of the form d< or >d selects all revisions dated later than d. If < or > is followed by = then the ranges are inclusive, not exclusive. A range of the form d selects the single, latest revision dated d or earlier. The date/time strings d, d1, and d2 are in the free format explained in co(1). Quoting is normally necessary, especially for < and >. Note that the - separator is a semicolon.

-l[lockers]
Prints information about locked revisions only. In addition, if the comma-separated list lockers of login names is given, it ignores all locks other than those held by the lockers. For example, rlog -L -R -lwft RCS/* prints the name of RCS files locked by the user wft.

-r[revisions]
Prints information about revisions given in the comma-separated list revisions of revisions and ranges. A range rev1:rev2 means revisions rev1 to rev2 on the same branch; :rev means revisions from the beginning of the branch up to and including rev; and rev: means revisions starting with rev to the end of the branch containing rev. An argument that is a branch means all revisions on that branch. A range of branches means all revisions on the branches in that range. A branch followed by a . means the latest revision in that branch. A bare -r with no revisions means the latest revision on the default branch, normally the trunk.

-sstates
Prints information about revisions whose state attributes match one of the states given in the comma-separated list states.

-w[logins]
Prints information about revisions checked in by users with login names appearing in the comma-separated list logins. If logins is omitted, the user's login is assumed.

-T

This option has no effect; it is present for compatibility with other RCS commands.

-V

Prints RCS's version number.

-Vn

Emulates RCS version n when generating logs. See co(1) for more.

-xsuffixes

Uses suffixes to characterize RCS files. See ci(1) for details.

     rlog prints the intersection of the revisions selected with the options -d, -l, -s, and -w, intersected with the union of the revisions selected by -b and -r.

-zzone

Specifies the date output format, and specifies the default time zone for date in the -ddates option. The zone should be empty, a numeric UTC offset, or the special string LT for local time. The default is an empty zone, which uses the traditional RCS format of UTC without any time zone indication and with slashes separating the parts of the date; otherwise, times are output in ISO 8601 format with time zone indication. For example, if local time is January 11, 1990, 8 P.M. Pacific Standard Time, eight hours west of UTC, then the time is output as 1990/01/11 04:00:00 with -z, as 1990-01-11 20:00:00-0800 with -zLT, and as 1990-01-11 09:30:00+0530 with -z+0530.

EXAMPLES

rlog -L -R RCS/*
rlog -L -h RCS/*
rlog -L -l RCS/*
rlog RCS/*

The first command prints the names of all RCS files in the subdirectory RCS that have locks. The second command prints the headers of those files, and the third prints the headers plus the log messages of the locked revisions. The last command prints complete information.

ENVIRONMENT—RCSINIT

Options prepended to the argument list, separated by spaces. See ci(1) for details.

DIAGNOSTICS

The exit status is zero if and only if all operations were successful.

IDENTIFICATION

Author: Walter F. Tichy.
Manual Page Revision: 5.7; Release Date: 1994/03/17.
Copyright (C) 1982, 1988, 1989, Walter F. Tichy.
Copyright (C) 1990, 1991, 1992, 1993, 1994, Paul Eggert.

SEE ALSO

ci(1), co(1), ident(1), rcs(1), rcsdiff(1), rcsintro(1), rcsmerge(1), rcsfile(5)
Walter F. Tichy, RCS   A System for Version Control, Software—Practice & Experience 15, 7 (July 1985), 637–654.

BUGS

The separator for revision ranges in the -r option used to be - instead of :, but this leads to confusion when symbolic names contain -. For backward compatibility rlog -r still supports the old - separator, but it warns about this obsolete use.

Index

LICENSE AGREEMENT AND LIMITED WARRANTY

READ THE FOLLOWING TERMS AND CONDITIONS CAREFULLY BEFORE OPENING THIS SOFTWARE MEDIA PACKAGE. THIS LEGAL DOCUMENT IS AN AGREEMENT BETWEEN YOU AND PRENTICE-HALL, INC. (THE "COMPANY"). BY OPENING THIS SEALED SOFTWARE MEDIA PACKAGE, YOU ARE AGREEING TO BE BOUND BY THESE TERMS AND CONDITIONS. IF YOU DO NOT AGREE WITH THESE TERMS AND CONDITIONS, DO NOT OPEN THE SOFTWARE MEDIA PACKAGE. PROMPTLY RETURN THE UNOPENED SOFTWARE MEDIA PACKAGE AND ALL ACCOMPANYING ITEMS TO THE PLACE YOU OBTAINED THEM FOR A FULL REFUND OF ANY SUMS YOU HAVE PAID.

1.   **GRANT OF LICENSE:** In consideration of your payment of the license fee, which is part of the price you paid for this product, and your agreement to abide by the terms and conditions of this Agreement, the Company grants to you a nonexclusive right to use and display the copy of the enclosed software program (hereinafter the "SOFTWARE") on a single computer (i.e., with a single CPU) at a single location so long as you comply with the terms of this Agreement. The Company reserves all rights not expressly granted to you under this Agreement.

2.   **OWNERSHIP OF SOFTWARE:** You own only the magnetic or physical media (the enclosed SOFTWARE) on which the SOFTWARE is recorded or fixed, but the Company retains all the rights, title, and ownership to the SOFTWARE recorded on the original SOFTWARE copy(ies) and all subsequent copies of the SOFTWARE, regardless of the form or media on which the original or other copies may exist. This license is not a sale of the original SOFTWARE or any copy to you.

3.   **COPY RESTRICTIONS:** This SOFTWARE and the accompanying printed materials and user manual (the "Documentation") are the subject of copyright. You may not copy the Documentation or the SOFTWARE, except that you may make a single copy of the SOFTWARE for backup or archival purposes only. You may be held legally responsible for any copying or copyright infringement which is caused or encouraged by your failure to abide by the terms of this restriction.

4.   **USE RESTRICTIONS:** You may not network the SOFTWARE or otherwise use it on more than one computer or computer terminal at the same time. You may physically transfer the SOFTWARE from one computer to another provided that the SOFTWARE is used on only one computer at a time. You may not distribute copies of the SOFTWARE or Documentation to others. You may not reverse engineer, disassemble, decompile, modify, adapt, translate, or create derivative works based on the SOFTWARE or the Documentation without the prior written consent of the Company.

5.   **TRANSFER RESTRICTIONS:** The enclosed SOFTWARE is licensed only to you and may not be transferred to any one else without the prior written consent of the Company. Any unauthorized transfer of the SOFTWARE shall result in the immediate termination of this Agreement.

6.   **TERMINATION:** This license is effective until terminated. This license will terminate automatically without notice from the Company and become null and void if you fail to comply with any provisions or limitations of this license. Upon termination, you shall destroy the Documentation and all copies of the SOFTWARE. All provisions of this Agreement as to warranties, limitation of liability, remedies or damages, and our ownership rights shall survive termination.

7.   **MISCELLANEOUS:** This Agreement shall be construed in accordance with the laws of the United States of America and the State of New York and shall benefit the Company, its affiliates, and assignees.

8.   **LIMITED WARRANTY AND DISCLAIMER OF WARRANTY:** The Company warrants that the SOFTWARE, when properly used in accordance with the Documentation, will operate in substantial conformity with the description of the SOFTWARE set forth in the Documentation. The Company does not warrant that the SOFTWARE will meet your requirements or that the operation of the SOFTWARE will be uninterrupted or error-free. The Company warrants that the